The Death Penalty in the Eighties

The Death Penalty in the Eighties

An Examination of the Modern System of Capital Punishment

Welsh S. White

Ann Arbor   The University of Michigan Press

Copyright © by The University of Michigan 1987
All rights reserved
Published in the United States of America by
The University of Michigan Press and simultaneously
in Markham, Canada, by Fitzhenry & Whiteside, Ltd.
Manufactured in the United States of America

1990   1989   1988   1987   4   3   2   1

Library of Congress Cataloging-in-Publication Data

White, Welsh S., 1940–
   The death penalty in the eighties.

   Includes bibliographies and index.
   1. Capital punishment—United States.
2. United States. Supreme Court. I. Title.
KF9227.C2W44   1987   345.73′0773   87-5909
ISBN 0-472-10088-2 (alk. paper) 347.305773

To my mother, Mary L. Knight

Acknowledgments

During the past two years, I have interviewed a large number of lawyers who specialize in capital punishment cases. These lawyers have been unusually generous with their time and have supplied me with information and materials that have enabled me to obtain a much better understanding of our system of capital punishment. Among those to whom I am particularly indebted are Bob Ravitz, David Stebbins, Bruce Ledewitz, Norrie Gelman, David Wymart, Kevin McNally, Dick Winterbottom, Mark Donatelli, Adam Stein, Dennis Balske, Jack Boger, and Craig Haney.

I would also like to thank my colleagues and friends who assisted by reading and critiquing portions of the manuscript. Those who offered especially valuable suggestions include Al Alschuler, Jack Boger, Craig Haney, Tom Gerety, Yale Kamisar, and my wife, Linda.

Finally, I would like to thank Alan Blanco, Paul Kay, and Kathy Lance for their excellent research assistance; and LuAnn Driscoll, Barb Salopek, Shelly Vosachlo, Tracy Roman, and Karen Hawkins for their superb secretarial support.

Contents

Introduction

For the past decade, a new system of capital punishment has been in effect in this country. The modern era of capital punishment began in 1976 when, in *Gregg v. Georgia*,[1] the United States Supreme Court held that capital punishment as such was not unconstitutional but that certain safeguards must be imposed to ensure that there is not "a substantial risk [that] the [death penalty will] be inflicted in an arbitrary and capricious manner."[2] In *Gregg* and its companion decisions, the Court reviewed five death penalty statutes, holding that three were constitutional and two unconstitutional.[3]

The Court's 1976 decisions set the parameters for the current system of capital punishment. In addition, they more or less committed the Court to a further review of procedures employed in death penalty cases. In the decade following the 1976 decisions, the Court has rendered an unprecedented number of significant capital punishment decisions. As a result of these decisions, there are important differences between our present system of capital punishment and the one that existed prior to 1972.

The purpose of this book is to examine the modern system of capital punishment. Some of the chapters are especially focused on explaining how the present system works. Chapter 2, for example, is an examination of plea bargaining in capital cases, and chapter 3 concerns the penalty phase of a capital trial. These chapters will be of special interest to attorneys because in them I analyze specific cases and set forth some of the techniques that have been successfully used by defense counsel either in plea bargaining a capital case or in defending a capital defendant at the penalty trial. I anticipate that they will also be of interest to the general reader. The chapters are not only accounts of interesting capital trials, but also explanations of the implications of these cases and examinations of the interrelationship between plea bargaining and the conduct of the penalty trial and the modern system of capital punishment.

In other chapters I deal with specific issues or problems related to the administration of the death penalty. In chapter 6, for example, I examine the extent to which racial discrimination exists in capital sentencing, and in chapter 7 I consider how the modern system of capital punishment deals with the problems posed by defendants who would prefer to be executed rather than sentenced to life imprisonment. These chapters also include examinations of particular capital cases. Chapter 6 includes an account of the trial and execution of Roosevelt Green, a young black man who was involved in an interracial crime, and in chapter 7 I try to explain why Gary Gilmore chose to face a Utah firing squad rather than to contest the validity of his death sentence. In addition to describing what happened in particular cases, I also try to examine the issues in question from a broader perspective, focusing especially on the interaction between the particular issue and the administration of the death penalty. Thus, in chapter 6 I consider the implications of the modern system's tolerance of a certain degree of racial discrimination in capital sentencing, and chapter 7 includes a discussion of the interrelationship between defendants who elect capital punishment and the deterrent effect of the death penalty.

Most of the remaining chapters concern the Supreme Court's role in shaping the modern system of capital punishment. Chapter 1 is an overview of the most significant Supreme Court decisions and an assessment of their impact. Other chapters are examinations and analyses of narrower legal issues. Chapter 8 is a detailed critique of *Witherspoon v. Illinois* and *Lockhart v. McCree*, two Supreme Court cases that deal with issues arising from the government's use of death-qualified juries in capital cases; chapter 4 concerns the Supreme Court cases that involve the defendant's right to present mitigating evidence at the penalty trial; and chapter 5 is a discussion of some of the legal and psychological issues that arise when prosecutors present particular types of closing arguments at the penalty trial. In these chapters, I try to strike a balance between describing the doctrine as it currently exists and suggesting improvements.

My ultimate objective is to sufficiently inform the reader so that he or she will have a reasonably good understanding of how the modern system of capital punishment operates and some basis for judging whether or not this system is superior to the one it replaced. In providing this information, I will particularly strive to present data that will assist the reader in judging whether the Supreme Court decisions have in fact reduced the "risk [that] the [death penalty will] be inflicted in an arbitrary and capricious manner." If I am successful in this attempt, the reader will be in a good position to determine whether the promise held out by the Supreme Court in the *Gregg* case has been fulfilled.

NOTES

1. 428 U.S. 153 (1976).
2. *Id.* at 195.
3. On July 2, 1976, the Court handed down five capital punishment decisions. In addition to *Gregg*, the cases decided were: Proffitt v. Florida, 428 U.S. 242

(1976); Jurek v. Texas, 428 U.S. 262 (1976); Woodson v. North Carolina, 428 U.S. 280 (1976); and Roberts v. Louisiana, 428 U.S. 325 (1976).

CHAPTER 1

An Overview of the Modern
System of Capital Punishment

On May 13, 1986, Justice Blackmun told a group of
federal judges that "the excruciating agony" of last-minute death penalty
decisions had "haunted and debilitated the Court" during its most recent
session.[1] Justice Powell also said that "death penalty cases were straining
the Court, with requests for stays often filed only 24 hours before scheduled executions."[2] The anguish the justices experienced in deciding individual applications for stays of execution reflects some of the ironies and
ambiguities in our present system of capital punishment.

The irony stems in part from the nature of the decision that creates the
justices' inner turmoil. An application for stay of execution does not demand
a decision on the merits; it merely requests that the Court delay the execution of a condemned prisoner pending a decision—by either the Supreme
Court or some other court—whether inflicting the death penalty would violate the Constitution. Compared to deciding important constitutional issues
on the merits, ruling on stay applications would appear to be routine business. That Supreme Court justices experience greater personal anguish
when dealing with routine stay applications than when deciding constitutional issues of tremendous significance may seem anomalous.

But of course the decision to grant or delay a stay application has a
unique immediate impact. If the Court grants the stay application, the
condemned prisoner remains alive; if the Court denies the stay, the prisoner will usually be executed. The anguish the Court experiences in dealing with these applications thus probably stems from its realization that a
denial of the stay is likely to result in a defendant's immediate execution.
It is interesting, but not remarkable, that a decision that immediately and
irrevocably decides the fate of one individual may be more wrenching
than a decision that has important long-range consequences for many
people. Indeed, abolitionists have claimed for years that people who ap-
prove of capital punishment in the abstract may feel differently when they
confront the reality of an execution.[3] The Court's difficulty in dealing with
applications for stays may reflect the validity of this observation.

The justices' discomfort in dealing with stay applications is also

4

ironic because the Court has, in a sense, created the system in which requests for last-minute stays of execution are commonplace. During most of its history, the Court has not been involved in the administration of the death penalty;[4] and even in the late sixties and early seventies, when the Court began to consider stay applications, it was concerned not so much with deciding whether stays should be granted in specific capital cases as with deciding whether they should be issued in all capital cases until the central issues relating to the administration of capital punishment could be considered and decided.[5] In the last decade, however, the Court has established a new system of punishment, and as that system now operates, it is almost inevitable that applications for stays of execution will be presented to the Supreme Court in many if not most capital cases.

The Parameters of the Modern System

In demarcating the modern era of capital punishment, the key cases are *Furman v. Georgia,*[6] decided in 1972, and *Gregg v. Georgia,*[7] decided in 1976. Before 1972, our system of capital punishment was much less complicated than it is now. Most states provided that in capital cases the jury would adjudicate guilt and determine sentence in a single proceeding and that in determining sentence the jury would have unfettered discretion to impose or withhold the death penalty. If the defendant was charged with the capital offense of first-degree murder, for example, the jury would first decide whether to convict the defendant of that charge, acquit him, or convict him of a lesser included offense such as second-degree murder. If it convicted the defendant of the capital charge, it was required to decide whether he should be sentenced to death or to life imprisonment. In most jurisdictions, the jury made this decision without hearing further evidence and without any guidelines. Pursuant to this jury-discretionary system of capital punishment, about 100 defendants a year were sentenced to death during the two decades before 1972,[8] and until the Supreme Court imposed a de facto moratorium on capital punishment in the late sixties, about half of them were executed.[9]

In *Furman v. Georgia,*[10] the Supreme Court held that the jury-discretionary system of capital punishment was unconstitutional. In *Furman* the Court essentially decided that the death penalty had been applied so capriciously as to violate the Eighth Amendment.[11] The Court left open the question whether death penalties imposed pursuant to a different system of capital punishment would be constitutional.

Four years later, the Court's decision in *Gregg v. Georgia*[12] introduced a new era of capital punishment. In *Gregg* and its companion cases the Court held that punishment by death was not automatically or invariably unconstitutional but that to impose capital punishment, a state had to adopt safeguards to ensure that the death penalty would be imposed in a just and rational manner. The Court's 1976 decisions are subject to conflicting interpretations,[13] but at a minimum the Court indicated that any capital punishment scheme must include safeguards that are designed to address two concerns: first, reducing the extent to which the death penalty is arbitrarily applied; second, providing for individualized sentencing.

In *Gregg* itself the Court especially emphasized the importance of avoiding the arbitrary imposition of capital punishment. In the course of upholding Georgia's death penalty statute, the pivotal plurality opinion read *Furman* as "mandat[ing] . . . that [the sentencing authority's] discretion . . . be suitably directed and limited so as to minimize the risk" that the death penalty will be applied arbitrarily.[14] The plurality added that the best means of directing the sentencing jury's discretion is to provide a system that includes both a bifurcated trial and guidelines for the sentencing authority.[15] According to the plurality, the bifurcated trial is desirable because it allows the sentencing jury to consider a full range of information relating to the crime and the character of the defendant. But the plurality emphasized that this information will be useful to the jury only if "it is given guidance regarding the factors about the crime and the defendant that the State . . . deems particularly relevant to the sentencing decision."[16] Thus, the Court seemed to conclude that reducing the risk of the death penalty's arbitrary application is essential and that the best means of doing so is to channel the sentencing authority's exercise of discretion.

In *Woodson v. North Carolina,*[17] decided the same day as *Gregg,* the Court introduced the theme of promoting individualized sentencing. North Carolina's post-*Furman* statute imposed a mandatory death sentence on all defendants convicted of the crime of first-degree murder. The Court declared that such statutes were unconstitutional because of their "failure to allow the particularized consideration of relevant aspects of the character and record of each convicted defendant before the imposition upon him of a sentence of death."[18] It condemned mandatory capital punishment statutes because they treat "all persons convicted of a designated crime not as uniquely individual human beings, but as members of a faceless, undifferentiated mass to be subjected to the blind infliction of the penalty of death."[19]

As several commentators have noted,[20] the two goals articulated in the 1976 decisions are to some degree in conflict. If the paramount objective is to apply the death penalty even-handedly, then the emphasis should be on providing the sentencing authority with clear objective standards that may be applied the same way in case after case. A defendant who commits two murders and has a bad prior criminal record, for example, might always be sentenced to death; a defendant with no prior record who commits only one murder might always be spared. If the paramount objective is to promote individualized sentencing, however, then providing clear standards to be rigorously applied in case after case is impossible.

The defendant with a bad prior record who has committed two murders (or twelve murders) may not automatically be sentenced to death, for this would treat him as a member of a "faceless, undifferentiated mass to be subjected to the blind infliction" of the death penalty. Indeed, when all the circumstances relating to the crime and offender are taken into account, this murderer may be found to be less deserving of the death penalty than the defendant with a good prior record who has committed only one murder. Thus, the Court's 1976 cases reflected a tension between a desire for even-handed application of the death penalty and a desire for individualized sentencing in capital cases.

Although the Court never explicitly resolved this tension, *Lockett v. Ohio*,[21] decided two years later, seemed to indicate that promoting individualized sentencing was the higher of its two priorities. In *Lockett* the Court invalidated the death sentence of Sandra Lockett, a young black woman who was convicted of capital murder on the basis of her peripheral participation in a pawnshop robbery in which one of her confederates shot and killed the pawnshop operator. Since Lockett had no intention to kill and was not even present inside the pawnshop when the killing occurred, imposing the death penalty in this situation seemed harsh. Moreover, Ohio's death penalty statute compounded the harshness by limiting the number of relevant mitigating circumstances so sharply that Lockett was not even allowed to present her youth and her relatively minor role in the crime as factors to be considered in making the penalty determination.[22]

The Court could have decided the case in Lockett's favor on several relatively narrow grounds.[23] Instead, it issued a broad ruling that not only invalidated Ohio's death penalty statute but fundamentally changed the nature of the sentencing decision in capital cases. The Court held that in all but the rarest kind of capital case,[24] the sentencing authority must "not be precluded from considering, as a mitigating factor, any aspect of a defendant's character or record and any of the circumstances of the offense that the defendant proffers as a basis for a sentence less than death."[25]

The Court added that the sentencing authority must be allowed not only to consider these mitigating factors but also to give them "independent mitigating weight."[26] Thus, under *Lockett*, the commitment to individualized sentencing in capital cases became almost complete. Except, possibly, in the rarest kind of capital case, a capital defendant could never be sentenced to death solely on the basis of the crime committed. No matter how heinous the offense, the sentencing authority could not be prevented from considering any mitigating evidence that related to the crime or the offender and, based on this evidence, rendering its own independent judgment whether the death penalty should be imposed.

With *Lockett* decided, the framework for the modern system of capital punishment was in place. As Steven Gillers has said,[27] the objective of reducing the death penalty's arbitrary application was not eliminated, but it was subordinated to the goal of promoting individualized capital sentencing. *Gregg*'s approval of statutes that narrow the class of capital crimes to those in which one or more aggravating circumstances are present "potentially reduces the number of persons subject to arbitrary action simply by reducing the pool of capital defendants."[28] Once the pool of eligible defendants is narrowed,[29]

> *Lockett* makes an arbitrariness analysis largely inapplicable to the selection stage of capital sentencing. If two defendants who commit similar homicides receive different sentences, it is not because the sentencing process is arbitrary, freakish or discriminatory, but because no two defendants—considering "character, prior record [and] the circumstances of [the] offense"—are the same.[30]

Indeed, *Lockett* is premised on the view that two defendants who committed similar crimes could be differentiated on the basis of a single "relevant mitigating factor." Moreover, the sentencing authority has virtually unlimited discretion to decide whether evidence presented to it should be discounted, weighed only slightly in the balance, or treated as a significant mitigating factor.

Suppose that two defendants are both convicted of killing police officers under precisely similar circumstances. Suppose further that the two defendants are identical in every respect, except that defendant A has a low IQ and defendant B has a high IQ. Under *Lockett,* the sentencer must decide for itself whether *either* the low IQ or the high IQ should be viewed as a mitigating circumstance and, if so, how heavily it should weigh in the death penalty determination. Thus, if the same sentencer condemns defendant A and spares defendant B, or vice versa, under *Lockett* neither result can be condemned as arbitrary. In both cases, the sentencing authority acts within its legitimate authority in deciding that *either* the low IQ or the high IQ should be treated as a mitigating factor and afforded sufficient weight to tip the balance in the capital defendant's favor. Thus, by 1978, the Court seemed to take the position that once the pool of eligible defendants is narrowed, the recognition that each case is unique makes it virtually impossible to monitor the extent to which the death penalty is arbitrarily applied.[31]

Procedural Safeguards

During this same period, the Court began to insist that stringent procedures be employed in capital cases. Between 1976 and 1981, it decided at least nine cases that established new safeguards for capital defendants.[32] These cases may be divided into two distinct but overlapping categories. First, some of the decisions simply extend to the penalty phase certain constitutional protections that previously applied only at the guilt stage. Thus, in *Gardner v. Florida*[33] the Court essentially held that a capital defendant must be afforded an opportunity to confront witnesses who present evidence against him at the penalty stage.[34] In later cases the Court specifically held that both the privilege against self-incrimination[35] and the double jeopardy clause[36] must be applied at the penalty stage. These cases are apparently premised on the view that the analogy between the guilt trial and the penalty trial is close enough to require that at least some of the provisions of the Bill of Rights applied at the guilt stage be applied at the penalty stage as well.

The second group of decisions establishes special sentencing guidelines to be used for the purpose of enhancing "reliability in capital sentencing."[37] Thus, *Lockett* establishes the rule that the jury may properly consider any mitigating evidence in determining whether a death penalty should be imposed. *Godfrey v. Georgia*,[38] decided two years later, establishes a limiting principle on the use of aggravating circumstances. Citing *Furman*, the Court held that an aggravating circumstance may not be so broadly defined that it fails to impose any restraint or direction on the jury's exercise of discretion.[39] On the other hand, *Beck v. Alabama*,[40] decided in the same year as *Godfrey*, concerns restraints that unduly restrict the jury's exercise of discretion. *Beck* invalidates a provision that prohibited the trial judge from instructing the jury deciding guilt or innocence in a capital case on any possible lesser included offenses.[41] The Court's rationale was that removing the lesser offense option increases the "risk of an unwarranted conviction" because it puts pressure on the jury to convict defendant of the capital offense rather than acquitting him altogether.[42]

The first group of decisions is apparently premised on the view that in some respects the penalty trial is closely analogous to the guilt trial; the second group seems to result from the Court's realization that death is different. In each decision in the second group, the Court emphasized that the death penalty determination is different in kind from any other sentencing decision.[43] Because death is different, the Court deemed it appropriate to implement safeguards to make capital sentencing procedures more reliable. These procedural safeguards, then, impose on capital sentencing unique limitations, whose purpose is to make the selection of capital defendants who will be sentenced to death more reliable.

The New System in Operation

In 1982, Jack Greenberg, then director of the NAACP Legal Defense and Educational Fund, described the modern system of capital punishment as "a roller coaster system of capital justice, in which large numbers of people are constantly spilling into and out of death row, but virtually no actual executions take place."[44] The statistics supported his statement. Between 1976 and 1982, 1,240 defendants were added to death row and

841 were removed from it.[45] During the same period, only 6 defendants were executed, only 1 involuntarily.[46]

Perhaps the most remarkable statistic Greenberg mentioned was the rate of reversal in death penalty cases. On December 20, 1980, the death sentences of more than 60 percent of the 1,533 defendants who had been sentenced to death under statutes adopted after the Court's decision in *Furman* had been reversed.[47] As Greenberg said, this figure is "staggeringly high compared to the reversal rate in ordinary criminal cases."[48] In most states, the rate of reversal in noncapital felony cases is unlikely to exceed 1 percent.[49]

The high rate of reversal could be attributed in part to the Court's new decisions. The *Woodson* and *Roberts* cases, for example, together invalidated thirteen state death penalty statutes,[50] thereby sparing the lives of a substantial proportion of the death row population.[51] Other decisions that invalidated state death penalty statutes[52] or procedures that were widely employed in a particular state[53] had a dramatic effect on the death row population there.[54] But, as Greenberg pointed out,[55] many of the reversals came from other sources. In some cases, the Supreme Court or federal courts held that death penalties were invalid because the states were failing to comply with previously established constitutional doctrine.[56] In others, state supreme courts invalidated death penalties on the ground that they violated state constitutions.[57] And, in still others, the *convictions* of those sentenced to death were reversed by state or federal courts on various grounds.[58]

Another noteworthy aspect of the post-*Furman* system was the time it took to determine the validity of a death penalty. If the system as a whole could be an analogized to a roller coaster,[59] some of the individual rides were extremely long. In 1982, Greenberg observed that "[v]irtually all capital sentences and convictions that have been litigated to a conclusion have been reversed."[60] This statement was accurate: with the single exception of the *Spenkellink* case,[61] no capital sentence had been litigated to its conclusion unless it had either been reversed or the defendant had voluntarily chosen to forgo further appeals.[62] In fact, it was somewhat remarkable that John Spenkellink was executed against his will after only five and one-half years on death row.[63]

The long delay between death sentence and execution cannot be attributed entirely to the Court's post-*Furman* capital punishment decisions.[64] During the sixties, the Warren Court decided a series of cases that greatly expanded a criminal defendant's rights to seek collateral relief.[65] As a result, every criminal defendant convicted and sentenced to imprisonment or death has a right to appeal his conviction and sentence in the state courts, to seek collateral relief in the state courts, and, once his state remedies are exhausted, to attack his conviction and sentence by means of a writ of habeas corpus in the federal courts. Moreover, the defendant is not necessarily limited to one shot at each of these proceedings. If, for example, the defendant has already filed and been denied one writ of federal habeas corpus, he may file a second writ if he can show that the grounds alleged in the new writ were not available when the first one was filed.[66]

The Supreme Court cases establishing new rights for capital defendants had some impact in lengthening the litigation process, because they established new claims for defendants to raise and courts to consider. To take a hypothetical example, suppose that a Texas capital defendant was convicted and sentenced to death in 1975 and that the Texas Court of Criminal Appeals affirmed his conviction in 1976. In 1977, he sought but failed to obtain collateral relief in the Texas state courts. In 1978, he filed a petition for writ of habeas corpus in the federal district court. Shortly after that petition was filed, the Supreme Court decided *Lockett v. Ohio*,[67] which called into question the constitutionality of the Texas death penalty statute.[68] The defendant added a claim based on *Lockett* to the federal writ and, in accordance with federal habeas law,[69] the federal court dismissed the petition, requiring the defendant to bring the *Lockett* claim in the state courts so that they could have an opportunity to consider it. Suppose that in 1979 the Texas courts denied the defendant's *Lockett* claim and that in 1980 the defendant again presented that claim along with his other claims to the federal district court. In 1981, while the federal district court was considering his claims, the Supreme Court decided *Estelle v. Smith*,[70] which held that under certain circumstances the introduction of psychiatric testimony at the penalty trial is unconstitutional.[71] Since psychiatric testimony was introduced at the defendant's penalty trial, he added a *Smith* claim to his federal writ, and the case went to the state courts again so that they could consider this claim. In this way, consideration of defendant's claims could easily have stretched out over nine or ten years, even if the litigation process was relatively expeditious. Moreover, if the claims based on *Lockett* and *Smith* were rejected, subsequent Supreme Court decisions, such as *Adams v. Texas*[72] and *Caldwell v. Mississippi*,[73] could bounce the case back into the state courts so that claims based on these decisions could be considered.

It must be said that this scenario would not have been altogether typical. Given the backlog in the state and federal courts, it would be unusual for some of the defendant's claims to be disposed of so rapidly. For example, in most states, it would be almost unheard of for a state supreme court to decide a capital defendant's appeal in less than two years from the time his death sentence was imposed.[74] Moreover, it would be unusual for Supreme Court decisions to precipitate so many new rounds of litigation. In some cases, however, new rounds of litigation could result from other causes, such as newly discovered evidence or an allegation that the capital defendant's trial counsel was ineffective. Furthermore, even if the courts were not required to litigate new issues, litigation in capital cases is likely to be protracted for various reasons, including the backlog in state and federal courts, the delay occasioned by waiting for particular issues to be decided by the Supreme Court, and the complexity of the issues to be decided.

The Rush toward Execution

During the 1982 term, the Court began to demonstrate a new attitude toward capital punishment. The new attitude was suggested in the Court's treatment of certain applications for stays of execution[75] and was evident in the decisions on the merits handed down near the end of the term.[76] But the Court's shifting focus was perhaps most clearly expressed in a statement made by Justice Powell to a group of federal judges.

Before the 1982 term, Justice Powell had been instrumental in creating the modern system of capital punishment. He had been a member of the pivotal plurality that had set the parameters of the modern system in *Gregg, Woodson,* and *Lockett,* and he had voted with the majority in most of the cases establishing special safeguards for capital defendants.[77] In a speech given on May 10, 1983, however, Justice Powell indicated that he was deeply dissatisfied with the capital punishment system that he had helped create. First, in a very unusual discussion of a specific case, he explained why the Supreme Court had permitted the execution of John Louis Evans, a defendant who had sought two stays of execution in the federal courts hours before his execution.[78] In justifying the Court's reversal of a federal district judge's decision to grant Evans a stay, Justice Powell said that "[c]ounsel offered no explanation for the timing" of his application. He then added that "[p]erhaps counsel should not be criticized for taking every advantage of a system that irrationally permits the now familiar abuse of process. The primary fault lies with our permissive system, that both Congress and the Courts tolerate."[79] In still stronger language, Justice Powell went on to say that "[n]o lawyer or judge would suggest a rush to judgment in capital cases. . . . [But] [t]his malfunctioning of our system of justice is unfair to the hundreds of persons confined anxiously on death row. It also disserves the public interest in the implementation of lawful sentences."[80] He concluded by suggesting that either Congress and the courts should find a speedier way to handle death penalty appeals or the states should abolish capital punishment.[81]

The four capital punishment cases decided in 1983 showed that the Court was opting for the first of Justice Powell's alternatives. The decisions clearly evidenced a new attitude toward capital punishment. First, the results in themselves were significant. As Robert Weisberg has pointed out, "[I]n the previous seven years since the Court constitutionally restored the death penalty in *Gregg v. Georgia* . . . in all but one of the fifteen fully argued capital punishment cases decided on the merits it had vacated or reversed the death sentence."[82] In each of the four cases decided at the end of the 1982–83 term, however, the Court upheld the death penalty. Moreover, the tone of the Court's opinions was different. Although the court reiterated its commitment to fair and fair-seeming procedures in capital cases,[83] it now also emphasized that even in capital cases, "not every imperfection in the deliberative process is sufficient . . . to set aside a state court judgment."[84] Most important, the Court placed a bizarre twist on the meaning of its oft-repeated statement that death is different. It indicated that the fact that death is different from other sanctions may cause a capital defendant to lose rights rather than gain additional protections.

Barefoot v. Estelle[85] is the case that best illustrates the Court's shift in attitude. In *Barefoot*[86] the Court decided both a procedural issue and a substantive one. The procedural issue arose after a federal district court had denied a petition for habeas corpus filed by a capital defendant and the Fifth Circuit Court of Appeals had denied the defendant's application for a stay of execution, pending appeal of the district court's judgment. The defendant had filed his notice of appeal in the Fifth Circuit on November 24, 1982. The Texas courts had scheduled his execution for January 25, 1983. The Fifth Circuit received the defendant's application for a stay of execution on January 14, 1983. On January 17, the parties were directed to present briefs and oral arguments to the Fifth Circuit on January 19. The case was heard on January 19, and on January 20, the Fifth Circuit issued an opinion and judgment denying the stay.

Needless to say, this expedited procedure was very unusual. In most federal cases, the parties are allowed several months to brief and argue the issues presented, and unless the issue is clearly frivolous,[87] the circuit court does not render an opinion deciding the case until well after the oral argument. Moreover, the Fifth Circuit's decision in *Barefoot* was remarkable in that by denying the defendant's stay application without ostensibly ruling on the merits of his appeal,[88] the appeals court ruled that the defendant's execution could proceed even though the court with jurisdiction over his case had not yet formally determined whether his death sentence was valid.

Nevertheless, the Supreme Court decided that the Fifth Circuit's only procedural error was the trivial one of failing to state explicitly that it was affirming the judgment of the district court.[89] This formal error was not sufficient to invalidate the Fifth Circuit's judgment.[90] The Court held that appeals courts may properly adopt summary procedures in death penalty cases[91] and that the "practice of deciding the merits of an appeal, when possible, together with the application for a stay, is not inconsistent with our cases."[92] The Court emphasized that capital defendants should not be allowed to use federal habeas corpus as a means "to delay [their] execution[s] indefinitely."[93] And it added that from the government's perspective, death penalty cases are different from other cases in that "unlike a term of years, a death sentence cannot begin to be carried out by the State while substantial legal issues remain outstanding."[94] By placing such emphasis on the states' interest in securing rapid executions, the Court not only permitted but encouraged the federal courts to adopt procedures that would expedite appeals in capital cases and thereby hasten the rush toward execution.

The *Barefoot* case also decided a substantive issue. At the defendant's penalty trial, two government psychiatrists, James Grigson[95] and John Holbrook, testified in response to hypothetical questions that the defendant would probably commit further acts of violence and represent a continuing threat to society. The defendant claimed that this testimony should have been excluded on three grounds. His primary claim was that psychiatrists as a group are not competent to predict a person's future dangerousness. This claim was supported by an amicus brief submitted by the American Psychiatric Association in which it was stated that "the unreliability of psychiatric predictions of long-term future dangerousness is by now an established fact within the profession."[96] The defendant buttressed this claim by arguing that even if psychiatrists are not generally unreliable in predicting future dangerousness, they should not be permitted to testify about a defendant's future dangerousness when they have not personally examined the defendant. Finally, the defendant argued that in the particular circumstances of the *Barefoot* case, the psychiatrists' testimony was too unreliable to be admitted at the penalty trial.

The Court's response to the defendant's primary claim was remarkable. It did not dispute the American Psychiatric Association's view of psychiatric testimony relating to future dangerousness, but it said that even if the APA was correct, it did not matter: "Neither [defendant] nor the Association suggests that psychiatrists are always wrong with respect to future dangerousness, only most of the time."[97] The Court went on to say that even though psychiatric predictions of dangerousness are unreliable, permitting them to be presented to the penalty jury does not violate a capital defendant's constitutional rights because the defendant will be allowed an opportunity to impeach or discredit the psychiatrists and to present an opposing view.[98] One would have thought that the Court's commitment to enhancing reliability in capital sentencing would have led it to at least discuss whether unreliable evidence presented by expert psychiatrists would tend to mislead the sentencing jury. Surprisingly, however, the Court not only neglected to discuss this issue; it failed even to mention its commitment to enhancing reliability in capital sentencing.[99]

Thus, the *Barefoot* case signaled the beginning of a new phase in the modern era of capital punishment. The Court's procedural holding, together with its guidelines permitting the federal courts to adopt special "summary procedures" for "all or . . . selected cases in which a stay of a death sentence has been requested,"[100] created a legal climate in which capital defendants sentenced to death could be hastened toward execution. In addition, the Court's substantive holding indicated at least that its concern for enhancing reliability in capital sentencing was tempered by a recognition that the state should be allowed almost total freedom to decide what governmental evidence may be admitted at the penalty trial. Moreover, as some commentators suggested, the quartet of cases that included *Barefoot* could be read more broadly, perhaps as indicating that the Court was no longer interested in "telling the states how to administer the death penalty phase of capital murder trials"[101] or even as suggesting that the Court was moving toward abandoning its role of monitoring the procedures employed in capital cases.[102]

Capital Punishment in the Mid-Eighties

In the years since Justice Powell made his statement criticizing the modern system of capital punishment, the system has changed. The death row population has increased enormously, because more defendants have been added to death row and fewer have been removed. Figure 1 indicates the direction and magnitude of the change.[103]

Like motorists on a highway clogged by a major traffic jam, defendants traveling the road toward execution now are finding it difficult to exit, because some of the former departure points have been obstructed or eliminated. Those who are mired in this traffic jam cannot confidently predict whether they eventually will be executed or not, however, because the number of defendants who have actually been executed remains small. Since May, 1983, executions have picked up, but they still occur in fits and starts. Thus, in the last six months of 1983, there were four executions; in 1984, twenty-one; in 1985, eighteen; and in the first six months of 1986, eleven.

As the number of executions has increased, the significance of particular executions has decreased, at least in the eyes of the public. As two defenders who specialize in capital cases have said, "We have moved from Norman Mailer epics, to page 8, section B, clippings, to executions which go unreported."[104] Defendants executed in recent times have not commanded the media attention afforded Gary Gilmore, whose story was on the front pages of newspapers and magazines for weeks before his execution, or John Spenkellink, whose execution was reported on the front page of the *New York Times*. One reporter's account of a 1985 execution may speak to the implications of this change:

> Martin's death was cool and efficient, wrapped in ritual and surrounded by bureaucracy. He wasn't killed so much as processed.
>
> I felt less anxiety in watching a man die than I do at watching a flu shot administered. I felt as though I could watch 10 executions in a row while eating a pizza.

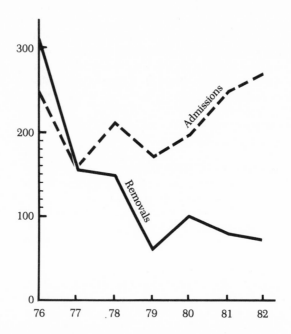

Fig. 1. Death row admissions versus removals, 1976–82.
Reprinted from U.S. DEP'T OF JUSTICE, NATIONAL PRISONER
STATISTICS REPORT, CAPITAL PUNISHMENT 1982, at 4 (1983).

> Somehow, I expected the taking of a life to be something more
> awesome. What I saw seemed to trivialize not only his life, but life
> in general.[105]

As executions become more commonplace, the significance of each condemned person's death may seem increasingly trivial. Ultimately, this
may promote a psychological trivialization of life in general.

Abolitionists had predicted that the resumption of executions would
lead to a public revulsion against the death penalty, but to date there has
been no sign of this. In fact, there are many indications that the public
appetite for capital punishment is increasing. Recent opinion polls show
that a substantial proportion of the population favors the death penalty,[106]
and events at executions indicate that some members of the public are
rabidly in favor of it. For example, at Thomas Barefoot's execution on
November 30, 1984, execution demonstrators "carried a cardboard model
of a hypodermic needle and chanted, 'hit me with your best shot.'"[107]
When Velma Barfield, the first woman to be executed under the modern

system of capital punishment, was electrocuted on November 2, 1984, a group of death penalty supporters "egged on the state" by shouting "'[h]ip, hip, hurrah . . . K-I-L-L . . . burn, bitch, burn.'"[108]

The strong public support for the death penalty has had an impact on the administration of capital punishment. According to defense attorneys, some prosecutors are more reluctant to plea bargain now than they were a few years ago, because they feel that in today's climate failure to seek the death penalty in certain types of cases could have a devastating effect on their political careers.[109] Moreover, at least one lawyer has said that the public support for the death penalty has placed another ironic twist on the Supreme Court's dictum that death is different. David Stebbins, an Ohio public defender, says that the Ohio State Supreme Court will be more receptive to attacks on a criminal defendant's conviction when the defendant has *not* been sentenced to death. The reason is that the Ohio Supreme Court, like other courts, is concerned about the political repercussions of reversing a death penalty.

As a result of this new political climate, in the mid-eighties prisoners are being added to death row faster than at any time since the thirties. Between December, 1980, and May, 1986, the population of death row climbed from 715[110] to 1,714,[111] an increase of almost exactly one thousand. Assuming the death row population continues to grow at the same rate, it might soon be necessary to execute "one person a day . . . [until] well into the 21st century"[112] simply to reduce the current backlog.

But in certain basic respects, the modern system of capital punishment has not changed. Contrary to the predictions of commentators,[113] the Supreme Court has not abandoned its role of regulating the system. The Court has continued to decide a large number of cases relating to the administration of the death penalty, and some of these cases have resulted in decisions expanding capital defendants' rights. In 1985, for example, *Ake v. Oklahoma*[114] held that an indigent capital defendant is entitled to the assistance of a psychiatrist in presenting an insanity defense, and *Caldwell v. Mississippi*[115] placed an important limitation on prosecutors' closing arguments at penalty trials.[116] In 1986, *Skipper v. South Carolina*[117] significantly expanded a capital defendant's right to present mitigating evidence at the penalty trial,[118] and *Ford v. Wainwright*[119] held that the states must establish procedures that will prevent the death penalty from being inflicted on condemned prisoners who are insane.

In comparison to earlier cases like *Lockett v. Ohio*[120] and *Estelle v. Smith*,[121] these decisions have not dramatically affected the administration of the death penalty. Nevertheless, they and other decisions[122] indicate that at least in certain contexts the Supreme Court retains its commitment to making capital sentencing more reliable. Moreover, the Court has not overruled or modified any of its post-*Gregg* decisions relating to capital punishment. The Court may be engaged in fine tuning our present system rather than reshaping it, but it has not ended its involvement in monitoring the administration of the death penalty.

The Court's continued involvement has had a considerable impact on the operation of the system. When the Court is considering a significant issue, for example, there will likely be a stay of execution in every capital case in which that issue is present. Even if the Court decides the issue adversely to the defendant, its consideration of the issue may delay a substantial number of executions for a substantial period of time.[123]

Although the legal framework of our capital punishment system remains the same, the death row population has increased significantly while the number of executions has increased moderately.[124] Why is this so? In his remarks at a recent judicial conference of the Second Circuit,[125] Justice Marshall suggested that the answer may lie in the Court's decisions restricting defendants' rights to collateral review rather than in those defining defendants' substantive rights.[126] In particular, Justice Marshall observed that in all criminal cases the Court has limited the availability of collateral review by "expanding the 'presumption of correctness' afforded state court findings, and by imposing rigid doctrines of procedural default that often turn on technical pleading rules at the expense of fundamental fairness."[127]

The Court's procedural default decisions may be especially significant. At trial, many capital defendants are represented by attorneys who are not well versed in the mechanics of capital trials or the rights of capital defendants. During the state court proceedings, they may fail to present or properly preserve federal constitutional claims that would be available to their clients. If the defendant is sentenced to death, at some later point he may be represented by an attorney more conversant with constitutional doctrine. This attorney will typically seek to attack the defendant's death penalty on the basis of claims not properly raised before. He will find, however, that two lines of decisions combine to present a significant obstacle.

First, the Court has held that a criminal defendant's failure to present or preserve federal constitutional claims in the state courts will ordinarily bar him from raising those claims in the federal courts unless he can show that they were not presented or preserved because of his attorney's ineffectiveness.[128] Second, in a significant 1984 decision,[129] the Court went further and indicated that even in capital cases, establishing ineffectiveness will be difficult because "[j]udicial scrutiny of counsel's performance must be highly deferential."[130] It held that a defense attorney's failure to present a possibly meritorious claim does not constitute ineffective assistance unless the omission was "outside the wide range of professionally competent assistance."[131] As Justice Marshall has said, the combined effect of these two lines of decision causes "many capital defendants [to] find that errors by their lawyers preclude presentation of substantial constitutional claims, but that such errors—with the resulting forfeitures of rights—are not sufficient in themselves to constitute ineffective assistance."[132]

The *Smith* Case

Justice Marshall might have added that some capital defendants have actually been executed after a procedural default precluded them from raising clearly meritorious constitutional claims. Perhaps the most dramatic example involves John Eldon Smith, who was executed in Georgia on December 15, 1983. Smith, along with his wife, Rebecca Machetti, was charged with blasting two people to death with a shotgun. Smith and Machetti were both tried in Bibb County, Georgia, Smith's trial commencing on January 27, 1975, and his wife's a few weeks later. Both were convicted of first-degree murder and sentenced to death.[133]

On January 21, 1975, just six days before the beginning of Smith's trial, the Supreme Court decided in *Taylor v. Louisiana*[134] that a conviction rendered by a jury selected by a system that leads to the underrepresentation of women is unconstitutional.[135] *Taylor* was potentially applicable to the cases of Smith and Machetti because at the time of their trials the Bibb County selection system allowed women but not men to opt out of jury service simply by requesting an exemption.[136] Neither Smith nor Machetti challenged the Bibb County jury selection system at or before trial, however. Smith's lawyer testified that the reason for his failure to raise the claim was that he was unaware of the *Taylor* decision at the time that Smith's trial began.[137]

Both Smith and Machetti sought collateral relief in the state courts. Both asserted the claim that women were underrepresented on the juries that convicted them.[138] In Machetti's case, the Georgia courts considered this claim on the merits and rejected it. When Machetti presented this same claim in her petition for federal habeas corpus, the federal court also considered her claim on the merits[139] but found it was valid.[140] Machetti was given a new trial. At the second trial, she received a sentence of life imprisonment.

Smith presented his claim that women were underrepresented on his jury after his wife had already obtained relief. In his case, the state courts held that Smith's failure to present this claim at or before trial, as required by Georgia law, precluded him from having it considered in a subsequent state proceeding. When Smith presented the same claim to the federal court, it held that his failure to raise the claim at the appropriate time in the state courts also precluded him from having it considered in the federal courts. Thus, Smith was executed despite the fact that before his execution it had been definitively determined that the jury that convicted him had been unconstitutionally selected. In fact, the same court that held that the jury selection system used at the time of Smith's trial was unconstitutional also held that Smith must be executed because he failed to raise this claim at the appropriate time.[141] Perhaps familiarity with the system of capital punishment developed in the post-*Barefoot* era led the majority to accept this result with equanimity. But, as the dissent suggested,[142] when measured against the fairness to capital defendants promised in the line of Supreme Court cases beginning with *Furman* and *Gregg,* the result in Smith's case seems anomalous.

Results in cases like *Smith* suggest that there is now more than one system of capital punishment. For some defendants, the safeguards established by the Supreme Court in its decisions since *Gregg v. Georgia*[143] provide substantial protection. At the capital trial, attorneys conversant with Supreme Court doctrine may be able to use the defendant's constitutional rights to avoid a death sentence.[144] Moreover, even if a death sentence is imposed, a capital defendant represented at trial by a knowledgeable and effective attorney will have a substantial possibility of having his death sentence reversed at some later point in the proceedings. On the other hand, capital defendants represented by attorneys who are not familiar with the modern system of capital punishment have substantially less chance of avoiding a death sentence at trial or successfully challenging it later on.

Moreover, as the *Smith* case demonstrates, other elements of chance are also involved. Defense counsel say that their chances of having a constitutional claim accepted or seriously considered by a state or federal court often depends on factors that have little to do with either the merits of the claim or whether it was raised at the appropriate time. For example, one of the most important considerations seems to be the pace of deliberation. If the federal courts consider the issues in a capital case in a summary procedure of the type approved in *Barefoot,* the capital defendant's constitutional claims are unlikely to prevail. On the other hand, the same constitutional claims will have a much better chance of success if they are considered in a context in which the parties are allowed an adequate opportunity to prepare and present their arguments and the court provides itself with an adequate opportunity to consider and decide them.

Conclusion

With its decisions in 1976, the Supreme Court created a system of capital punishment that was intended to operate more fairly and less arbitrarily than the old system of capital punishment. More than ten years later, it still may be somewhat early to evaluate the extent to which the Court has achieved its objective. During the first five years of the post-*Gregg* system, only one person was involuntarily executed; during the next five years, more people were executed, but only sporadically, at the rate of about ten per year. During these same ten years, however, the population on death row increased to the point where there are now more than seventeen hundred people awaiting execution. Until some substantial proportion of these cases is finally resolved, no definitive judgment on our system of capital punishment is possible.

Nevertheless, some things seem clear. First, in the space of ten years, the Supreme Court has changed its approach in some respects. Although the 1976 death penalty decisions emphasized the importance of applying the death penalty even-handedly, the Court's later cases attached less significance to that objective and more to the goal of promoting individualized sentencing in capital cases. Moreover, the Court's early cases articulated a strong commitment to maintaining fair and fair-seeming procedures in capital cases, but later cases often seemed more concerned with providing procedures that would speed the capital defendant's journey toward execution.

But it would be an oversimplification to suggest that the Court is simply adopting a more permissive attitude toward the use of capital punishment. Rather, its view of capital punishment is deeply ambivalent. Indeed, decisions decided no more than a year apart often seem to manifest totally different priorities. For example, in 1985, the Court decided both *Caldwell v. Mississippi*[145] and *Wainwright v. Witt*.[146] In *Caldwell*, it ruled in a capital defendant's favor and repeatedly emphasized the "heightened need for reliability" in capital sentencing.[147] In *Witt*, it decided against a capital defendant[148] and never articulated any concern for imposing special safeguards in capital cases. These differences may be attributed in part to divisions within the Court,[149] but even individual justices seem sometimes to fluctuate in their approach to dealing with death penalty issues. In 1982, for example, Justice O'Connor articulated one of the strongest statements made by any justice in support of a proposition that capital defendants should be afforded a process that will minimize the possibility of error in capital sentencing.[150] Yet in 1983 she joined in Justice White's opinion holding that the United States Court of Appeals may process capital defendants' appeals through procedures that allow little time for consideration of even nonfrivolous constitutional issues.[151]

The Court's ambivalence may be accounted for by the fact that it is genuinely torn by issues relating to capital punishment. Most of the justices continue to be concerned with providing fair procedures in capital cases, but their concern is tempered by their increasing awareness of the strong public support for capital punishment. Moreover, individual justices who suffer excruciating agony when deciding whether a particular defendant's execution should be temporarily postponed feel increasing frustration with a capital punishment system that allows some executions to be postponed almost indefinitely.

The system of capital punishment is at a crossroads. Justice Blackmun's May 13, 1986, statement suggests that the Court would like to escape from the anguish of deciding whether particular defendants will be executed. In fact, however, the Court's responsibility for dealing with this kind of issue seems likely to increase. In the near future, it will play an important part in deciding the fate of the more than seventeen hundred prisoners on death row. Beyond that, the Court seems committed to continuing its effort to regulate our system of capital punishment. Thus, it will continue to be involved in deciding which defendants will be selected for execution, how many will be selected, and under what circumstances the selection will take place.

NOTES

1. N.Y. Times, May 13, 1986, § A at 10.
2. *Id.*
3. *See, e.g.,* M. MELTSNER, CRUEL AND UNUSUAL: THE SUPREME COURT AND CAPITAL PUNISHMENT 62 (1973) [hereinafter cited as MELTSNER].
4. Before 1968, the only issues relating to capital punishment considered by the Court concerned the means by which the death penalty may be administered after a valid death sentence has been imposed. *See* Francis v. Resweber, 329 U.S. 459 (1947) (second electrocution, conducted after first had failed to kill defendant, held not in violation of Eighth Amendment cruel and unusual punishment clause); Andres v. United States, 333 U.S. 740 (1948) (hanging held permissible form of execution); Wilkenson v. Utah, 99 U.S. 130 (1878) (shooting held permissible form of execution).
5. During this period, executions were held in abeyance pending the Court's decisions in several cases challenging first the constitutionality of procedures employed in capital cases and, later, the constitutionality of the death penalty itself. *See generally* MELTSNER, *supra* note 3, at 214–46.
6. 408 U.S. 238 (1972).
7. 428 U.S. 153 (1976).
8. *See* 408 U.S. at 291 (concurring

opinion of Brennan, J.) (observing that during the period 1961–70 an average of 106 defendants per year were sentenced to death).
9. During the years 1950 to 1967, an average of 53 persons per year were executed. The yearly execution figures were as follows:

1950	82	1959	49
1951	105	1960	56
1952	83	1961	42
1953	62	1962	47
1954	81	1963	21
1955	76	1964	15
1956	65	1965	7
1957	65	1966	1
1958	49	1967	2

See U.S. DEP'T OF JUSTICE, NATIONAL PRISONER STATISTICS REPORT, CAPITAL PUNISHMENT 1930–70, at 8 (1971).
10. 408 U.S. 238 (1972).
11. For an excellent in-depth discussion of the *Furman* holding, *see* Weisberg, *Deregulating Death,* 1983 SUP. CT. REV. 305, 314–17 [hereinafter cited as Weisberg].
12. 428 U.S. 153 (1976).
13. *See generally* Weisberg, *supra* note 11, at 318–22.
14. 428 U.S. at 198 (plurality opinion of Stewart, J., Powell, J., and Stevens, J.).
15. *Id.* at 195.
16. *Id.* at 192.
17. 428 U.S. 280 (1976).
18. *Id.* at 303 (plurality opinion of Stewart, J., Powell, J., and Stevens, J.).
19. *Id.* at 304 (plurality opinion of

Stewart, J., Powell, J., and Stevens, J.).

20. *See, e.g.,* Weisberg, *supra* note 11, at 325–28; Liebman & Shepard, *Guiding Capital Sentencing Discretion Beyond the "Boiler Plate": Mental Disorder as a Mitigating Factor,* 66 GEO. L.J. 757 (1978).

21. 438 U.S. 586 (1978).

22. Ohio's statute provided that upon a finding that a defendant was guilty of aggravated murder (*i.e.,* murder and one of the statutorily specified aggravating circumstances) the sentencer was required to impose the death penalty unless it found by a preponderance of the evidence that one of the three following mitigating circumstances was present:
    1. The victim of the offense induced or facilitated it.
    2. It is unlikely that the offense would have been committed, but for the fact that the offender was under duress, coercion, or strong provocation.
    3. The offense was primarily the product of the offender's psychosis or mental deficiency, though such condition is insufficient to establish the defense of insanity. *Id.* at 612–13 (plurality opinion of Burger, C.J.).

23. For example, the Court could have decided that the defendant should have been allowed to attempt to persuade the sentencer that her relatively minor role in the crime was a mitigating factor calling for a sentence less than death. *See id.* at 614–17 (Blackmun, J., concurring). Alternatively, it could have decided that imposing the death penalty on the facts presented in *Lockett* was cruel and unusual punishment, because the penalty was disproportionate to the offense.

See id. at 624 (White, J., concurring).

24. In a footnote, the Court indicated that mandatory capital punishment might be permissible "when a prisoner—or escapee—under a life sentence is found guilty of murder." *Id.* at 604 n.11.

25. *Id.* at 604.

26. *Id.* at 607.

27. *See* Gillers, *Deciding Who Dies,* 129 U. PA. L. REV. 1, 26–31 (1980) [hereinafter cited as Gillers].

28. Gillers, *supra* note 27, at 27.

29. In many jurisdictions, the narrowing process is virtually insignificant, because taken as a whole, the statutory aggravating circumstances are so expansive that at least one of them could be found in almost any traditional first-degree murder case. *See, e.g.,* W. WHITE, LIFE IN THE BALANCE 30–31 (1984).

30. Gillers, *supra* note 27, at 29–30.

31. The Court's decision in *Furman* did seem to indicate, however, that some effort would be made to monitor the extent to which the death penalty is discriminatorily applied. For further discussion of this issue, see chap. 6.

32. For an account of the first seven of these decisions, see Gillers, *supra* note 27, at 121–24. *See also* Estelle v. Smith, 451 U.S. 454 (1981) and Bullington v. Missouri, 451 U.S. 430 (1981), discussed *infra* in text at notes 35–36.

33. 430 U.S. 349 (1977).

34. *Id.* at 356. The Court held that the petitioner was denied due process of law when the death sentence was imposed, at least in part, on the basis of information contained in a confidential presentencing report that he had no

opportunity to rebut or explain. The Court emphasized that a state could *not* justify the use of this information on grounds that a full disclosure would be time consuming, that sentencing judges can properly exercise their discretion in weighing secretive information, or that investigators must be allowed to assure their sources of confidentiality so that they can continue to obtain relevant but sensitive material.

35. *See* Estelle v. Smith, 451 U.S. 454 (1981).
36. *See* Bullington v. Missouri, 451 U.S. 430 (1981).
37. Lockett v. Ohio, 438 U.S. at 601.
38. 446 U.S. 420 (1980).
39. *Id.* at 427.
40. 447 U.S. 625 (1980).
41. *See id.* at 628–29. Under the Alabama death penalty statute, the trial judge was prohibited from giving the jury the option of convicting the defendant of a lesser included offense. The jury had the choice of either convicting the defendant of the capital crime, in which case it was required to impose the death penalty, or acquitting him, which would have allowed him to escape all penalties. After conviction, the trial judge was required to hold a hearing on aggravating and mitigating circumstances; after the hearing the judge could refuse to impose the death penalty or affirm its imposition.
42. *Id.* at 637.
43. *See, e.g., id.* at 637. ("[D]eath is a different kind of punishment from any other which may be imposed in this country"); Godfrey v. Georgia, 446 U.S. 420, 427 (1980) (the uniqueness of the penalty of death requires that "the sentencer's discretion be guided by clear and objective

standards, that provide specific and detailed guidance for imposing the death sentence"); Lockett v. Ohio, 438 U.S. 586, 604 (1978) ("[T]he penalty of death is qualitatively different from any other sentence").

44. Greenberg, *Capital Punishment as a System,* 91 YALE L.J. 908, 926 (1982) [hereinafter cited as Greenberg].
45. *See* U.S. DEP'T. OF JUSTICE, NATIONAL PRISONER STATISTICS REPORT, CAPITAL PUNISHMENT 1982, at 4 (1983).
46. For an account of the first seven executions, *see* Streib, *Executions Under the Post-Furman Capital Punishment Statutes: The Halting Progression from "Let's Do It" to "Hey, There Ain't No Point in Pulling So Tight,"* 15 RUT. L. REV. 399 (1984) [hereinafter cited as Streib].
47. Greenberg, *supra* note 44, at 918.
48. *Id.*
49. *See, e.g., id.* at 918 (noting that in California, during the 1979–80 fiscal year, 0.8 percent of all felony convictions were reversed).
50. At the time *Woodson* was decided, there were 109 prisoners on death row in North Carolina alone. *See* DEATH ROW, U.S.A., July 2, 1976, at 4–5 (published by NAACP Legal Defense and Educational Fund, Inc.).
51. *See generally* Richey, *Death Penalty Statutes: A Post–Gregg v. Georgia Survey and Discussion of Eighth Amendment Safeguards,* 16 WASHBURN L.J. 497, 506 (1977).
52. *E.g.,* Lockett v. Ohio, 438 U.S. 586 (1978).
53. *E.g.,* Adams v. Texas, 448 U.S. 38 (1980).
54. The Court's decision in Estelle v. Smith, 451 U.S. 454 (1981), for example, invalidated many of the

then-existing death sentences in Texas. *See generally* Note, 10 Am. J. Crim. L. 73 (1982).

55. Greenberg, *supra* note 44, at 919.
56. *See, e.g.,* Adams v. Texas, 448 U.S. 38 (1980) (Texas jury selection procedure in capital cases was in violation of Witherspoon v. Illinois, 391 U.S. 510 (1968)); Washington v. Watkins, 655 F.2d 1346 (5th Cir. 1981) (process by which state of Mississippi secured death sentence was in violation of *Lockett*).
57. *See, e.g.,* District Attorney for Suffolk Dist. v. Watson, 381 Mass. 648, 411 N.E.2d 1274 (1980) (death penalty is invalid under state constitution).
58. *See, e.g.,* Ashlock v. State, 367 So.2d 560 (Ala. Crim. App. 1978) (trial judge's refusal to give defense-requested instruction on weighing credibility of government witness mandated reversal of conviction); Ochoa v. State, 573 S.W.2d 796 (Tex. Crim. App. 1978) (conviction for capital murder reversed on ground that police obtained defendant's statement in violation of *Miranda*).
59. *See supra* text at note 44.
60. Greenberg, *supra* note 44, at 919.
61. John Spenkellink was executed in Florida on May 25, 1979.
62. *See* Streib, *supra* note 46.
63. Spenkellink was sentenced to death on December 20, 1973, and was executed on May 25, 1979. *See* Spenkellink v. Wainwright, 578 F.2d 582, 586 (1978).
64. There were instances of capital defendants remaining on death row for long periods before 1972. For example, Caryl Chessman languished on California's death row for nearly twelve years before being executed on May 2, 1960. *See* W. Kunstler, Beyond a Reasonable Doubt? The Origi-

nal Trial of Caryl Chessman 292–98 (1961).
65. *See generally* Chism, *In Defense of Modern Federal Habeas Corpus for State Prisoners,* 21 De Paul L. Rev. 682 (1973); Meador, *The Impact of Federal Habeas Corpus on State Trial Procedures,* 54 Va. L. Rev. 286 (1966).
66. *See, e.g.,* Sanders v. United States, 373 U.S. 1 (1963) (second or later petition for habeas corpus will not be barred unless grounds alleged in petition were previously denied on merits or successor petition constituted an "abuse of the writ").
67. 438 U.S. 586 (1978).
68. For a discussion of *Lockett's* possible application to the Texas statute, see Hertz & Weisberg, *In Mitigation of the Penalty of Death: Lockett v. Ohio and the Capital Defendant's Right to Consideration of Mitigating Circumstances,* 69 Calif. L. Rev. 317, 328–41 (1981).
69. *See* Rose v. Lundy, 455 U.S. 509 (1982).
70. 451 U.S. 454 (1981).
71. *Smith* held that the admission of a psychiatrist's testimony at the penalty phase violated defendant's Fifth Amendment privilege, because he was not advised before the pretrial psychiatric examination that he had a right to remain silent and that any statement he made could be used against him at a capital sentencing proceeding.
72. 448 U.S. 38 (1980).
73. 105 S. Ct. 2633 (1985).
74. A random sampling of five California death penalty cases indicates that in every case there was a lapse of at least three years between the imposition of the death sentence and the California Supreme Court's disposition of the

appeal. *See* People v. Frank, 38
Cal. 3d 711, 700 P.2d 415, 214
Cal. Rptr. 801 (1985) (defendant
sentenced to death in 1980, supreme court heard his mandatory
appeal in 1985); People v. Boyd,
38 Cal. 3d 762, 700 P.2d 782,
215 Cal. Rptr. 1 (1985) (defendant sentenced in 1981, appeal
heard in 1985); People v. Harris,
36 Cal. 3d 36, 679 P.2d 433, 201
Cal. Rptr. 782 (1984) (defendant
sentenced in 1981, appeal heard
in 1984); People v. Easely, 34
Cal. 3d 858, 671 P.2d 813, 196
Cal. Rptr. 309 (1983) (defendant
sentenced in 1974, appeal heard
in 1983); People v. Davenport, 41
Cal. 3d 247, 710 P.2d 861, 221
Cal. Rptr. 794 (1985) (defendant
sentenced in 1981, appeal heard
in 1985).
75. *See infra* note 78.
76. *See* Zant v. Stephens, 462 U.S.
862 (1983); Barefoot v. Estelle,
463 U.S. 880 (1983); Barclay v.
Florida, 463 U.S. 939 (1983);
California v. Ramos, 463 U.S. 992
(1983).
77. In fact, before 1982, Bullington v.
Missouri, 451 U.S. 430 (1981),
was the only case establishing a
safeguard for a capital defendant
in which Justice Powell did not
vote with the majority.
78. John L. Evans III was convicted
of murder and sentenced to die
on April 22, 1983. Forty hours
before his scheduled execution he
filed an appeal with the Supreme
Court. Twenty minutes after they
rejected his claim, Evans filed a
new petition with the federal district court and won a temporary
stay of execution. At the request
of the state of Alabama the Supreme Court lifted the stay, permitting Evans to be executed. *See*
N.Y. Times, May 13, 1986, § A at
10.

79. N.Y. Times, May 10, 1983, § A at
10.
80. *Id.*
81. *Id.*
82. Weisberg, *supra* note 11, at 305
n.1.
83. *See, e.g.,* Zant v. Stephens, 462
U.S. 862, 884–85 (1983).
84. *Id.* at 884.
85. 463 U.S. 880 (1983).
86. For an excellent discussion of all
four cases, see Weisberg, *supra*
note 11, at 343–60.
87. In *Barefoot* all parties conceded
that the issue raised by the defendant was not frivolous. *See,
e.g.,* 463 U.S. at 908 (dissenting
opinion of Marshall, J.).
88. The Fifth Circuit did discuss the
constitutional claims raised by the
defendant and indicated that it
believed those claims were without merit. At the beginning of its
opinion, however, the court stated
that the question to be decided in
ruling on the stay application was
"the likelihood of success of [the
defendant's] appeal." Barefoot v.
Estelle, 697 F.2d 593, 595 (5th
Cir. 1983). The Court added that
"[t]here should be a substantial
case on the merits of any serious
legal question involved in the appeal to warrant staying the decision below." *Id.*
89. 463 U.S. at 891 (1983).
90. *Id.* at 891.
91. *Id.* at 894.
92. *Id.*
93. *Id.* at 887.
94. *Id.* at 888.
95. Grigson was no stranger to Texas
penalty trials. In June, 1981,
Time observed that Grigson had
acquired the nickname Dr. Death
after his progovernment testimony
helped persuade Texas penalty
juries to impose the death penalty
in numerous capital cases. *See*
TIME, June 1, 1981, at 64.

96. 463 U.S. at 919 (dissenting opinion of Marshall, J.).

97. *Id.* at 901.

98. *Id.* But, as the dissent pointed out, even in noncapital criminal cases the Court has prohibited the government from admitting certain categories of evidence on the grounds that the evidence is unreliable and prejudicial. *Id.* at 916 (dissenting opinion of Blackmun, J.). In Foster v. California, 394 U.S. 440 (1969), for example, the Court had held that an unreliable identification prompted by suggestive police procedures could not be admitted. Moreover, coerced confessions were initially excluded from evidence because the Court considered them evidence unreliable but at the same time likely to have a highly persuasive effect on the jury. *See, e.g.,* Jackson v. Denno, 378 U.S. 368, 383 (1964) (observing that the "premise underlying the *Stein* opinion [Stein v. New York, 346 U.S. 156 (1953)] [was] that the exclusion of involuntary confessions is constitutionally required solely because of the inherent untrustworthiness of a coerced confession"); *see generally* Y. KAMISAR, POLICE INTERROGATION AND CONFESSIONS: ESSAYS IN LAW AND POLICY 1–25 (1980). These earlier cases obviously had rejected the view that the adversary process will always allow the jury to make an accurate evaluation of evidentiary reliability.

As several commentators have pointed out, there is a particular danger that juries will misgauge the probative value of evidence presented by scientific or medical experts: "The major danger of scientific evidence is its potential to mislead the jury; an aura of scientific infallibility may shroud the evidence and thus lead the jury to accept it without critical scrutiny." 463 U.S. 926 (1983) (dissenting opinion of Blackmun, J.) (quoting Giannelli, *The Admissibility of Novel Scientific Evidence: Frye v. United States, a Half-Century Later,* 80 COLUM. L. REV. 1197, 1237 (1980)). *See also* J. ROBITSCHER, THE POWERS OF PSYCHIATRY 187–88 (1980); Cocozza & Steadman, *Prediction in Psychiatry: An Example of Misplaced Confidence in Experts,* 25 SOC. PROBS. 265, 272–73 (1978).

99. The dissent called the majority to task for this omission, 463 U.S. at 924 (dissenting opinion of Blackmun, J.), but the majority made no response.

100. *Id.* at 894.

101. Weisberg, *supra* note 11, at 305.

102. *See* Gillers, *Proving the Prejudice of Death-Qualified Juries After Adams v. Texas,* 47 U. PITT. L. REV. 219, 253: "The next decade may see capital punishment issues in some measure exiled to the extra-constitutional limbo they inhabited before 1968; hands off must be a rather tempting policy given the increasing death row population, and strong pro-execution sentiment voiced in the legislatures and anticrime campaigns."

103. For further discussion of the rate at which the death row population has increased, see text *infra* at notes 110–12.

104. K. MCNALLY & G. ROBINSON, CLOSE ENOUGH FOR GOVERNMENT WORK: THE "NEW" DEATH PENALTY AND ITS HIDDEN COSTS 14 [hereinafter cited as MCNALLY & ROBINSON].

105. *Eyewitness to an Execution,* New Orleans Times Picayune, Jan. 7, 1985, at A9 (*quoted in* MCNALLY

& ROBINSON, *supra* note 104, at 14).

106. The Gallup Poll reported in February, 1985, that 72 percent of Americans favor the death penalty for murder. This is the highest figure since 1936, and only twenty years ago 45 percent of the public favored the death penalty and 43 percent were opposed. See Silas, *The Death Penalty: The Comeback Picks Up Speed,* 71 A.B.A. J. April, 1985, at 48–51. Moreover, the campaign to unseat Rose Bird, California's first woman chief justice, showed that those who favor the death penalty feel strongly about this issue. Bird was opposed for confirmation because she voted to reverse death sentences in all of the fifty-five death penalty cases to come before her during her nine-year tenure on the court. On November 4, 1986, the death penalty proponents made Bird "the first member of the [California Supreme Court] to be rejected under the 50-year-old confirmation law." TIME, Nov. 17, 1986, at 53.

107. LT (10/30/84) (*quoted in* McNALLY & ROBINSON, *supra* note 104, at 9)

108. Reston, "Invitation to a Poisoning," VANITY FAIR, Feb., 1985, at 82 (*quoted in* McNALLY & ROBINSON, *supra* note 104, at 9).

109. For a discussion of plea bargaining in capital cases, see chap. 2.

110. *See* Greenberg, *supra* note 44, at 917.

111. DEATH Row, U.S.A., May 1, 1986, at 1.

112. McNALLY & ROBINSON, *supra* note 104, at 16; *See also* Streib, *supra* note 46, at 487 (observing that even if the rate of actual executions reaches the all-time high of 1935 [199 executions], if the death sentencing rate continues at about the same pace [approximately two hundred per year], "[t]he result will be the continuation of an irreducible five to ten years backlog of condemned prisoners on death row. If the actual execution rate rises to only fifty per year, which is more likely, then the population on death row will double every decade").

113. *See supra* text at notes 101–2.

114. 105 S. Ct. 1087 (1985).

115. 105 S. Ct. 2633 (1985).

116. For a discussion of *Caldwell,* see chap. 5.

117. 106 S. Ct. 1669 (1986).

118. For a discussion of *Skipper,* see chap. 4.

119. 54 U.S.L.W. 4789 (1986).

120. 438 U.S. 586 (1978).

121. 451 U.S. 454 (1981).

122. *See, e.g.,* Turner v. Murray, 106 S. Ct. 1683 (1986) (capital defendant accused of interracial crime is entitled to have prospective jurors informed of victim's race and questioned on issue of racial bias).

123. For example, the chief reason there were so few executions during the first few months of 1986 was that the Supreme Court was considering Lockhart v. McCree, 106 S. Ct. 1758 (1986), a case that considered the constitutionality of convictions imposed by death-qualified juries. While the decision in *McCree* was pending, stays of execution were in effect for hundreds of defendants who might have been benefited by a favorable decision in *McCree.*

124. *See supra* text at notes 103–12.

125. *See* Marshall, *Remarks on the Death Penalty Made at the Judicial Conference of the Second Circuit,* 86 COLUM. L. REV. 1 (1986)

[hereinafter cited as Marshall].

126. Marshall, *supra* note 125, at 3.

127. *Id.* at 2–3.

128. *See generally* Tague, *Federal Habeas Corpus and Ineffective Representation of Counsel: The Supreme Court Has Work to Do,* 31 STAN. L. REV. 24–25 (1978).

129. Strickland v. Washington, 104 S. Ct. 2052 (1984).

130. *Id.* at 2065.

131. *Id.* at 2066.

132. Marshall, *supra* note 125, at 3.

133. Smith v. Kemp, 715 F.2d 1459 (11th Cir. 1983).

134. 419 U.S. 522 (1975).

135. *Taylor* specifically held that a selection system that provided that a woman should not be selected for jury service unless she had previously filed a written declaration of her desire to be subject to jury service was unconstitutional. But in reaching this result, the Court emphasized that the state or county may not adopt any jury selection system that results in "the systematic exclusion of women." *Id.* at 533. In Duren v. Missouri, 439 U.S. 357 (1979), the Court held that a jury selection system that allowed women to "opt out" of jury service was unconstitutional.

136. 715 F.2d at 1470.

137. Since the *Taylor* decision was decided only six days before the beginning of Smith's trial, it might have been very difficult for Smith's attorney to be aware of it. Most practicing attorneys try to keep abreast of recent Supreme Court decisions by reading *United States Law Week,* a source that reports on Supreme Court decisions as well as other legal developments. But the report of a case in *Law Week* is often not delivered to subscribers until about a week after the case has been decided.

138. Machetti asserted this claim in her first application for state postconviction relief, which was filed in 1978. Smith, on the other hand, first asserted the claim in his second petition for state postconviction relief, which was filed in 1982.

139. Under the Supreme Court's decision in Warden v. Hayden, 387 U.S. 294 (1967), after the state court had considered Machetti's claim on the merits, the federal court was required to do the same.

140. Machetti v. Linahan, 679 F.2d 236 (11th Cir. 1982).

141. *See* 715 F.2d at 1471.

142. *See id.* at 1476 (Hatchett, J., concurring and dissenting).

143. 428 U.S. 153 (1976).

144. For further discussion of how this may come about, see chap. 3.

145. 105 S. Ct. 2633 (1985).

146. 105 S. Ct. 844 (1985).

147. *See, e.g.,* 105 S. Ct. at 2640.

148. Modifying its 1968 decision in Witherspoon v. Illinois, 391 U.S. 510 (1968), the Court held that the proper standard for determining when a prospective juror in a capital case may be excluded for cause because of his views on capital punishment is whether the juror's views would prevent or substantially impair the performance of his duties as a juror in accordance with his instructions and oath. *See* 105 S. Ct. at 847.

149. Two justices, Brennan and Marshall, adhere to the position that capital punishment is cruel and unusual punishment in all situations. Justice Rehnquist invariably and justices White, Burger, and O'Connor generally vote for the government in death

penalty cases. The other justices are the swing votes, changing their votes depending on the particular issue presented.

150. *See* Oklahoma v. Eddings, 455 U.S. 104, 118 (1982) (concurring opinion of O'Connor, J.).

151. *See supra* text at notes 85–94.

CHAPTER 2   **Plea Bargaining and the Death Penalty**

In arguing that the capital punishment statutes enacted after *Furman v. Georgia*[1] were unconstitutional, Anthony Amsterdam told the Court that in practice the new statutes would produce the same random pattern of death penalties that had been found to exist under the pre-*Furman* system. He argued that because the new statutes would necessarily operate in a criminal justice system that is "honeycombed with discretion," the sentencing guidelines contained in the statutes would not fundamentally change the character of the death penalty decision. As under the old system, the responsible decision makers would be free to exercise virtually unlimited discretion in determining which of the eligible capital offenders should be sentenced to death.

Amsterdam emphasized particularly the impact of plea bargaining. In most jurisdictions somewhere between 70 and 90 percent of serious criminal cases end in guilty pleas,[2] many of them as a result of plea bargains. In capital cases, the prosecutor may be even more likely to engage in plea bargaining; and in practice there are few if any checks on his decision whether to offer a plea bargain in any particular capital case. Thus, Amsterdam argued that the prosecutor's exercise of this discretion was one factor that would skew the extent to which the new statutes were even-handedly applied.

In *Gregg v. Georgia*,[3] the argument that the new statutes would not fundamentally alter the nature of the death penalty's application was rejected. Speaking for a plurality of four justices, Justice White specifically addressed the claim relating to the effect of plea bargaining.

> Petitioner also argues that decisions made by the prosecutor—
> either in negotiating a plea to some lesser offense than capital
> murder or in simply declining to charge capital murder—are stan-
> dardless and will inexorably result in the wanton and freakish
> imposition of the penalty condemned by the judgment in *Furman*.
> . . . This is untenable. Absent facts to the contrary, it cannot be
> assumed that prosecutors will be motivated in their charging deci-

31

sion by factors other than the strength of their case and likelihood that the jury would impose the death penalty if it convicts. Unless prosecutors are incompetent in their judgments, the standards by which they decide whether to charge a capital felony will be the same as those by which the jury will decide the questions of guilt and sentence. Thus, defendants will escape the death penalty through prosecutorial charging decisions only because the offense is not sufficiently serious; or the proof is insufficiently strong.[4]

Thus, Justice White concluded that in the absence of evidence to the contrary, it must be assumed that the prosecutor's winnowing of capital cases through the charging (or plea-bargaining) process will mirror the jury's determination of which capital defendants shall be spared.

The Prosecutor's and Defense Attorney's Roles in Plea Bargaining

Justice White's premise, of course, is that in determining whether the death penalty will be charged, prosecutors will be influenced by the same factors as the jury will be in determining whether the death penalty will be imposed. In the context of plea bargaining, however, this premise is very dubious. The vast empirical literature relating to plea bargaining[5] indicates that it operates pursuant to dynamics that are totally different from those that apply in criminal trials. This literature has not focused specifically on plea bargaining with capital defendants. Over the past two years I have conducted numerous interviews with defense counsel who specialize in capital cases. These interviews indicate that the likelihood of a plea bargain in a capital case will be dramatically affected by factors that have nothing to do with the nature of the crime or the strength of the evidence against the defendant.

First, the place where the alleged capital crime is committed appears to be extremely important. Differences in plea-bargaining policies between prosecutors in different states is to be expected, of course, because of the differences in the various state statutes. Defense counsel indicate, however, that there are vast differences between the policies adopted by different prosecutors in the same state. For example, Bruce Ledewitz, a Pennsylvania law professor with wide experience in capital cases, stated that from 1982 to 1984 the policy of the Allegheny County (Pittsburgh) district attorney's office was to allow nearly every capital defendant an opportunity to plead guilty. On the other hand, during the same period, the policy of the Philadelphia district attorney's office was to refuse to bargain in almost every capital case. According to Kentucky public defenders Kevin McNally and Mike Wright, a similar dichotomy exists in the state of

Kentucky. Prosecutors in some counties will routinely offer plea bargains in almost all capital cases; prosecutors in other counties will not.

The policy of offering nearly every capital offender an opportunity to plead is more widespread than one might think. David Stebbins, the death penalty coordinator of the Ohio Public Defender's Office, identified several places in Ohio, including Cuyahoga County (Cleveland), in which the prosecutor routinely allows capital defendants an opportunity to plead to lesser offenses. Bob Ravitz, a statewide public defender in Oklahoma, says that in most parts of Oklahoma prosecutors will allow pleas in nine out of ten capital cases so long as they are assured that the defendants will "not be released on parole any time soon." And David Wymart, the chief trial deputy for Colorado, says that the policy of pleading down capital cases applies throughout the state. Wymart says that since the latest Colorado death penalty statute was enacted in 1979 there have been thousands of capital cases but that he can think of only six in which the defendant was not allowed an opportunity to plead to a lesser offense.

Moreover, in almost every jurisdiction, prosecutors in small counties will be extremely likely to offer a plea bargain in nearly all capital cases. For the most part, this is simply a matter of economics. Given the limited space and personnel available, the small counties are generally very reluctant to invest four weeks or more in the trial of a capital case. For example, Stebbins told of a situation in which a judge in a small county put considerable pressure on the prosecutor to plea bargain a double murder case. According to Stebbins, the judge was simply horrified by the expense that would be involved in the two capital trials. He told the prosecutor that the county was already over its budget and could not afford the additional expense. Eventually, the prosecutor offered the defendant an opportunity to enter pleas in both cases.

The possibility of plea bargaining will also depend on the lawyers involved in the case, both the prosecutor and defense counsel. The prosecutor's attitude toward plea bargaining will be affected not only by his own values and experience[6] but also by his political situation at the time the case arises. Nearly every defense counsel I talked to echoed the view of Bob Ravitz, who said that in predicting the likelihood of a plea bargain offer in a capital case often the most important factor is whether the prosecutor involved is "within two years of an election." Several attorneys went on to say that they would consider the impact of an upcoming election in shaping their plea-bargaining strategy. For example, Dick Winterbottom and Mark Donatelli, public defenders in Sante Fe, New Mexico, said that in one case the prosecutor was facing a primary election so there was no offer of plea bargain. The defenders managed to delay the trial of the case until after the primary, at which time a plea bargain was offered and accepted. Winterbottom and Donatelli said that in other highly charged cases they would move for the recusal of the local prosecutor because a special prosecutor from the state attorney general's office would be less subject to political pressure and therefore more likely to enter into plea negotiations. This tactic too was often successful.

Defense attorneys have other ways of inducing plea offers in capital cases. One widely employed strategy is to file many pretrial motions. Defense counsel say that some prosecutors are lazy and most do not like to spend a lot of time litigating such motions, so that filing them will nearly always facilitate plea bargaining.

According to defense counsel, some types of pretrial motions are likely to be particularly effective. David Wymart said he knows that if he can file a successful motion for change of venue a plea offer will be forthcoming. The reason is that Colorado prosecutors don't like to be placed in a strange setting, away from their homes, and they will go to some lengths to avoid the prospect of temporarily moving to a different county for the trial of a capital case. Wymart and other attorneys also said that any pretrial motion that seems likely to result in major expense for the prosecutor will also facilitate plea bargaining. Thus, a pretrial motion for the appointment of a defense psychiatrist[7] or to obtain mitigating evidence from another country[8] will be particularly likely to be effective.

Adam Stein of North Carolina says that in appropriate cases the best strategy for inducing a plea bargain is to convince the prosecutor that you (the defense counsel) know more about trying a capital case than he does. Bob Ravitz echoes this view, adding that if the prosecutor knows that he is up against an experienced, effective defense counsel, this in itself will make it more likely that he will offer a plea. Other attorneys say that in specific situations more subtle techniques may be appropriate. Dennis Balske, legal director of the Southern Poverty Law Center in Montgomery, Alabama, said that in some cases it is vitally important to contact members of the victim's family in the hope that they may be persuaded to tell the prosecutor that they do not want the death penalty or at least that it is not important to them that the death penalty be imposed. Several defense attorneys mentioned this technique and said that it could have a major impact. In other cases, defense attorneys have tried to use the somewhat analogous technique of establishing contact between the prosecutor and members of the defendant's family. Dick Winterbottom and Mark Donatelli recalled one case in which they purposely arranged to have the defendant's particularly beguiling four-year-old son be in close proximity to the prosecutor during the preliminary stages of a capital case. When the prosecutor learned who the little boy was, he was shocked; shortly after that, he offered the defendant a chance to plead to a noncapital charge.

Of course, it is impossible to mention all the techniques defense counsel will use to facilitate plea bargaining. Much depends on the particular style and personality of defense counsel.[9] All of the most effective attorneys rely on a great deal of preparation, probing to find the weak point in the prosecutor's case. Beyond that, different attorneys use charm, logic, intimidation, and many other techniques to convince the prosecutor that the case should be plea bargained. They will use different approaches depending on their personalities and the particular circumstances presented. Although it may be impossible to specify their techniques in more detail, it is clear that some defense attorneys are remarkably skilled at inducing plea offers. Indeed, some claim that the best of them will be able to induce a plea offer in nearly every capital case, regardless of the circumstances.

These observations show that the prosecutor's decision to plea bargain is certainly not based exclusively on his assessment of the nature of the alleged capital offense or the strength of the government's case. Indeed, the existing literature suggests that these factors are of secondary importance. Prosecutors have offered plea bargains even in cases where the defendant's crime seems especially heinous and the evidence of his guilt is strong.

The Bundy Case

As one example, consider the case of Ted Bundy. Bundy was perhaps the most notorious of the so-called serial murderers.[10] After being pursued by law enforcement officials for several years,[11] he was finally charged with capital crimes committed in Florida, a state that is perhaps more committed than any other to the proposition that capital punishment is a necessary part of our criminal justice system.[12] Bundy was charged in Tallahassee, Florida, with one of what was known as the Chi Omega killings, in which four girls were viciously attacked while they were sleeping in a college sorority house. The assailant beat the girls with a club so severely that blood was spattered on the ceiling of the sorority house, strangled one of them with nylon pantyhose, and bit one of them on the buttocks with such force that it caused extensive injuries to her rectum and vagina. As a result of the attack, two of the girls died.[13] By the time Bundy was charged with the murder of one of them, the state already had a strong case against him, including the testimony of several witnesses who could place him near the scene of the crime, and it had every reason to believe that its case would become significantly stronger.[14] In addition, Florida authorities in Pensacola had charged him with the abduction and murder of a thirteen-year-old girl named Kimberly Leach, another chilling crime[15] that also appeared to be supported by strong evidence.[16] And, finally, based on their pursuit of Bundy over several years, law enforcement officials had obtained compelling evidence that he had perpetrated dozens of other killings in various parts of the country.[17]

But despite all these facts, which would seem to demand that the death penalty be sought, the Florida prosecutors in Tallahassee and Pensacola joined in offering Bundy an opportunity to avoid the death penalty in exchange for pleas of guilty that would include a full confession to the Florida murders.[18]

The Capital Defendant's Role in Plea Bargaining

The next stage of the Bundy case is also illuminating. It identifies another factor that is vital in determining which capital defendants will in fact avoid the death penalty by entering into a plea bargain. Bundy refused the prosecutor's offer. He refused it even after Millard Farmer, a defense attorney widely known for his skill in dealing with capital cases, exercised all of his considerable powers of persuasion to induce him to accept it. Why did Bundy decline the prosecution's plea offer? His own explanation was elicited by two authors who interviewed him extensively:

> Suddenly, it dawned on me that Millard had gotten his foot in the door in some devious way to put me in a position of accepting a plea bargain. I felt like he was conceding that I was guilty. And if you look at the cases he takes, that's essentially what he does, just avoids the death penalty. I didn't consider myself in that category.[19]

Those who are most familiar with Ted Bundy, including his lawyers, have claimed that by the time he refused the plea bargain Bundy was severely mentally disturbed, so much so that he was not competent to stand trial[20] and should not have been held legally responsible for his most recent homicidal acts.[21] These claims cannot be taken as established, because they were never accepted in a court of law. Nevertheless, given the context of the case, including the strength of the evidence against him, Bundy's statement on its face shows a serious lack of judgment. He had already obliquely confessed to the crimes charged.[22] Aside from that, the evidence against him was very strong. Moreover, even if he somehow managed to be acquitted of the capital charges, there was ironclad evidence relating to enough noncapital charges to ensure that he would be sent to prison for life in any event.[23] And Bundy did not seem to be one of those prisoners who feel that the death penalty is preferable to life imprisonment. He unequivocally stated that he was afraid of Florida's electric chair and wanted to avoid it.[24] Thus, he had everything to gain and nothing to lose by accepting the plea bargain. But because of his warped judgment he was unable to see this, and as a result he was sentenced to death.

In this respect, Bundy's case is not atypical. According to defense attorneys, many capital defendants refuse to enter into plea bargains even though it seems clearly in their interest to do so. According to defense attorneys, these cases fit into various categories. Bundy exemplifies the defendant who has serious mental problems. Other defendants, although not seriously disturbed, still lack the judgment to make a rational choice. Several attorneys stated that some capital defendants will be very reluctant to accept a plea offer because they feel it simply does not fit their macho image. By admitting their guilt they feel they are in some sense submitting to authority.

Other capital defendants have a special revulsion against confessing specific aspects of their crime. Robert and Susan Morrow, private attorneys in Harris County, Texas, recounted a particularly sad case that illustrates this point. The defendant was charged with the rape, kidnap, and murder of his niece, a girl in her early teens. Since the facts involved were somewhat grisly, defense attorneys were concerned that the case would result in a death penalty if it went to trial. After considerable effort, they got the prosecutor to dismiss the capital charge and agree to a sentence of life imprisonment in exchange for a plea of guilty to the rape charge. The defendant, however, balked at this because he was ashamed to admit that he had raped his own niece. He said he would be willing to plead guilty to kidnapping, but not to rape. The prosecutor was unwilling to alter the terms of the bargain, and in the end, the defendant went to trial, was convicted, and was sentenced to death.

Subtler types of psychological factors may also be involved. Several attorneys noted that some capital defendants revel in the notoriety that comes with a capital charge. They are reluctant to accept a favorable plea bargain because they know that once the capital charge is gone they will no longer be the center of attention. Kevin McNally added that in some cases the attention the capital defendant is seeking is of a much more personal sort. In order to gain a capital defendant's trust, a defense attorney needs to gain his confidence. Thus, he needs to do more than show that he is a competent attorney who has vigorously prepared the case. He also needs to establish a rapport with the defendant and so must spend a lot of time with him, talking to him and ministering to even his insignificant needs. But the time spent in establishing a rapport may have a double-edged effect. The defendant will trust his attorney and be more likely to be guided by his advice, but at the same time he may be even more reluctant to accept a plea offer because he knows that doing so will cause his attorney to pay less attention to him.

Despite this possibility, McNally and other attorneys emphasize that it is vitally important for a defense attorney to establish rapport.with the capital defendant. Otherwise, the attorney will probably not be in as good a position to defend a capital charge, and he will certainly not be in as good a position to induce the defendant to accept a plea bargain. Even under the best of circumstances, capital defendants who are offered a plea bargain are in a wrenching situation. They have an opportunity to avoid the death sentence, but in its place they will face the near certainty of being sent to prison for a long time, possibly even for the rest of their lives. Moreover, most defendants do not have a realistic view of the criminal justice system. They tend to be overly optimistic, believing that their attorneys can accomplish more than is in fact possible. Thus, even in a good attorney-client relationship the attorney may find it extremely difficult to persuade a capital defendant to accept a favorable plea bargain. If the defendant doesn't trust his attorney to begin with, the attorney's efforts to induce a plea are likely to be ineffective and counterproductive. Thus, the rapport or trust between the capital defendant and his attorney is yet another factor that will affect the likelihood that a particular plea bargain offer will be accepted.

The Lockett Case

If the Bundy case shows that prosecutors will be willing to plea bargain with capital defendants even when the death penalty may seem entirely appropriate, the experience of Sandra Lockett indicates that capital defendants who refuse a plea bargain may be sentenced to death even though in the circumstances the penalty may seem particularly inappropriate.[25] Lockett was prosecuted for murder as a result of her involvement in the killing of a pawnshop owner. According to the state's evidence, Lockett, Al Parker, and two others discussed various ways of obtaining money. Lockett suggested the idea of a robbery and led the group to the pawnshop. There was never any talk about killing anybody. During the holdup, Lockett stayed outside in the car. In the pawnshop, Parker held a gun on the victim, the victim grabbed for it, and the gun accidentally went off, killing the victim. Parker and his companions fled. Parker rejoined Lockett in the car, and the two of them drove away.[26]

Before trial, Lockett was offered an opportunity to plead guilty to voluntary manslaughter and aggravated robbery if she would cooperate with the state.[27] After the government had "prepared its case"[28] (*i.e.*, obtained the testimony of Parker in exchange for a plea bargain), it made Lockett a slightly less generous offer. She would be allowed to avoid any possibility of the death penalty by pleading guilty to aggravated murder. Both of these offers were rejected. Lockett subsequently went to trial, was found guilty of aggravated murder with two specifications, and was sentenced to death.[29]

As Charles Black has said, the Lockett case "spins off many problems."[30] On the most obvious level, it seems anomalous that Lockett should be sentenced to death when her involvement in the killing was so minimal. She did not fire the shot that killed the pawnshop operator, she did not intend that he should die, and she was not even present when he was killed. If the new system of capital punishment is designed to select only the most heinous criminals for execution, it seems ironic that Sandra Lockett was one of those selected.[31]

The irony is heightened when Lockett's death penalty is considered in the context of the plea bargaining that took place in that case. Since Parker was the actual killer of the pawnshop owner, it would seem that if anyone should receive the death penalty it should be him. Yet Parker entered into a plea bargain under which he pled guilty to murder and testified on behalf of the government; in exchange, he received a life sentence. Lockett, on the other hand, went to trial and was sentenced to death.

Since plea bargaining is an accepted part of our criminal justice system, perhaps we must recognize that defendants who go to trial and are convicted will often receive harsher sentences than more culpable defendants who plea bargain. Nevertheless, this aspect of our system seems particularly distasteful when the less culpable defendant who goes to trial receives the death penalty. As Black has said:

> To all practical intents and purposes, this woman is going to be
> killed because she insisted on being tried. Again, it may be inevitable that people who insist on being tried be punished more severely
> than those who do not. I am inclined to think plea bargaining
> cannot and perhaps even should not be eradicated. But is not death
> too great a punishment for refusal to enter into this process?[32]

Of course, all defendants who are executed after refusing plea bargains that would spare their lives are in a sense being "killed because [they] insisted on being tried." For a defendant like Bundy, this policy may seem tolerable because at least he appears to be a particularly heinous offender. Allowing Bundy an opportunity to escape the death penalty might seem like dubious policy; the sentence of death appears unexceptional. For a defendant like Sandra Lockett, however, the inappropriateness of the death penalty highlights the problems with the policy that led to its imposition. By any reasonable standard, the death penalty for a defendant like Lockett appears too severe. The prosecutor presumably could have declined to seek the death penalty even though the defendant declined the two plea bargains, but he chose not to do so. From the government's perspective, the goal of reserving the death penalty for only the most heinous offenders was subordinated to the policy of imposing the maximum penalty on capital defendants who refuse to plea bargain. Thus, the policy of plea bargaining—a policy that is justified primarily on the ground that it conserves judicial resources[33]—apparently has the effect of leading to the imposition of death sentences on defendants who by any objective criteria do not deserve to be executed.

As in Bundy's case, it may be useful to ask why a defendant like

Lockett would decline the plea bargains offered. In Lockett's case, however, the answer seems relatively simple. Presumably, she declined the offers because she or her lawyer thought she could do better at trial. As Black points out,[34] three of the seven judges on the Ohio Supreme Court thought that since Lockett was only in the car when the killing occurred, she could not be guilty of any form of homicide. Lockett and her attorney must have believed that they could convince an Ohio jury or trial judge of this as well. Thus, Lockett's decision not to plead was not irrational but was probably based on a sound assessment of the probabilities of the outcome at trial.

But this merely highlights another irony in the system. Most capital defendants will be offered a plea bargain, but because of the way the criminal justice system operates, the likelihood that a capital defendant will accept one is probably inversely related to her assessment of the chances of obtaining a favorable outcome at trial.[35] A less guilty-seeming defendant like Lockett, for example, is probably less likely to accept a plea bargain than a more guilty-seeming defendant like Parker. A defendant in Parker's position will be aware that the plea bargain offers him as favorable an outcome as he is likely to receive if he goes to trial. A defendant in Lockett's position, on the other hand, may rationally believe that the jury's disposition of her case will likely be more favorable than the plea offered by the prosecutor. Thus, the defendants who rationally believe that they have chances of obtaining a favorable outcome at trial—a group that includes some of the least culpable capital defendants—are more likely to go to trial; as a result, their chances of receiving the death penalty are increased.

Critique

If the view I have presented of plea bargaining in capital cases is accurate, Justice White's assumption concerning its impact on the selection of capital offenders is incorrect. Both the prosecutor's willingness to offer a capital defendant a plea bargain and the defendant's willingness to accept it will be critically affected by factors that do not relate to the nature of the crime charged or to the strength of the government's case. Thus, the Court's conclusion that the death penalty will not be arbitrarily applied is suspect. Since plea bargaining is widely employed in capital cases, its effect on the selection of those sentenced to death will be pervasive, and it will dramatically skew the extent to which the death penalty is evenhandedly applied.

This conclusion suggests serious questions about the constitutionality of our present system of capital punishment. Justice White's opinion upholding the constitutionality of the post-*Furman* capital sentencing schemes was expressly premised on certain assumptions about the way in which prosecutors would behave under those schemes. To show that those assumptions are factually wrong is to call the constitutionality of the schemes into question. As I have already indicated,[36] however, the Court in recent cases has departed so far from the letter and spirit of *Furman* that it cannot realistically be expected to view plea bargaining's skewing of the even-handed administration of the death penalty as a concern of constitutional dimension. Nevertheless, the data I have presented do raise new questions about the fairness of our system of capital punishment.

Moreover, a clear perception of plea bargaining in capital cases highlights some of the problems relating to plea bargaining in general. Two related problems that seem particularly worthy of discussion are, first, plea bargaining's effect on a defense attorney's ability to serve his client and at the same time operate in an ethically proper fashion and, second, plea bargaining's effect on the attorney-client relationship. Both problems arise in any plea-bargaining situation, but they are particularly evident when the stakes are highest, as they are in a capital case.

The conflict between an attorney's ability to serve his client and to behave in an ethically proper fashion arises when he feels certain that it is in his client's interest to accept a plea but the client insists that he does not want to do so. The ABA Standards Relating to the Defense Function state that the ultimate decision on what plea should be entered should be made by the client rather than the attorney.[37] Although this standard does not specify the amount of persuasion that attorneys may exert to induce a plea, most attorneys would agree that once the situation has been fully explained to the defendant and the defendant has indicated that he would prefer to plead not guilty, the proper course for the attorney is to prepare to go to trial.

Most of the defense attorneys I interviewed stated that they would generally follow this rule. Nearly every one also stated, however, that the possibility of the death penalty casts a shadow over the proceedings, making it more difficult for them simply to accept the client's judgment. Moreover, when pressed, most attorneys remember cases in which they were decidedly unwilling to accept the client's judgment. Before allowing a defendant to go to trial and face the prospect of a likely death sentence, they would exert significant pressure to get him to change his mind.

David Wymart of Colorado explained the type of pressure he would exert in particularly vivid terms. He said that in dealing with a defendant who is reluctant to accept a favorable bargain, "[y]ou have got to strip him of all hope." Wymart went on to say that in order to break down capital defendants' powers of resistance, "I will be brutal with them. I will tell them that if their case goes to trial their kids will be famous because there's not the slightest chance of avoiding the death sentence." Wymart added that in acting this way with the defendant he feels a "kind of schizophrenia" because in order to induce a favorable plea offer he will at the same time be telling the prosecutor that if the case goes to trial there isn't the slightest chance that the death penalty will be imposed.

Other attorneys did not describe the pressure they impose on defendants so dramatically, but they said that in some cases they would "lean pretty hard" on the capital defendant and that they would on occasion tell him that if the case went to trial, the death penalty would be "inevitable" and that he would be "foolish not to accept" the prosecutor's plea offer. They also said that in appropriate cases they would bring in the defendant's friends or family members and try to get them to persuade the defendant to accept the prosecutor's plea offer by impressing him with the magnitude of the threat he was facing.

The ethical problem presented is not unique to defense attorneys representing capital defendants. Albert Alschuler's illuminating study of plea bargaining[38] indicates that defense attorneys confront exactly the same dilemma when dealing with defendants who are reluctant to accept favorable plea bargains in noncapital cases.[39] In capital cases, however, the presence of a possible death sentence heightens the usual tensions and creates new ones. In many cases the psychological effect of a possible death penalty may render the defendant less capable of rationally evaluating the alternatives available to him. If this is the case, the problems for an attorney who is seeking to explain the benefits of a favorable plea bargain offer are obviously compounded. In addition, the death penalty may also have a profound effect on the defense counsel's conduct. To a criminal defense attorney perhaps the most devastating experience imaginable is the prospect of having a client executed when you feel that you could have done something more to save his life. Thus, the defense attorney's perception that a capital defendant's life is in his hands may make it more difficult for him to strike a reasonable balance between yielding the defendant a proper degree of decision-making autonomy and taking action that appears to be in the defendant's ultimate best interest.

The tensions created by plea bargaining are also likely to have a deleterious effect on the attorney-client relationship. As I have already noted,[40] when the defense attorney and the capital client do not have much rapport to begin with, the attorney's effort to induce a plea may totally destroy the relationship. The client is likely to experience a sense of betrayal. He may feel that the defense attorney never was concerned with representing his interests or that the attorney is in fact an agent of the government.

But even when the defense attorney has established a good relationship with his capital client, attempting to induce a guilty plea may seriously undermine that relationship. Dick Winterbottom and Mark Donatelli of New Mexico told about one case in which this happened. The defendant was charged with perpetrating some particularly grisly murders during the course of a prison riot. After negotiations, the prosecutor offered the defendant an opportunity to avoid the capital charge in exchange for a plea that would result in a life sentence with parole eligibility in thirty years. Under the circumstances, the defenders thought this was an excellent offer, and they urged their client to accept. The defendant maintained that he was innocent of the charge, but the defenders believed that the prosecution would be able to present a compelling case against him at trial. In their own words, they "leaned on him pretty hard" to accept the plea. They told him that this was the best way to have a chance to come out young enough to still enjoy life. They talked about the bad conditions on death row and about the long-term effects of living there. They said to him, among other things, "[Y]ou aren't rational because of where you're living. Trust us." They also involved his girlfriend in trying to convince him that a guilty plea was the only sensible alternative. They worked long and hard on the defendant and his girlfriend, but the defendant held firm. He had started out liking the defenders but ended up distrustful. He believed that they were trying to elicit his guilty plea so that they could get someone else off. By the time the case went to trial, his antagonistic attitude made it more difficult for Winterbottom and Donatelli to defend him. Nevertheless, from the defendant's point of view, the case had a happy ending. The case went to trial and defendant was convicted and received a life sentence. On appeal, however, the conviction was reversed, and he was eventually allowed to plead guilty to a lesser charge and received a sentence of six years, to be served concurrently with a sentence he was already serving.

Again, Alschuler's study indicates that plea bargaining may also have a deleterious effect on the attorney-client relationship in noncapital cases.[41] But the tensions created by the possible death sentence are likely to compound this effect. Counsel's eagerness to avoid the death penalty may warp his judgment and cause him to use tactics that may seem especially inappropriate to the defendant. Moreover, as the case recounted by Winterbottom and Donatelli illustrates, counsel's obligation to explain the realities of capital punishment—for example, the psychological effect of being incarcerated for years on death row—may create tensions that would not otherwise exist. As the bearer of the bad tidings, he may end up being the target of the defendant's anger and denial.

The ultimate result is that attorneys for capital defendants are often placed in excruciatingly difficult positions. Defending a capital client at trial is a job that requires extraordinary skill and sensitivity under the best of circumstances. In addition to preparing to meet the government's case, the defense attorney needs to establish an especially close rapport with his client so that, if the situation calls for it, he will understand the defendant well enough to be able to present the strongest possible arguments in favor of sparing his life.[42] Given this demanding task, most defense counsel would prefer to focus their energies exclusively on preparing for trial. Under our present system, however, this is not possible: Defense counsel must often also engage in plea bargaining. In doing so, he may not only dissipate some of the energy he would like to focus on preparing for trial; in some cases it may also undermine the rapport he has established with his client, making it more difficult for him to mount a successful argument for life in the event that the case does go to trial.

Possible Solutions

It is much easier to identify the problems of plea bargaining than it is to propose effective solutions. However, two ideas deserve to be mentioned: imposing guidelines on the prosecutor and abolishing plea bargaining in capital cases. Both have serious drawbacks.

Requiring the prosecutor to follow guidelines in deciding which capital cases could be plea bargained would reduce his exercise of discretion. Certain categories of capital cases would be defined as those in which the death penalty *must* be sought. Thus, for example, the prosecutor might be instructed that no plea bargaining would be permitted in situations in which a defendant who had a prior conviction for a serious felony was charged with the capital murder of a police officer. If rigorously applied, the guidelines would tend to reduce the extent to which the death penalty was arbitrarily applied, because the prosecutor and defense counsel would have less freedom to avoid the possibility of a death sentence by plea bargaining.

From a substantive point of view, however, imposing specific plea bargaining guidelines would present serious difficulties. In *McGautha v. California*,[43] Justice Harlan's majority opinion carefully examined the problem of imposing sentencing guidelines in capital cases. He concluded that implementing specific sentencing guidelines would in fact be counterproductive, because "the factors which determine whether the sentence of death is the appropriate penalty in particular cases are too complex to be compressed within the limits of a simple formula."[44] In *Gregg v. Georgia*,[45] the Court questioned some of Justice Harlan's analysis[46] but nevertheless concluded that in capital cases the sentencing authority should be provided with general rather than specific guidelines.[47] Moreover, since *Gregg* the Court has gone even further in insisting that specific guidelines that would narrowly restrict the sentencer's exercise of discretion are constitutionally unnecessary and inappropriate.[48] Thus, under our present system of capital punishment, the statutes do provide guidelines for the sentencing authority, but in accordance with the Court's decisions, the guidelines are not specific. Instead, they are formulated so that in making the death penalty decision the sentencer may properly consider any aggravating or mitigating factor that bears on the character of the offender or the circumstances of the offense. In accordance with

Justice Harlan's analysis, the idea of providing the sentencer with specific guidelines that may be easily applied has been rejected.

If specific sentencing guidelines are inappropriate for the sentencer, they should also be inappropriate for the prosecutor. Justice Harlan's rationale applies equally in both cases. The point of his analysis is that because the factors relevant to capital sentencing are so complex, the cases in which a death sentence should be imposed cannot be separated from the eligible pool of capital cases by any simple formula. If it is futile to use a simple formula to identify the most heinous cases for the sentencer, it is equally futile to do so for the prosecutor.

If detailed guidelines for the prosecutor are inappropriate, the approach of using guidelines to control his exercise of plea-bargaining discretion in capital cases is probably doomed to failure. Imposing very general guidelines on the prosecutor's right to offer a plea bargain would almost certainly be ineffective, because it would not impose any real check on his exercise of discretion. For example, it would be nearly meaningless to tell him not to offer a plea bargain in any case in which the statutorily defined aggravating circumstances clearly outweigh any mitigating circumstances relating to the crime or the offender. Because the judgment involved is so subjective, in any given capital case the prosecutor could legitimately conclude that the statutorily defined aggravating circumstances did not in fact outweigh the relevant mitigating circumstances. The guidelines would not impose an effective check on his exercise of discretion.

A more extreme approach would be to prohibit the prosecutor from plea bargaining in capital cases entirely. Once a capital charge was brought, the prosecutor would not be permitted to offer the defendant any inducement in exchange for a guilty plea, and a capital defendant who chose to plead guilty would not thereby avoid the possibility of a death sentence. If the defendant pled guilty to a noncapital charge, he would still be tried for the capital offense; and if he pled guilty to the capital offense, he would still be subjected to a penalty trial at which the sentencer would determine whether the death penalty should be imposed. If effectively implemented, this approach would solve any problems that stem from plea bargaining in capital cases—if plea bargaining disappeared, the problems associated with it would disappear too.

But there would be difficulties with this approach also. First, if the rule would apply only *after* a capital charge was brought, it would probably have only a minimal effect. The prosecutor plays a major role in deciding whether there will be a capital charge. In some jurisdictions, he makes the decision unilaterally; in others, he has de facto control over what is theoretically the grand jury's charging decision. Thus, to forbid prosecutors from bargaining after a capital charge is filed would simply cause them to bargain before. That might cause some administrative difficulties, but it would not fundamentally alter the nature of plea bargaining in capital cases.

The rule could be broadened so as to apply before as well as after the filing of a capital charge. But that would result in the utterly impracticable consequence that no potential capital charge could be bargained. Even the strongest opponents of plea bargaining have recognized that the practice cannot be totally or partially abolished unless other changes in our criminal justice system are made at the same time.[49] In this particular case, the most obvious point is that abolishing plea bargaining in capital cases would place a severe strain on the limited resources allocated to the trial of criminal cases. David Stebbins's story about the small county judge who insisted that a capital case be plea bargained because the county could not afford to pay for a capital trial illustrates this point. The trial of almost any capital case is very expensive. If the government were forced to try all of the capital cases that are now plea bargained, probably few if any counties would be able to afford it. The strain on ordinary resources such as courtroom space, court personnel, prosecutors, and public defenders would be immense. And this does not even take into account the extraordinary expenses that are often associated with the trial of a capital case, such as providing for special security measures at trial, sequestering the jury, and furnishing indigent capital defendants with expert witnesses.[50] Thus, abolishing plea bargaining in capital cases would not be feasible without the expenditure of significant additional resources. And given the present political climate, it is doubtful that any additional resources are available for this purpose.

Conclusion

Plea bargaining in capital cases will continue to be a powerful factor in determining which of those charged with capital offenses will ultimately be sentenced to death. So long as it is, the resulting impact on our system of capital punishment will be significant. The legal apparatus, including the detailed capital sentencing statutes and the procedural protections provided by the Supreme Court, suggests that our system is committed to a careful selection process under which aggravating and mitigating factors relating to each capital crime will be carefully evaluated and, ultimately, the most heinous capital offenders will be sentenced to death. In theory, the application of the death penalty to these offenders will promote penological goals, by ensuring that the worst offenders receive their just deserts or by providing an example that will deter other offenders. But the experience of defense attorneys suggests that the most heinous capital offenders can often avoid the death penalty by entering a guilty plea. Indeed, an examination of the system as it actually operates suggests that in fact the most important function of the death penalty may be to facilitate prosecutors' efforts to induce guilty pleas. That makes things easier for the prosecutor, but it has deleterious effects on our system of justice. Plea bargaining in capital cases makes it less likely that the death penalty will be applied even-handedly or that imposing it will achieve any of the penological goals it was intended to serve.

NOTES

1. 408 U.S. 236 (1972).
2. *See generally* D. NEWMAN, CONVICTION: THE DETERMINATION OF GUILT OR INNOCENCE WITHOUT TRIAL 3 (1966).
3. 428 U.S. 153 (1976).
4. *Id.* at 224–25.
5. *See, e.g.,* M. HEUMANN, PLEA BARGAINING (1978); D. NEWMAN, CONVICTION: THE DETERMINATION OF GUILT OR INNOCENCE WITHOUT TRIAL; Schulhofer, *Is Plea Bargaining Inevitable?*, 97 HARV. L. REV. 1037 (1984); Alschuler, *The Defense Attorney's Role in Plea Bargaining*, 84 YALE L.J. 1179 (1975); Alschuler, *The Prosecutor's Role in Plea Bargaining*, 86 U. CHI. L. REV. 50 (1968).
6. According to defense attorneys, sometimes less experienced prosecutors will be less inclined to enter into plea negotiations. Apparently this is because they are likely to be more impressed with the heinous nature of capital cases. For example, Robert and Susan Morrow of Harris County, Texas, recalled a young woman prosecutor who for a time viewed felony-murder capital cases (*e.g.,* a burglary case in which the victim was stabbed to death) as too serious to plea bargain, even though they were being routinely plea bargained by other prosecutors in the same county.
7. Pursuant to the Supreme Court's decision in Ake v. Oklahoma, 105

S. Ct. 1087 (1985), an indigent capital defendant who demonstrates that his mental condition is likely to be a significant issue at the guilt or penalty trial is entitled to the appointment of a defense psychiatrist.
8. For example, Wymart told of a case in which the prosecution offered a plea after the defendant filed a motion to bring in witnesses from Mexico who would testify to events relating to the defendant's troubled personal history. Pursuant to Lockett v. Ohio, 438 U.S. 586 (1978), the defendant has a right to present mitigating evidence to the jury. The Court has not yet ruled, however, on the question whether an indigent capital defendant is entitled to funds for the purpose of obtaining mitigating evidence that would otherwise be unavailable.
9. Cf. Skolnick, *Social Control in the Adversary System*, 11 J. CONFLICT RESOLUTION 52, 60–62 (1967) (various approaches adopted by defense attorneys may be attributed in part to fact that some defense attorneys, including most public defenders, will be "cooperative" with prosecutors, while others will not).
10. A serial murderer is loosely defined as one who kills a series of people who are unknown to him at different times and in different places. Bundy, for example, is believed to

have killed at least thirty-six people over an eight-year period in three different states.

11. *See generally* S. MICHAND & H. AYNESWORTH, THE ONLY LIVING WITNESS: A TRUE ACCOUNT OF HOMICIDAL INSANITY (1983) [hereinafter cited as MICHAND & AYNESWORTH]; A. RULE, THE STRANGER BESIDE ME (1981).

12. In proportion to its population, Florida has imposed more death sentences and performed more executions than any other state. As of July 31, 1986, the numbers were 244 death sentences and 16 executions. In addition, Robert Graham, Florida's governor since 1978 (recently elected to the United States Senate) has made numerous public statements in support of the death penalty.

13. *See* MICHAND & AYNESWORTH, *supra* note 11, at 215–23.

14. Eventually the state was able to present compelling physical evidence, including testimony from bite mark experts who testified to their opinion that Bundy inflicted the marks on the victim's buttocks. *See* MICHAND & AYNESWORTH, *supra* note 11, at 209.

15. Kimberly Leach was abducted by a strange man while she was walking toward a school gym in order to retrieve her purse. *Id.* at 232. Fifty-seven days later her severely mutilated body was found hidden in the woods. *Id.* at 247–49.

16. At trial, physical evidence established that Bundy's clothing, the victim's clothing, and the interior of the white van Bundy had been driving probably came into contact. *Id.* at 288.

17. *See id.;* A. RULE, THE STRANGER BESIDE ME (1981).

18. *See* MICHAND & AYNESWORTH, *supra* note 11, at 256.

19. *Id.* at 256.

20. *Id.* at 258.

21. *Id.* at 280.

22. *Id.* at 245–46.

23. *Id.* at 250.

24. *Id.* at 246.

25. For an excellent account and analysis of the *Lockett* case, see Black, *The Death Penalty Now,* 51 TUL. L. REV. 429 (1977) [hereinafter cited as Black].

26. State v. Lockett, 49 Ohio St. 2d 48, 358 N.E.2d 1062 (1976).

27. *Id.* at 52, 358 N.E.2d at 1066.

28. *Id.*

29. *Id.* On appeal, the Ohio Supreme Court affirmed Lockett's conviction and death sentence. *Id.* at 62, 358 N.E.2d at 1075. The United States Supreme Court reversed Lockett's death sentence, however. *See* Lockett v. Ohio, 438 U.S. 586 (1978). For a discussion of the Supreme Court's decision in *Lockett,* see chap. 1.

30. Black, *supra* note 25, at 435.

31. In Enmund v. Florida, 458 U.S. 782 (1982), the Court held that the death penalty imposed on an accomplice to a robbery who neither took life, attempted to take life, nor intended to take life was in violation of the Eighth Amendment. Sandra Lockett appears to fall within the scope of the *Enmund* holding, because it was never determined that she took, attempted to take, or intended the taking of another's life.

32. Black, *supra* note 25, at 435.

33. *See generally* Enker, *Perspectives on Plea Bargaining,* in TASK FORCE REPORT: THE COURTS 108, 112 (1967).

34. Black, *supra* note 25, at 432.

35. Some would dispute this proposition, arguing that the likelihood that a capital defendant will accept a plea bargain will not be related

to the strength of the case against her, because the prosecutor will take into account the strength of the government's case in setting the terms of the plea bargain. Thus, a capital defendant who rationally believes she has a chance of obtaining a favorable outcome at trial will still be as likely as other capital defendants to accept a proffered plea bargain, because the terms of the bargain will reflect the defendant's likelihood of obtaining a favorable outcome.

But this analysis fails to consider the fact that defendants who perceive the chance of a favorable outcome may be more likely to risk the uncertainties of litigation. A capital defendant who believes there is a fair chance of acquittal or conviction for involuntary manslaughter will be loath to accept a plea to voluntary manslaughter. Even though the defendant realizes that the voluntary manslaughter offer accurately discounts the risks of litigation, she would probably prefer to gamble on the possibility of a more favorable result. On the other hand, a rational capital defendant who knows that there is little or no chance of a favorable result will be inclined to accept a plea that will avoid the death penalty even though it results in a sentence of life imprisonment. This defendant will be less likely to feel that acceptance of the plea forecloses an option that should not be foreclosed.

36. *See* chap. 1.
37. *See* ABA Project on Standards for Criminal Justice, Standards Relating to the Defense Function § 3.3 comment at 207–8 (1970).
38. Alschuler interviewed defense attorneys in each of ten large cities, obtaining valuable information relating to plea bargaining practices, *see* Alschuler, *The Prosecutor's Role in Plea Bargaining,* 36 U. Chi. L. Rev. 50 (1968); Alschuler, *The Trial Judge's Role in Plea Bargaining* (pt. 1), 76 Colum. L. Rev. 1059 (1976), as well as the defense attorney's perspective on tactical and ethical problems that arise in the plea bargaining context, *see* Alschuler, *The Defense Attorney's Role in Plea Bargaining,* 84 Yale L.J. 1179 (1975). These interviews were part of a larger study that also examined the role of the prosecutor and trial judge in plea bargaining as well as the feasibility of devising an alternative to a system of justice that relies heavily on plea bargaining. *See* Alschuler, *Implementing the Criminal Defendant's Right to Trial: Alternative to Plea Bargaining,* 50 U. Chi. L. Rev. 931 (1983).
39. *See* Alschuler, *The Defense Attorney's Role in Plea Bargaining,* 84 Yale L.J. 1179, 1306–13 (1975) [hereinafter cited as Alschuler].
40. *See supra* text following note 35.
41. *See* Alschuler, *supra* note 39, at 1311–13.
42. *See generally* Goodpaster, *The Trial for Life: Effective Assistance of Counsel in Death Penalty Cases,* 58 N.Y.U. L. Rev. 299 (1983).
43. 402 U.S. 183 (1971).
44. *Id.* at 205 (quoting from Model Penal Code § 201.6 comment 3 at 71 (Tent. Draft No. 9, 1959).
45. 428 U.S. 153 (1976).
46. *Gregg*'s pivotal plurality opinion interpreted Justice Harlan's opinion as concluding that "standards to guide a capital jury's sentencing deliberations are impossible to for-

mulate." *Id.* at 196 n.47. In rejecting this conclusion, the plurality
expressly relied on the same provisions of the Model Penal Code that
Justice Harlan relied on to establish that *narrow* capital sentencing
standards are inappropriate. Thus,
the Court essentially agreed with
Justice Harlan's conclusion that
specific sentencing guidelines that
will narrowly channel the penalty
jury's discretion are inappropriate
but disagreed with his further conclusion that general guidelines are
also of little benefit.

47. *Id.* at 193–95.

48. *See, e.g.,* Barclay v. Florida, 463
U.S. 939 (1983); Zant v. Stephens,
462 U.S. 862 (1983).

49. *See, e.g.,* Alschuler, *Implementing
the Criminal Defendant's Right to
Trial: Alternatives to Plea Bargaining,* 50 U. CHI. L. REV. 931
(1983).

50. *See, e.g.,* Ake v. Oklahoma, 105 S.
Ct. 1087 (1985) (indigent capital
defendants are entitled to appointment of defense psychiatrist when
their mental state is likely to be
significant issue at guilt or penalty
phase).

CHAPTER 3

The Penalty Trial

The most visible by-product of the modern era of capital punishment is the penalty trial. Before *Furman v. Georgia*,[1] most states provided for unitary capital trials in which the jury adjudicated guilt and punishment in a single proceeding. Since 1976, however, the capital trial has been divided into two parts: first there is a guilt trial in which the jury decides whether the defendant is guilty of a capital offense; if the jury finds the defendant guilty, the case proceeds to the penalty phase, in which the jury (or, in a few states,[2] the judge) determines whether the defendant should be sentenced to life imprisonment or death.

Although the precise issues to be determined in the penalty trial vary from jurisdiction to jurisdiction, under nearly all of the current death penalty statutes "the judge or jury finds and considers certain 'aggravating' and 'mitigating' facts about the defendant's crime or character and then sentences him to either execution or life imprisonment."[3] Another common element of every jurisdiction's penalty trial is that in accordance with the Supreme Court's decision in *Lockett v. Ohio*,[4] the defendant is afforded an almost unlimited opportunity to present mitigating evidence relevant to the circumstances of the crime or the character of the offender. Most jurisdictions also provide that the sentencer should render a verdict of death if but only if the aggravating circumstances outweigh the mitigating circumstances.[5] The jurisdictions vary, however, in the extent to which they provide guidance to the sentencer, some providing only modest direction by referring to some of the aggravating and mitigating circumstances that may properly be considered and others "purporting to control the sentencer's deliberation through a highly complex verbal formula."[6]

From the Supreme Court's perspective, the penalty trial was designed to alleviate two of the major problems that existed in the pre-*Furman* system. Under the old system, the jury that adjudicated the defendant guilty of a capital crime was required to decide immediately whether a sentence of death or life imprisonment should be imposed. They were given no standards to assist them in making this discretionary judgment. The absence of guidelines was viewed as a major reason for the arbitrary and capricious imposition of the death penalty.

The procedure at the penalty trial was intended to remedy the problems stemming from an absence of guidelines. Requiring the sentencer to make its death penalty determination on the basis of a weighing of the aggravating and mitigating circumstances was designed to reduce the pool of those eligible for the death sentence[7] and to inject a greater degree of rationality into the sentencing process.

The second problem with the pre-*Furman* system concerned its failure to provide the jury with information relevant to the sentencing decision. Because the pre-*Furman* trial was focused on the issue of guilt, the parties' opportunity to present evidence relevant to penalty was limited. Evidence offered by the government to establish the defendant's bad character or prior criminal record would generally be excluded as prejudicial, since it would not have a material bearing on the question of guilt. And although the defense might have greater freedom to present mitigating evidence, the fact that the jury would consider this evidence in deciding on guilt would often operate as a constraint. For example, evidence of defendant's troubled childhood or mental and emotional problems might tend to establish that the death penalty should not be imposed, but it would probably also be perceived as incriminating. When confronted with this dilemma,[8] the defense generally chose not to present the mitigating evidence to the jury.

The addition of the penalty trial lessens the restraints imposed on the prosecutor and eliminates the defendant's dilemma. At the penalty phase, the government is free to offer any evidence relevant to a statutorily defined aggravating circumstance, and the defense is permitted to present evidence that is relevant not only to a statutorily defined mitigating circumstance but also to *any* circumstance the defense claims is mitigating.[9] Assuming the parties take advantage of their opportunities, the jury will be provided with a fuller exposure to the circumstances of the offense and the personal characteristics of the offender. In the Court's view, this will lead to the imposition of death sentences that are more accurate, in the sense that they are based on a fuller assessment of relevant information.

The twofold purpose of the penalty trial, then, is to reduce the arbitrary imposition of the death penalty and to promote individualized sentencing in capital cases. Does it achieve those goals? A careful examination of the procedure may provide some answers to that question.

The Penalty Jury's Verdict

On the surface, the penalty trial seems quite analogous to the guilt trial that precedes it. In both, the parties present evidence and argument to the jury in the context of an adversary proceeding. The rules of evidence are applicable, the government is required to establish its case by meeting a certain burden of proof,[10] and the jury is required to render or recommend a verdict by applying substantive standards. Moreover, the Supreme Court has held that many of the procedural safeguards that are constitutionally required at the guilt stage are also applicable at the penalty stage.[11] Thus, the penalty trial seems designed to place the death penalty decision within the framework of our adversary system, to make sure that the advantages that accrue from the adversary fact-finding system at an ordinary trial will also be present at the penalty phase of a capital case.

But the issues to be decided at the guilt and penalty phases are critically different. At the guilt trial, the jury's essential task is to determine objective facts. They must answer specific questions about the defendant's conduct at the time of the alleged crime. Did he kill the victim? If so, did he have the required mental state at that time? Was he acting in self-defense at the time of the killing? Some of these questions may be extremely difficult, but the jury may answer them by making objective determinations about the facts relating to the crime.

The jury's decision at the penalty trial involves some assessment of objective facts, but it also involves something more. The jury is asked to determine whether aggravating and mitigating circumstances are present and then to weigh each set of circumstances against the other. Determining whether aggravating circumstances are present is essentially objective. They must consider, for example, whether the victim was a police officer,[12] whether the murder was committed during a felony,[13] and whether the defendant was previously convicted of a felony.[14] These are questions that may be answered by establishing historical facts.[15]

When it comes to the mitigating circumstances, however, the jury's task is more complex. Statutes generally define mitigating circumstances in a way that requires the jury to make subjective judgments. For example, the jury must decide whether the defendant played a relatively minor role in a crime[16] and whether he was under the influence of extreme mental or emotional disturbance at the time of a killing.[17] These are questions that may not be resolved by simply determining historical facts. *Relatively minor* and *extreme* do not quantify a level of criminal participation or a degree of mental or emotional disturbance. The jury must make value judgments on how little criminal participation is relatively minor and how much mental or emotional disturbance is extreme. Moreover, based on the Supreme Court's decision in *Lockett,* the jury is not limited to dealing with statutorily defined mitigating circumstances.[18] They must also exercise their independent judgment to determine whether other evidence proffered by the defense should be treated as a mitigating circumstance. For example, if the defendant presents convincing testimony that he was severely abused when he was a child, the jury will have to decide whether that is a mitigating circumstance. And finally, most of the statutes provide no guidelines to assist the jury in weighing aggravating circumstances against mitigating circumstances.[19] Thus, in determining whether any particular combination of aggravating circumstances will outweigh any particular combination of mitigating circumstances, the jury is required to make a further value judgment.

In fact, in recent cases the Supreme Court has recognized that aggravating and mitigating circumstances may serve only a minimal function in guiding the jury.[20] Aggravating circumstances do narrow the class of offenders eligible for the death penalty; but once it is determined that a particular offender is eligible for capital punishment, aggravating and mitigating circumstances do not circumscribe the jury's discretion. They only direct it toward some factors to be considered. Essentially, the jury has the same kind of task as it had under the pre-*Furman* statutes. Once it determines that at least one statutorily defined aggravating circumstance is present, it must make a moral judgment about whether the death penalty should be imposed.

The Role of Counsel at the Penalty Trial

The nature of the issue presented at the penalty trial has important implications for defense counsel. The attorney's role in that arena is not so much to litigate facts as to direct a morality play. According to defense attorneys who specialize in capital cases, the best way to be successful at the penalty stage is to present a dramatic psychohistory of the defendant to the jury. Defense counsel must gather together a massive amount of material pertaining to the defendant and present it to the jury in a way that will explain where the defendant has come from and why he has become the man he is now. This dramatic presentation has less to do with establishing specific mitigating circumstances than with presenting the defendant in a way that will provoke the jury's understanding and empathy.[21] As one expert in the field put it, "[I]n capital cases, the prosecutor's approach is typically to hold up the crime and have that alone represent the defendant; at the penalty trial, the defense tries to provide the defendant's actions with a context so that the jury will see and understand him as a human being."[22]

Unfortunately, many attorneys who represent capital defendants do not understand the significance of the penalty trial. The typical defense attorney has had little or no prior experience in dealing with capital cases and does not understand that there is a vast difference between representing a defendant in an ordinary criminal trial and representing a capital defendant in the penalty trial. As a result, many attorneys do not even begin to prepare for the penalty trial until after their clients have been adjudicated guilty of a capital crime—and as David Stebbins has said, "By then, it's too late." Even if the attorney obtains a short continuance from the court, he will never have enough time to gather all the material that needs to be presented at the penalty trial.

Because defense counsel often fail to understand the dynamics of the penalty trial, there has been a surprisingly large number of cases in which defendants have been executed after their attorneys presented little or no mitigating evidence at their penalty trials. Perhaps the best-known case involves John Spenkellink, who in 1979 became the first person in more than a decade to suffer involuntary execution. His crime did not seem particularly heinous. In 1973 Spenkellink, a drifter and ex-convict, picked up a hitchhiker named Joseph Szymankiewicz, another former convict. Szymankiewicz, who was older and tougher, forced Spenkellink to have sexual relations with him. Later, Spenkellink discovered that his traveling companion had stolen his money. They fought, and Spenkellink shot Szymankiewicz to death.

At the penalty phase of Spenkellink's capital trial, evidence could have been introduced that might have not only awakened the jury's sympathy for Spenkellink but also helped them understand why he became involved in criminal activity.[23] Spenkellink's father had been a World War II hero. Later, he suffered from psychological problems, apparently as a result of his experience in the war. Spenkellink admired his father. At the age of eleven, however, he suffered the traumatic experience of finding his father dead on the garage floor, a victim of asphyxiation. After that event, Spenkellink began a career of minor crime. Prison psychiatrists who examined him over the years wrote that his criminal behavior was due in large part to his father's suicide and that he was amenable to treatment. Unfortunately, however, none of this evidence was presented at the penalty trial. The jury had no real opportunity to develop any empathy for Spenkellink. Under these circumstances, their decision to impose the death penalty for a relatively nonheinous capital offense is less inexplicable.

The Spenkellink case is not an isolated phenomenon. From recent times, a number of similar examples could be cited.[24] For example, in 1984 Johnny Taylor was executed in Louisiana after his attorney failed "to adduce any testimony or to make any argument to the jury at the sentencing stage."[25] And in 1986 Daniel Thomas was executed in Florida after his attorney made a strategic choice to present no background information relating to the defendant but rather "to remain consistent in the eyes of the jury by continuing his guilt phase strategy of appealing to the concept of reasonable doubt that Thomas had committed the crimes rather than trying to play on the jury's sympathy."[26]

Experienced capital defense attorneys agree that the problem identified by Thomas's counsel is an important one. A defense attorney does have to consider whether he will appear consistent in the eyes of the jury. For example, if an attorney argues at the guilt phase that her client is innocent and then at the penalty stage has the defendant testify that he committed the offense and is sorry, she is likely to lose credibility with the jury. Defense attorneys who specialize in capital cases emphasize that it is vitally important for defense counsel to adopt an overall strategy that will enable her to retain credibility at the penalty trial if her client is convicted of the capital crime. But attorneys with wide experience in capital cases say that less experienced attorneys often strike the balance in the wrong way, by shaping their strategy at the penalty stage in light of the strategy they adopted at the guilt stage. More experienced attorneys assert that in most capital cases, defense counsel should shape strategy at the guilt trial in light of the strategy that would be most likely to prevail at the penalty stage.

Dennis Balske of Alabama, who has tried dozens of capital cases in various parts of the country, says that the lawyer's primary focus should generally be on the penalty trial, because "in most capital cases the defense just doesn't have any chance of winning at the guilt stage." Balske adds that he does not mean that the defense should concede guilt at the guilt phase. In appropriate cases, counsel can argue that the defendant should be convicted of a lesser included offense rather than the capital offense or that there is reasonable doubt about all the offenses charged. But if the evidence of the defendant's guilt is overwhelming, as it often is, counsel should not vigorously argue that the defendant is innocent. Such arguments are likely to be not only futile but counterproductive, because they may destroy defense counsel's credibility with the jury. Balske says that in many capital cases defense counsel's best strategy will be to take a low-key approach at the guilt trial, suggesting to the jury that the defense is not really contesting many of the facts presented by the prosecutor. If the defendant is found guilty of the capital offense, counsel should assume a more dynamic role at the penalty trial, suggesting that the important phase of the case is about to begin. In this way, she may be able to establish a rapport with the jury and convince them that the penalty trial is in fact the critical stage of the proceedings.

But even attorneys who understand the dynamics of a capital trial may be ill equipped to assume the role demanded of them in that setting. First, even if the attorney understands the importance of presenting the defendant's life story to the jury, she may not be able to unearth all the necessary information. As I have already noted,[27] many capital defendants are hostile and uncommunicative; some have severe mental problems; and some feel so ashamed of their criminal acts that they are reluctant to talk to anyone about their crimes or their background. Some are even uncertain whether they want to avoid the death penalty.[28] Obviously, defense counsel cannot expect a capital defendant to provide her with leads to helpful mitigating evidence during the first interview. In many cases counsel must be both patient and psychologically astute to develop the rapport that will finally elicit that information. But lawyers are not trained as psychologists, and criminal defense attorneys are not noted for their patience. Thus, in some cases defense counsel's failure to present persuasive mitigating evidence at the penalty trial may be attributed directly to her failure to develop a meaningful rapport with the capital defendant.

Even if the lawyer is able to establish some rapport with the defendant, amassing all the necessary information about the defendant's background will take a great deal of legwork. Someone will need to talk to the people who knew the defendant during the various stages of his life—family members, friends, teachers, psychiatrists—and who can trace the path of his life for the jury. Most defense counsel simply do not have the time to find or interview these witnesses. So unless the defense is granted funds for an investigator—and in many states it is not[29]—gathering information for the penalty trial will be problematic.

Moreover, even if the defense is able to compile the information on the defendant's background, how should it be presented to the jury? Simply giving the jury a mass of facts and opinions may confuse them. They need help in interpreting the data and in assessing its relevance. The lawyer must try to condense a great deal of material so that it can be presented as a coherent story that explains the defendant's life—where he came from and how he came to be the person he is. The ability to put someone's life story together requires a talent that is not in the typical criminal defense attorney's repertoire. Some defense attorneys have developed this skill, but most would be able to present the defendant's story more effectively if they had the help of an interpretive psychologist who could assist them in collecting and organizing the material to be presented and in interpreting (or explaining) the material in a way the jury will understand. Again, however, the extent to which funds are available to supply interpretive psychologists for capital defendants varies from state to state.[30]

The Role of the Interpretive Psychologist

The role of the interpretive psychologist can be very significant. Craig Haney, who is a professor of psychology at the University of California at Santa Cruz, is an interpretive psychologist with impressive credentials. He has testified in many penalty trials in California and other states and has analyzed the backgrounds and social histories of more than sixty defendants accused of either multiple killings or extremely heinous capital offenses. Haney says that the interpretive psychologist's primary goal is to establish empathy, understanding, and compassion between the jury and the defendant. When the defendant has been adjudicated guilty of atrocious crimes, this may appear to be a difficult task. But Haney maintains that even in the worst cases empathy can be established if the jury gets a sense that in some important respects the defendant's life is similar to theirs and at the same time comes to understand why the defendant's deviant behavior occurred.

In order to bring the defendant to life before the jury, it is important to show that his life is connected to other lives. Thus, Haney and other experts say that in appropriate cases they sketch scenes that show the fabric of the defendant's life—triumphs and successes as well as failures and obstacles. Defense counsel may introduce pictures of the defendant with his family or with friends at his high school graduation. Similarly, if the defendant is married or has children, the defense will often have the defendant's wife or children testify at the penalty trial. In some cases merely having the defendant's child appear on the witness stand can be enough to evoke the jury's empathy for the defendant. Bob Ravitz, a defense attorney from Oklahoma, recalls one case in which the jury was overcome by emotion after they heard the defendant's small daughter testify that she "loved her Daddy" and that her Daddy "bought her dresses and ice cream." According to Ravitz, after the jury heard the little girl speak, they were psychologically incapable of imposing the death penalty.

But in addition to showing the defendant's connection to other lives, the defense counsel or interpretive psychologist must explain why the defendant is different from other people. The interpretive psychologist will try to identify a central problem or several themes that help explain the defendant's deviance. The problem or themes may be a history of child abuse or any early injury that caused brain damage or simply the defendant's relationship with other members of his family. The psychologist's goal will be to show the ways in which the defendant is himself a victim. He may be different from other people, but the differences are often a result of factors that are beyond his control.

Of course, there is a tension between showing the defendant's connection to other lives and at the same time explaining the source of his problems. If the jury perceives the defendant as essentially deviant and defective, they will not be likely to develop much empathy for him. Thus, the psychologist must try to tread a narrow line between giving the jury a full and accurate picture of the defendant's deviance and illustrating the important ways in which the defendant is not dissimilar from them and is a human being who deserves to live.

The Case of the Trail-side Killer

What follows is an account of a penalty trial in a capital case. It is atypical, and I have chosen to discuss it here for precisely that reason. The typical capital case would probably be tried in a southern state. It would involve a defendant who killed one or two victims and a penalty trial in which counsel was not assisted by an interpretive psychologist and in which only a small amount of mitigating evidence was presented. This case was tried in California, one of the few states that provides capital defendants with funds that enable them to hire both an investigator and an interpretive psychologist. The crimes for which the defendant was accused achieved such notoriety that the perpetrator became known as the trail-side killer. At his trial, David Carpenter was convicted of having killed two persons, and there was testimony that indicated he was also responsible for five other killings. At the penalty trial, Carpenter's defense attorney was assisted by Craig Haney and several other experts. Haney recalls that the case was probably the most demanding of any he has ever participated in.[31] The trial record in Carpenter's case bears Haney out. The defense case at the penalty trial lasted for about two weeks, and the transcript of the complete trial covers more than twenty thousand pages.

At Carpenter's guilt trial, the government attempted to establish the facts that had earned the defendant his nickname. Over a two-year period between 1979 and 1981, women hiking in the parks of northern California were surprised by a slightly built white man in his late forties. Some of the women were raped, then murdered. A jury convicted Carpenter of murdering two women in national parks located in Santa Cruz, California. Evidence was then presented that he was implicated in five other similar crimes in parks located in Marin County, California. Carpenter was on trial for the murders occurring in Santa Cruz, but the prosecution was allowed to introduce evidence of the additional crimes as aggravating circumstances to be considered by the sentencing jury at the penalty phase (even though he had not yet been tried for or convicted of those crimes).

In preparing the defendant's case at the penalty trial, Haney and other members of the defense team interviewed literally hundreds of witnesses. Their goal was to provide a detailed social history of the defendant in the form of a psychobiography that would humanize Carpenter, expose the jury to the formative events of his life, and help them to better understand the causes of his criminal behavior. They were remarkably successful. They found witnesses who could testify to Carpenter's experiences over a period of more than forty years, back to the time when he was a young child. In addition, by examining institutional records and old newspaper clippings, they were able to present documents that corroborated key portions of their witnesses' testimony and shed further light on Carpenter's life.

The social biography that emerged was an extraordinary one. David Carpenter was raised in an extraordinarily abusive family environment. He was beaten so badly as a child that a number of his teachers noticed the bruises that frequently covered his body and reported this fact to the authorities. David was ashamed of the beatings and would avoid changing his clothes for gym class to prevent other students from seeing the marks.

At the age of four or five, Carpenter developed a stutter that would plague him for the rest of his life. It was so severe that it made it difficult for him to communicate. His parents beat him for stuttering. When he was slightly older, the neighborhood children picked on him incessantly, partly because he was an outsider who stuttered and partly because he was physically weak. His father then beat him because he was not able to handle himself physically with the other children.

Carpenter was subjected to emotional abuse as well. His parents set impossible standards for him and rejected and humiliated him when he inevitably failed to meet them. His mother stood over him with a stick, forcing him to practice his musical instruments rather than play with his friends. His needs for affection were rebuffed, and Mrs. Carpenter characterized him as "too clingy," and "constantly under foot, like a dog." Childhood friends remember often seeing him banished to the kitchen, where he ate alone after having violated one of the bizarre and rigid rules that governed the Carpenter dinner table. One of Carpenter's teachers, who had had Carpenter as a student forty-five years before, testified at the penalty trial that she remembered him well. She said that she could never forget him because "[h]is face and eyes have haunted me ever since he sat in my class. He always looked terrified."

When Carpenter was about thirteen or fourteen, he ran away from home. A short time later he was apprehended by the police when he broke into some cabins in Santa Cruz county in order to obtain food. The probation officer assigned to Carpenter's case concluded that the boy was a victim of the most extreme child abuse he had ever witnessed and that he had to be taken away from his parents.

Unfortunately, at that time there were few alternatives for a child who needed to be removed from his family. Eventually, Carpenter was placed in the Napa State Mental Hospital. The conditions at Napa State were horrible. In fact, Haney and his investigator, Margaret Ericson, were able to discover a contemporaneous New York Times exposé on the barbaric conditions of the unit in which Carpenter was confined. According to the investigative journalist who wrote the article, the children in that unit were chained to tables and confined in straitjackets and given no real treatment or meaningful help of any kind. The only therapy provided Carpenter at this institution was known as hydrotherapy. Hydrotherapy involved rushing water over a patient for hours at time. Haney said that even forty years later Carpenter would visibly tremble whenever he talked about his memories of this "treatment." To their credit, however, the staff members at Napa recognized that they were not providing Carpenter with the help he needed. They released him on the condition that he be provided with intensive one-to-one psychotherapy. For some reason, however, the juvenile probation department failed to follow up, and Carpenter never received any such treatment.

At the age of sixteen or seventeen, David Carpenter was sent to the Preston School of Industry, a quasi-military "reform" school. Preston was also known for its abusive practices and for its absence of treatment programs. Students who misbehaved were severely beaten. Haney was able to uncover legislative reports that were critical of the sadistic practices and the lack of psychological services that existed at Preston during the period when Carpenter was confined there.

Carpenter was released from Preston in his late teens. Over the next eight or nine years, he appeared to make a more or less normal adjustment to society. He took a job working as a bursar on a steam freighter. In this very structured, quasi-institutional environment, he appears to have performed very well. In his early twenties he married, had children, and was a good provider for his family.

But when he reached his late twenties things began to break down. His wife objected to his being away at sea so much, so he quit his job as a bursar and took an onshore job with the same company. In order to make more money he also took a second job working extra hours in his father's delivery business. The strain of working and living in normal society brought him closer to the emotional breaking point. Then, in the course of his employment, he had a confrontation with his father and was subjected to a public humiliation. Immediately after this event, he drove away in a truck, and while in a state of great agitation he encountered a woman who was his coworker. He abducted the woman, took her to a wooded area on federal property, and struck her with a hammer, severely injuring her.

After pleading guilty to the federal charges against him, Carpenter was subjected to an extensive presentence investigation. Several psychiatrists examined him, and they all reached the same conclusions. They said that he was suffering from very severe psychological problems, especially with respect to his sexual identity. They also said that, as his prior record indicated, he was not essentially a criminal and should be amenable to treatment. They all recommended that he be sentenced to three to five years and given extensive treatment while incarcerated.

The judge, however, ignored these recommendations. He sentenced Carpenter to fifteen years' imprisonment at McNeil Island. McNeil Island was a maximum security federal institution that did not provide any kind of treatment or therapy for its inmates. During his nine years on McNeil Island, Carpenter saw a therapist only once and then only for a fifteen- to twenty-minute evaluation. That therapist, a psychiatrist, was impressed by the fact that Carpenter had been reading books on psychology in order to cure his own problems while incarcerated. He concluded that Carpenter was motivated to change but had received no treatment that would help him deal with his psychological problems.

Carpenter was released from McNeil Island after nine years of incarceration. He had received none of the treatment that had been unanimously recommended when he was sentenced, and no arrangements were made for him to receive any kind of therapy once released. He was soon able to obtain a job and established a reputation as a reliable worker. Within three or four months, however, he committed a series of rapes, including two in Santa Cruz county. He was arrested in that county and brought before a state court judge. The psychological reports showed the same thing as before. They concluded that Carpenter was a man with severe psychological problems who was amenable to treatment. This time the judge seemed to take the psychiatrists' recommendations seriously. He told Carpenter that he considered him "redeemable" and that he was sending him to an institution with a recommendation that he receive intensive therapy. The judge did in fact write a letter in which he recommended that Carpenter be given therapy, but he forgot to attach it when he wrote to the correction authorities. Carpenter was sent to a maximum security state institution where, again, no treatment facilities were available. Later the judge tried to rectify his mistake, but it took time. After serving three or four years of his sentence without treatment, Carpenter was transferred to Vacaville, an institution where he was able to obtain treatment. During the last two years of his state sentence, when Carpenter was in his mid-to-late forties, he received group therapy for three hours a week. Despite the recommendations of a string of psychiatrists and psychologists, this was the only treatment that Carpenter ever received in nearly twenty years of incarceration. Shortly after he was released from prison in 1979, the trail-side killings began.

At the penalty trial, the defense presented Carpenter's history in great detail. Haney says that Carpenter's life was not presented as merely a series of events, however. Particular periods were focused upon in order to develop certain themes. Haney says that in this case he concentrated particularly on the periods in which Carpenter was institutionalized in federal and state penitentiaries (especially his nine years on McNeil Island), because he wanted to emphasize to the jury that "the specific ways in which society and the criminal justice system had failed this guy." He wanted the jury to see that Carpenter's problems arose in part from the horrendous abuse he was subjected to as a child and that although prescriptions had been given for dealing with these problems the criminal justice system had almost completely failed to act on them.

In addition, the defense presented witnesses who testified to Carpenter's behavior while in prison. The purpose was to show that although Carpenter might by then have been incapable of behaving himself in normal society, he could make a real contribution to society in prison. His prison record was extraordinarily good. In fact, during his many years in institutions, he was not once cited for any type of misbehavior. Moreover, witnesses testified that Carpenter made positive contributions in the prison. He restrained people in arguments, engaged in constructive activities, and served as an advisor and role model to younger inmates. In short, his past conduct in prison indicated that if he were given a life sentence, he would not only pose no threat to society but would make positive contributions to the prison population.

In response to the defense's presentation at the penalty trial, the government, of course, emphasized the fact that Carpenter had been convicted of killing two victims and that evidence had been presented suggesting that he was responsible for five more murders. In his closing argument, the prosecutor placed pictures of the victims in various parts of the courtroom and directed his comments to these pictures as he spoke to the jury about the aggravating circumstances in the case. In addition, he called two expert witnesses to respond to some of the evidence and analysis presented by the defense at the penalty trial.

Thomas Szasz, a well-known psychiatrist who has written books attacking the concept of mental illness,[32] told the jury that in his opinion crime is a "product of evil" and nothing else. Elaborating on this theme, he testified that Carpenter's criminal acts should not be attributed to his background of abuse, to his psychological problems, or to the record of institutional failure; rather, he should be executed for his crimes because "people choose to be bad."

Stanton Samenow, a psychologist with a national reputation,[33] presented similar testimony. Samenow told the jury that criminals are a "breed apart" and in essence are "born evil." Although neither of the doctors had examined Carpenter or heard any of the testimony about his background, the prosecution used them to argue that he was not fit to live.

At the conclusion of the presentation of evidence, the defense asked the judge to specifically instruct the jury that they could use particular aspects of Carpenter's background (such as the fact that he had been subjected to extreme child abuse) as mitigating circumstances. The judge refused; instead, he read to the jury the provisions from the California statute that set forth the factors to be considered by the sentencer in determining penalty. These provisions include factors such as the "age of the defendant at the time of the crime,"[34] whether or not "defendant acted under extreme duress," and whether the defendant was "under the influence of extreme mental or emotional disturbance at the time of the crime." In addition, the final provision adds, as another factor to be considered, "[a]ny other circumstance which extenuates the gravity of the crime even though it is not a legal excuse for the crimes."[35]

The penalty jury deliberated for a full week. Then they returned with a verdict of death. Haney says that the jurors were obviously emotionally torn; some of them were in tears when they delivered their verdict. After the trial, some of the jurors said that they had been very impressed with and affected by the evidence presented by the defense at the penalty trial, but they didn't know what to do with it. One said, "[W]e didn't know if any of the things that happened to the defendant could be mitigating circumstances. We thought that mitigating circumstances had to relate to the crime committed and the testimony about the defendant's background didn't relate to that." So, even though some members of the jury were extremely moved by the social biography that the defense presented, they imposed the death penalty on the defendant, apparently because they believed it was required by the California statute.

Analysis

In retrospect, it does not seem surprising that Carpenter was sentenced to death. After all, he was convicted of having murdered two innocent victims and was implicated in five other similar crimes. But when I asked why this was one of the few cases on which he has worked in which the defendant received the death penalty, Haney emphasized two additional factors. First, he said that the defense's inability to have Carpenter tell the penalty jury that he was sorry for his criminal acts—a problem that arose because Carpenter consistently maintained that he was not involved in the trail-side killings—was damaging because a personal expression of remorse would have made it easier for the jury to see Carpenter as a person, a member of the human community rather than a monster. Second, Haney emphasized that the jury's confusion about the definition of a mitigating circumstance, which was perhaps precipitated by the judge's failure to charge as the defense requested, may have made a critical difference.

If Haney's analysis is correct, the question arises whether the addition of the penalty trial has changed the system's inability to consistently select the most heinous offenders for execution. If the heinousness of the offender is determined solely by the seriousness of the offense, then certainly a person who rapes and murders a number of innocent victims must be viewed as one of our most heinous offenders. Yet, according to Haney, if the penalty trial had gone somewhat differently, Carpenter's jury might have been moved to spare his life in spite of his crimes.

Of course, the Carpenter case could also be evaluated from a different perspective. The basis for the Supreme Court's decision in *Lockett* is that a jury must not judge offender's heinousness merely by considering the circumstances of the crimes committed. As later cases make clear,[36] the jury must also be allowed to consider, as possible mitigating circumstances, any evidence relating to the defendant's background. When the mitigating circumstances in Carpenter's case are considered, then perhaps Carpenter's place on the scale of heinousness drops sharply. In other words, it may be that the death penalty decision in Carpenter's case was a close one only because the background evidence presented by the defense was unusually compelling.

I asked Haney about this possibility. He replied that Carpenter's penalty trial was unusual in that the defendant's life story was so well documented and so carefully presented. He said that the type of background evidence presented was not entirely atypical. Elaborating on this, he said, "[P]eople who commit extraordinary crimes have extraordinary backgrounds and are responding to extraordinary circumstances. Our society does not encourage people to think about crime, especially violent crime, in this way. So capital juries have to be educated about the defendants whose lives they sit in judgment of. But, if you look hard enough, the explanations and the understanding will come."

Haney added that except in California, the defense is generally not able to present this kind of background material because they are not provided with the time or funds that will enable them to collect it. He said that unless someone is able to spend hundreds of hours interviewing witnesses and going through documents, "the defense can do little more than scratch the surface. That is why you see penalty trials in which the defense presents no mitigating evidence or in which only the defendant's mother is called to testify." Haney also said that when the defense is able to present a complete picture of the defendant's background, the jury is often so moved by the evidence that they will be inclined to spare the defendant's life. Whether the jury actually does so, however, may depend on intangible factors, such as how the jury understands the term *mitigating circumstance*.

All this suggests that the addition of the penalty trial has not done much to reduce the extent to which the death penalty is arbitrarily applied. The statutes that require the prosecution to prove at least one aggravating circumstance does result in a marginal reduction of the pool of eligible capital offenders.[37] Beyond that, however, it appears that the selection of capital offenders for execution will depend more on the dynamics of each particular penalty trial than on the exact nature of the aggravating and mitigating circumstances presented. If the defense is able to present a complete picture of the defendant at the penalty trial, then it may be that no amount of aggravating circumstances will be sufficient to guarantee the death penalty. Rather, the question of whether the death penalty will be imposed will depend on intangibles, such as the extent to which the jury feels empathy with the defendant or the precise nature of the trial judge's instructions. On the other hand, when the defense fails to present a complete case at the penalty trial, the death penalty may be imposed even if the defendant's capital crime would not be viewed as particularly heinous by any reasonable standard.[38] Thus, to some extent, the addition of the penalty trial only exacerbates the disadvantaged position of a defendant who for whatever reason is unable to present a full picture of his background to the penalty jury.

The Defendant's Failure to Express Remorse

Both of the factors identified as possibly precipitating a death penalty decision in the Carpenter case are interesting. Haney's statement that Carpenter's failure to express remorse at the penalty stage could have made a difference is consistent with the views expressed by many defense attorneys. For example, Bruce Ledewitz of Pennsylvania said, "If possible, it is always desirable to have the defendant tell the penalty jury he is sorry for the crimes he committed. If the defendant seems sincere, his expression of remorse will often have a telling effect with the jury." Ledewitz added that if the defendant does not express remorse at the penalty hearing, the prosecutor may take advantage of it in his closing argument. In Pennsylvania, at least, it has been held permissible for the prosecutor to comment on the defendant's failure to express remorse at the penalty trial.[39]

Under the pre-*Furman* system, the question of a capital defendant expressing remorse to the jury was not likely to arise. Since the issues of guilt and penalty were generally determined in a single proceeding, a capital defendant who wished to express remorse would be confronted with a particularly difficult dilemma. By expressing remorse for the crime committed, he would perhaps influence the jury favorably on the issue of sentence, but at the same time he would be likely to convict himself of the capital offense. Thus, the addition of the penalty trial has greatly widened the capital defendant's opportunity to express remorse. As a result, whether and how a defendant expresses remorse is now an important factor in determining whether he will receive the death penalty.

This may appear to be a salutary development. Certainly, a defendant should not be placed in a position where he has to incriminate himself if he chooses to express his remorse to the jury. Moreover, it seems perfectly reasonable for the penalty jury to weigh the defendant's expression of remorse in deciding whether they will impose the death penalty. Historically, a guilty person's confession and expression of remorse has been viewed as a necessary first step in the process of rehabilitation.[40] Moreover, unlike a guilty plea entered pursuant to a plea bargain,[41] a capital defendant's expression of remorse at the penalty trial may be evaluated on its own terms. A penalty jury that believes the defendant's expression of remorse is insincere is free to disregard it or even to weigh this evidence of hypocrisy against the defendant. When the penalty jury believes that the defendant is genuinely sorry for what he has done, it seems perfectly appropriate for them to take that into account in deciding whether the death penalty should be imposed.

There is some danger, however, that too much weight will be given to this factor. It may be true that a sincere expression of remorse is a step toward rehabilitation. But when a defendant is led to believe that remorse will gain him something, evaluating his sincerity may be much more difficult. Capital defendants who express remorse at the penalty trial have usually been advised by counsel that this kind of testimony may save them from execution. When an expression of remorse is made under these circumstances, the jury may find it difficult to determine whether the defendant's statement is genuine or is being made to manipulate their feelings.

Moreover, what about the capital defendants who decline to express remorse at the penalty trial? Are they less likely candidates for rehabilitation? In some cases, at least, the reverse may be true. A defendant who wants to be spared execution[42] but nevertheless, despite his attorney's advice,[43] refuses to express remorse for his crime at the penalty trial may be pursuing this unprofitable course of action either because he is ashamed to talk about the crime he committed or because he believes he is not guilty.

Certain types of offenders are quite likely to be too ashamed of their crimes to even admit them, much less express remorse about them. The case in which a defendant refused a favorable plea bargain because he was ashamed to admit that he had raped his niece is a good example. Alschuler's interviews with defense counsel indicate that it is not at all atypical:

> "[M]urderers are often people who have led entirely respectable lives until a single traumatic moment," said Boston Attorney Joseph S. Oteri. "It is the hardest thing in the world for them to admit their guilt." Other attorneys suggested that the blocks to confession erected by sex criminals are even more formidable. In an effort to preserve a favorable image of himself, a defendant might succeed in truly blotting out the moment of his crime.[44]

Many capital defendants, of course, are both murderers and sex criminals. Thus, it is not surprising that some of them are unwilling to express remorse for their crimes at the penalty trial.

Is a defendant who is unwilling to express remorse because of shame likely to be a poor prospect for rehabilitation? Any judgment concerning the likelihood of an offender's rehabilitation is speculative, but it could be argued that the offender's sense of shame is better evidence of genuine remorse than an expression of contrition at the penalty trial. So, if remorse is indeed the first step toward rehabilitation, a defendant's inability to express his remorse should not necessarily be held against him.

Capital defendants who believe they are not guilty fit into more than one category. Some are in fact merely "blotting out the moment of [their] crime[s]." But some may actually be innocent. There are documented cases of innocent defendants who were sentenced to death and/or executed.[45] Some of them, in fact, took place quite recently.[46] If an innocent defendant were convicted of a capital crime and then told that his life might be spared if he testified before the penalty jury and expressed remorse for the crime he committed, he might well respond, "I wish I could do that; but I didn't commit the crime, so I don't know enough about it to make an intelligible expression of remorse."[47]

In summary, the modern penalty trial has significantly enlarged the capital defendant's opportunity to express remorse and has made issues relating to the defendant's expression of remorse far more significant than they were under the pre-*Furman* system. Defense attorneys and other experts believe that an expression of remorse can make a difference in the outcome of a penalty trial. As a result, penalty juries often do have an opportunity to consider a defendant's expression of remorse, and in some cases they may also be exposed to the prosecutor's adverse comment on a defendant's failure to express remorse. Nevertheless, an evaluation of the reasons why capital defendants do or do not express remorse suggests that

the ostensibly simple words "I'm sorry" have paradoxical implications—
and that they may not deserve as much weight as penalty juries seem to be
giving them.

The Meaning of Mitigating Circumstances

Craig Haney's description of the *Carpenter* jury's confusion over the
meaning of a mitigating circumstance highlights another aspect of the
modern penalty trial. From Haney's account, it appears that the jury may
have felt torn between following their gut feelings, which might have lead
them to spare the defendant, and performing the kind of legal arithmetic
that led them to impose the death penalty.

Robert Weisberg's description of what occurs in penalty trials indicates that it may not be unusual for penalty juries to feel that they are
confronted with this type of dilemma. Weisberg shows that at least in
California, prosecutors often premise their closing arguments on the claim
that the jury is *not* required to make a moral decision in deciding whether
the death penalty will be imposed. The prosecutor typically begins her
closing argument by emphasizing that the jury does have guidelines for
determining whether the death penalty should be imposed.[48] Then she
goes through the various circumstances, stressing particularly aggravating ones that are present and mitigating ones that are not.[49] In her conclusion, "[T]he prosecutor reviews the aggravating and mitigating circumstances and literally performs legal arithmetic, adding them up on the
board, and showing that the aggravating outweigh or outnumber the mitigating."[50] Then the prosecutor emphasizes the significance of this result:

> You have a scale in front of you. One is for aggravation and one is
> for mitigation. If the scale tips towards mitigation, then you are
> bound by law to impose the sentence of life without possibility of
> parole. But if on the other hand that scale tips at all towards the
> factors in aggravation outweighing the circumstances in mitigation,
> then you are bound by law to impose the sentence of death in this
> case.[51]

Weisberg shows that the California trial judge's standard instructions
to the penalty jury lend credence to the prosecutor's argument. The judge
instructs the jury "to take account of and be guided by the aggravating
and mitigating circumstances" and that "if it finds the aggravating outweigh the mitigating it must choose a death sentence."[52] Weisberg even
found one California case[53] in which, after hearing these instructions, the
jury asked the judge whether it would be permissible for them to show
mercy and sentence the defendant to life imprisonment even though they
found that the aggravating circumstances outweighed the mitigating

ones. The judge responded by merely repeating the instruction: "[I]f you conclude that the aggravating circumstances outweigh the mitigating circumstances, you should impose a sentence of death."[54]

The dilemma perceived by California penalty juries is in fact a false one. Under the Supreme Court's decisions, a penalty jury must be allowed to decide for itself whether any evidence pertaining to the crime or the character of the offender should be considered a mitigating circumstance. Moreover, a jury can weight a mitigating circumstance in any way it wishes. For example, a jury sympathetic to the defendant because of his troubled family background could properly find that the troubled background constituted a mitigating circumstance and that that one mitigating circumstance outweighed all of the aggravating circumstances established by the prosecution.

Nevertheless, the fact that the penalty jury sometimes perceives a dilemma is itself significant. It shows the paradoxical consequences of the Court's efforts to provide rationality in capital sentencing. Under the new system, the jury receives more guidance, and it has an opportunity to receive much more information about the character of the capital defendant. Ironically, however, these changes have in some respects created a more chaotic system. Under the pre-*Furman* system, the jury rendered a moral decision; it reached into its gut to decide whether death was the appropriate punishment for the defendant. Now, however, the jury is sometimes torn between rendering a moral decision and applying a legal formula they don't quite understand.

Conclusion

The penalty trial has had mixed success in alleviating the two problems it was designed to correct. The modern version of the penalty trial does make it possible for the jury to learn a great deal more about the defendant. As a result of the Supreme Court's decisions, the defense has an opportunity to present an enormous amount of material on background and character. As the *Carpenter* case illustrates, when the defense takes advantage of this opportunity, the modern jury is allowed to view the defendant from a perspective that was not available to the pre-*Furman* jury. On the other hand, in many cases the defense fails to present any significant mitigating evidence at the penalty trial. According to experts in the field, this can be attributed not to an absence of favorable mitigating evidence but to either a lack of resources or defense counsel's failure to understand the dynamics of the penalty trial. Thus, the penalty trial promotes individualized sentencing in capital cases, but it also exacerbates the disparity in capital defendants' representation at trial, which in turn may be expected to exacerbate the death penalty's uneven application.

The consequences of the Court's effort to inject guidelines into the capital sentencing process may be even more disappointing. The guidelines were originally intended to provide the jury with standards, thereby reducing the extent to which the death penalty is arbitrarily imposed. Inevitably, the goal of reducing arbitrariness (by providing the jury with standards) comes into conflict with the goal of promoting individualized sentencing (by permitting the defendant to argue that any information relating to his character or background may be treated as a mitigating circumstance). As a result of the tension between these two goals, the penalty jury's perception of its role is likely to be confused, and in fact the jury's actual role in capital sentencing seems less clear than it was under the pre-*Furman* system. The addition of a penalty trial that includes guidelines for the jury has provided the jury with standards—but at a cost. The jury understands that it must consider and weigh specific factors, but it will often be confused about its ultimate role in capital sentencing.

NOTES

1. 408 U.S. 238 (1972).
2. The judge makes the final death penalty decision in seven states: Alabama (see ALA. CODE § 13A-5-47 (1982 Supp. 1985)), Arizona (see ARIZ. REV. STAT. ANN. § 13-703 (Supp. 1985)), Florida (see FLA. STAT. ANN. § 921.141 (West 1985)), Idaho (see IDAHO CODE § 19-2515 (Supp. 1985)), Indiana (see IND. CODE. ANN. § 35-50-2-9 (Burns 1985)), Montana (see MONT. CODE ANN. § 46-18-301 (1985)), Nebraska (see NEB. REV. STAT. § 29-2522 (R.S. Supp. 1984). In Florida and Indiana, the jury makes a recommendation of life or death, but this does not bind the judge.
3. Weisberg, *Deregulating Death*, 1983 SUP. CT. REV. 305, 306 [hereinafter cited as Weisberg]. One important exception to this pattern is the Texas statute. That statute, which was held to be constitutional in Jurek v. Texas, 428 U.S. 262 (1976), provides that once a defendant is convicted of capital homicide, the penalty jury

is required to answer three questions. If it answers each one affirmatively, the death penalty must be imposed. See TEX. CODE CRIM. PROC. ANN. art. 37.071 (Vernon Supp. 1986).
4. 438 U.S. 586 (1978).
5. See, e.g., 42 PA. CONS. STAT. ANN. § 9711 (Purdon 1982) ("verdict must be sentence of death if the jury unanimously finds at least one aggravating circumstance and no mitigating circumstances or if the jury unanimously finds one or more aggravating circumstances which outweigh any mitigating circumstances").
6. Weisberg, *supra* note 3, at 307.
7. Most of the statutes provide that the death penalty may not be imposed unless the sentencer finds at least one aggravating circumstance. See, e.g., GA. CODE ANN. § 17-10-31 (1982); IND. CODE ANN. § 35-50-2-9 (Burns 1985); ILL. ANN. STAT ch. 38, § 9-1 (Smith-Hurd 1985).
8. In Crampton v. Ohio, a companion case to McGautha v. California,

402 U.S. 183 (1971), a capital defendant claimed that forcing him to face this dilemma was unconstitutional. The Court, however, rejected this claim.

9. *See* Lockett v. Ohio, 438 U.S. 586, 606 (1978). The Court noted that there might be an exception to this rule in a very narrow category of cases. It declined to decide whether mandatory capital punishment might be constitutional when imposed on a prisoner or escapee with a life sentence who is convicted of murder. *See id.* at 603 n.11.

10. In most jurisdictions, the government is required to establish aggravating circumstances beyond a reasonable doubt. *See, e.g.,* GA. CODE ANN. § 17-10-30 (1982); ILL. ANN. STAT. ch. 38, § 9-1 (Smith-Hurd 1985); IND. CODE ANN. § 35-50-2-9 (Burns 1985).

11. *See, e.g.,* Smith v. Estelle, 451 U.S. 454 (1981) (privilege against self-incrimination is applicable at penalty trial); Bullington v. Missouri, 451 U.S. 430 (1981) (double jeopardy clause is applicable at penalty trial).

12. *See, e.g.,* GA. CODE ANN. § 17-10-30 (1982); MONT. CODE ANN. § 46-18-303 (1985); 42 PA. CONS. STAT. ANN. § 9711 (Purdon 1982).

13. *See, e.g.,* ALA. CODE § 13A-5-49 (Supp. 1985); GA. CODE ANN. § 17-10-30 (1982); 42 PA. CONS. STAT. ANN. § 9711 (Purdon 1982).

14. *See, e.g.,* ALA. CODE § 13A-5-49 (Supp. 1985); ARIZ. REV. STAT. ANN. § 13-703 (Supp. 1985); GA. CODE ANN. § 17-10-30 (1982).

15. Weisberg points out that procedural and substantive complications are likely to arise when the prosecutor seeks to prove at the penalty trial that the defendant has previously committed violent crimes. *See* Weisberg, *supra* note 3, at 335–38.

16. *See, e.g.,* ALA. CODE § 13A-5-51 (Supp. 1985); ARIZ. REV. STAT. ANN. § 13-703 (Supp. 1985); MONT. CODE ANN. § 46-18-304 (1985).

17. *See, e.g.,* ALA. CODE § 13A-5-51 (Supp. 1985), MONT. CODE ANN. § 46-18-304 (1985).

18. *See supra* text at note 9.

19. The Georgia statute is perhaps the best example. *See* GA. CODE ANN. 17-10-30 (1982). In Zant v. Stephens, 462 U.S. 862 (1983), the Court explained the statute's operation as follows: "In Georgia, unlike some states, the jury is not instructed to give any special weight to any aggravating circumstances, to consider multiple aggravating circumstances any more significant than a single such circumstance, or to balance aggravating against mitigating circumstances pursuant to any special standard." *Id.* at 873–74.

20. *See* Zant, 462 U.S. at 879 (aggravating circumstances specified in a state death penalty statute may serve function of merely "narrowing the category of persons convicted of murder who are eligible for the death penalty").

21. *See infra* text at notes 30–35.

22. This statement was made to me by Craig Haney on February 21, 1986. For a discussion of Haney's qualifications as an expert in the operation of the penalty trial, *see infra* text at notes 30–31.

23. For one account of the Spenkellink case, *see* Clark, "Spenkellink's Last Appeal," *Nation,* Oct., 1979, at 385, 404–14, *reprinted in* THE DEATH PENALTY IN AMERICA 224–33 (H. Bedau ed. 3d ed. 1982) [hereinafter cited as Bedau].

24. For recent cases in which the defense presented little or no mitigat-

ing evidence at the penalty trial, *see, e.g.,* Straight v. Wainwright, 772 F.2d 674 (11th Cir. 1985) (no mitigating evidence presented); Dillon v. Duckworth, 751 F.2d 895 (7th Cir. 1984) (very little mitigating evidence presented); Milton v. Procunier, 744 F.2d 1091 (5th Cir. 1984) (no mitigating evidence presented); Porter v. Raleigh, 478 So. 2d 33 (Fla. 1985) (no mitigating evidence presented).

25. Taylor v. Maggio, 727 F.2d 341, 349 n.10 (1984).
26. Thomas v. Wainwright, 767 F.2d 738, 746 (11th Cir. 1985).
27. *See* chap. 2.
28. For a discussion of some of the issues that arise as a result of this class of defendants, *see* chap. 7.
29. For the most part, state statutes provide funds for investigators, psychologists, or other assistance at the penalty trial only when the defense can meet the burden of proving that the services are "necessary for an adequate defense." Defining necessary and adequate is left to the trial court's sound discretion. *See, e.g.,* ALA. CODE § 15-12-21(d) (Supp. 1985); ARIZ. REV. STAT. ANN. § 13-4013 (1978); FLA. STAT. ANN. § 939.07 (West 1982); IDAHO CODE § 19-852 (1982); KAN. STAT. ANN. § 22-4508 (1977); KY. REV. STAT. §§ 31.110, .200 (1978); LA. CODE CRIM. PROC. ANN. art. 875 (West 1983); MONT. CODE ANN. § 46-18-111 (1985); N.C. GEN. STAT. § 7A-450, 7A-454 (Supp. 1984); OHIO REV. CODE ANN. § 2929.024 (Page 1984); S.D. CODIFIED LAWS ANN. § 19-15-9 (Supp. 1984); TEX. CODE CRIM. PROC. ANN. art. 26.05 (Vernon 1985). In exercising their discretion, most state trial courts have been reluctant to grant funds to defendants at the penalty phase.

Often their reasoning is that although investigation and psychological profiles may be helpful, they are certainly not necessary to provide an adequate defense. A few states are even more restrictive in granting funds to penalty trial defendants. These states abide by the "necessary for an adequate defense" criteria but also limit the amount a trial court can grant. *See, e.g.,* ARK. STAT. ANN. § 43-2419 (Supp. 1985); GA. CODE ANN. § 17-12-60 (1977). The one significant exception to this restrictive system of "necessary for an adequate defense" is California. In California the court "will grant a defendant funds for an investigator or psychologist as long as the request seems reasonable to the trial court." *See, e.g.,* CAL. PENAL CODE § 987.9 (West 1977). The rationale for this unique position is that when the life of a defendant is at stake, courts and legislatures must realize that all relevant information regarding the defendant's past or character is crucial to an adequate defense, and the state must provide the funds for investigation so this information can be brought to light. Keenan v. Superior Court, 30 Cal.3d 750, 640 P.2d 108, 180 Cal. Rptr. 489 (1982). The distinction between California and the other states can be attributed in part to the statutory language (reasonable v. necessary) and in part to the way the courts have interpreted that language.

30. *See supra* note 29.
31. Much of the following account of the case is drawn from Haney's statements to me during two interviews, the first on July 14, 1985, and the second on February 21, 1986.
32. *See, e.g.,* T. SZASZ, THE MYTH OF

Mental Illness: Foundations of a Theory of Personal Conduct (1974).

33. Samenow was the only psychologist appointed to President Reagan's crime commission.

34. Cal. Penal Code § 190.3(i) (West 1978).

35. *Id.* at § 190.3(k).

36. *See, e.g.,* Eddings v. Oklahoma, 455 U.S. 104, 115 (1982) (for sixteen-year-old defendant, "evidence of a turbulent family history, of beatings by a harsh father, and of severe emotional disturbance is particularly relevant").

37. The reduction is only marginal because, as I have said elsewhere, "Under most statutes . . . the aggravating circumstances taken together are so broad that almost any traditional first-degree murder case could be found to include at least one of them."W. White, Life in the Balance: Procedural Safeguards in Capital Cases (1984) (footnote omitted).

38. *See supra* text at notes 22–23.

39. *See* Commonwealth v. Travaglia, 502 Pa. 474, 467 A.2d 288 (1982). For a discussion of the legal issue presented when a court allows the prosecutor to comment on the defendant's failure to express remorse, *see* chap. 5.

40. This theme has been widely expressed in both legal and literary writings. A person who fails to show remorse is thought to be proud of his crimes and not ready for rehabilitation. *See, e.g.,* N. Hawthorne, The Scarlet Letter (1850).

41. For a discussion of the argument that a guilty plea evidences remorse, *see* Alschuler, *The Changing Plea Bargain Debate,* 69 Cal. L. Rev. 652, 661–69 (1981) [hereinafter cited as Alschuler].

42. Some capital defendants do not want to be spared execution. For a discussion of some of these issues involved with respect to these defendants, *see* chap. 7.

43. Of course, there will be cases in which the defendant's attorney does not advise him to express remorse at the penalty trial. The attorney might believe that an expression of remorse would be inconsistent with the defendant's posture at the guilt trial, or she simply might not share the prevailing view that an expression of remorse is desirable.

44. Alschuler, *supra* note 41, at 667.

45. *See generally* H. Bedau & M. Radelet, Miscarriages of Justice [to be published]; Bedau, *supra* note 23, at 234–41. Bedau notes that it is particularly difficult to document wrongful executions because "[o]nce the convicted capital offender is dead, it becomes virtually impossible to set the record straight." *Id.* at 237.

46. *See id.* at 239–41 (recounting the story of Freddie Pitts and Wilbur Lee, who were released in 1975, after being sentenced to death and spending twelve years in prison, most of it in death row, for a crime they didn't commit).

47. *See,* A. Scaduto, Scapegoat: The Lonesome Death of Bruno Richard Hauptmann (1976). Accused and convicted of kidnapping and killing the Lindbergh baby, Hauptmann maintained his innocence until he was executed. At trial, he testified that the reason he showed no remorse or sorrow on the stand was because he was innocent. He told the prosecutor that he had never been on the Lindbergh premises or seen the child and that he was incapable of feeling sorry for something he had

not done and knew nothing about.

48. *See* Weisberg, *supra* note 3, at 376.
49. *Id.* at 377.
50. *Id.*

51. *Id.* at 377–78.
52. *Id.* at 371.
53. The case was People v. Neely, No. 40424 (Cal. Super. Ct., El Dorado Cty., Dec. 15, 1982).
54. Weisberg, *supra* note 3, at 371.

CHAPTER 4

The Defendant's Right to Present Evidence and Argument at the Penalty Trial

As the trail-side killer's case indicates,[1] a capital defendant who is afforded a broad right to present evidence at the penalty trial may take advantage of this opportunity and present a compelling case of mitigation. In many jurisdictions, however, the state courts have been less liberal than the California courts in allowing capital defendants to introduce mitigating evidence.[2] So it may be particularly important to determine how the Supreme Court decisions limit a state court's right to bar mitigating evidence at the penalty trial.

Two groups of Supreme Court cases are significant: those that pertain to the state courts' right to exclude mitigating evidence as irrelevant and the single case that pertains to the state courts' right to exclude relevant mitigating evidence as unreliable. Other specific evidentiary questions bear on this issue, too, as does the question of what limits may be imposed on defense counsel's closing argument at the penalty trial.

The Standard of Relevance: *Lockett, Eddings,* and *Skipper*

Ostensibly, *Lockett v. Ohio*[3] does not deal with the admissibility of evidence. But by defining what is constitutionally relevant to the death penalty determination, *Lockett* makes it clear that the capital defendant has a broad right to present mitigating evidence at the penalty trial. In invalidating Ohio's capital punishment statute, *Lockett* held that in all but the rarest capital cases, "the sentencer [may] . . . not be precluded from considering, *as a mitigating factor,* any aspect of a defendant's character or record and any of the circumstances of the offense that the defendant proffers as a basis for a sentence less than death."[4] That the defendant has a constitutional right to have the sentencer consider any evidence that relates to his character, his record, or the circumstances of his offense

75

implies that he has a concomitant right to introduce such evidence at the penalty trial. Thus, *Lockett* implicitly holds that a capital defendant has a constitutional right to introduce at the penalty trial any evidence that is relevant to his character, his record, or the circumstances of his offense.

Of course, the significance of the right established in *Lockett* turns on the content given to the terms *character, record,* and *circumstances of the offense.* In a footnote, the *Lockett* court states that nothing in its opinion "limits the traditional authority of a court to exclude, as irrelevant, evidence not bearing on the defendant's character, prior record, or the circumstances of his offense."[5] Taken by itself, this footnote might seem to imply that a state trial judge may apply state rules of evidence in determining questions of relevance. This approach would allow the state courts to undermine the effect of *Lockett* by simply interpreting *character, record,* and *circumstances of the offense* very narrowly. If, for example, the state's "traditional" rule is that a person's troubled childhood is not relevant to his character, the state trial judge would be free to exclude evidence that the defendant was subjected to extreme child abuse.

In *Eddings v. Oklahoma*[6] and *Skipper v. South Carolina,*[7] the Court made it clear that the rule established in *Lockett* cannot be so easily eviscerated. In *Eddings* the sixteen-year-old defendant pled guilty to capital murder. At the penalty hearing before a judge, he introduced extensive evidence relating to his background, including the fact that he was the product of a broken home and had been neglected by his mother and subjected to severe physical punishment by his father. At the conclusion of the evidence, the judge found that the aggravating circumstances outweighed the mitigating circumstances and imposed the death sentence. In weighing the aggravating and mitigating circumstances, the judge specifically said that "in following the law . . . [he could not] consider the fact of this young man's violent background."[8] The Supreme Court held that this death penalty was invalid under *Lockett* because the sentencer "refuse[d] to consider, *as a matter of law,* . . . relevant mitigating evidence."[9] The Court added that under the circumstances of this case evidence of the defendant's troubled background was "particularly relevant."[10]

In *Skipper,*[11] the defendant was convicted of capital murder and rape. At the penalty trial, he was prevented from presenting testimony by two jailers and one "regular visitor to the prison" that he had "made a good adjustment" during his time in jail. In holding that the exclusion of this evidence was in violation of the Eighth Amendment the Court further expanded the capital defendant's right to present mitigating evidence at the penalty trial. It concluded that the proffered evidence shed light on the defendant's "probable future conduct if sentenced to life imprisonment" and that "a defendant's disposition to make a well-behaved and peaceful adjustment to life in prison is itself an aspect of his character that is by its nature relevant to the sentencing determination."[12] Thus, the Court determined that evidence relating to the defendant's conduct after the crime in question could also be relevant to his character.

The *Skipper* opinion was also significant because the Court for the first time identified at least one situation in which the state courts could properly exclude mitigating evidence offered by a capital defendant. In a footnote to his majority opinion in *Skipper,* Justice White observed that the Court had "no quarrel with the statement of the Supreme Court of South Carolina that 'how often [the defendant] will take a shower' is irrelevant to the sentencing determination."[13] In the majority's view, the evidence offered in *Skipper* was distinguishable from evidence relating to the defendant's "personal hygiene practices" because the inferences to be drawn from it were "'mitigating' in the sense that they might serve 'as a basis for a sentence less than death.'"[14]

Eddings and *Skipper* show that the federal courts will have the final word in deciding what evidence is relevant to the defendant's character or record or the circumstances of the offense. Moreover, they indicate that the Court's traditional deference to state rules of evidence will not prevent it from applying a liberal standard in determining issues of relevance. In determining what is relevant to the defendant's character, *Eddings* indicates that the Court may look to the past—taking into account evidence of the defendant's troubled childhood—and *Skipper* indicates that it may look to the future—taking into account events that took place after the defendant's crime or even events that help predict his future conduct.

More importantly, *Skipper* intimates that the standard for determining whether mitigating evidence offered by the defendant is relevant is whether the evidence "might serve 'as a basis for a sentence less than death.'" Taken together with the Court's example of the type of evidence that would *not* be relevant to the penalty determination,[15] that language suggests that the standard of relevance will be broad enough to include any evidence that a reasonable juror *might* view as significant enough to tip the balance in the capital defendant's favor. How often a person takes a shower would not, of course, influence a reasonable juror's judgment. But any evidence relating to meaningful events in the defendant's life might. If the defendant had had childhood blackouts,[16] for example, or had engaged in commendable activities in his youth or while in prison, a reasonable juror might view these events as significant enough to be weighed in the defendant's favor and, in a close case, to form the "basis for a sentence less than death."

Moreover, *Skipper*'s iteration of the standard suggests that in ruling on issues of relevance, courts should focus less on whether the evidence is directly related to the defendant's character or the circumstances of the offense and more on whether the evidence could be viewed as significant. Testimony by members of the defendant's family that they will miss him if he is executed, for example, should not be excluded on the ground that it is not relevant to the defendant's character.[17] The testimony does have a bearing on the defendant's character in the sense that it reflects the impact he has had on those close to him, and a reasonable juror could certainly view it as a basis for sparing his life.

In general, then, the Supreme Court has indicated that the state courts' discretion to exclude defense mitigating evidence as irrelevant to the penalty determination is severely circumscribed. The federal courts will make their own determination of whether the evidence offered is relevant to the defendant's character or the circumstances of the offense, and based on *Skipper,* it appears that they should not exclude mitigating evidence as irrelevant unless it is clear that a reasonable juror could not view it as significant enough to form the "basis for a sentence less than death."

The Standard of Reliability: *Green v. Georgia*

If *Eddings* and *Skipper* impose restrictions on the state court's authority to exclude mitigating evidence on the grounds of irrelevance, *Green v. Georgia*[18] shows that the state court's power to exclude on the ground that the evidence does not meet traditional standards of reliability will also be subject to limitations.

In *Green,* Roosevelt Green and Carzell Moore were charged jointly with rape and murder. Moore was tried first and sentenced to death. Green was then convicted of first-degree murder. At the penalty trial, Green sought to prove that he was not present when the victim was killed. He attempted to introduce the testimony of Thomas Pasby, who had testified for the state at Moore's trial. According to Pasby, Moore confided to him that he had killed the victim, shooting her twice after ordering the defendant to run an errand.

One of the most basic rules of evidence is that hearsay will be excluded unless it fits within an exception to the hearsay rule. Hearsay is generally defined as testimony about an out-of-court statement that is offered in evidence to prove the truth of the matter asserted.[19] Pursuant to this definition, Pasby's testimony about Moore's statement was hearsay. The statement was made out of court and the testimony was being offered to prove the truth of the facts asserted by the declarant.

Following its traditional evidentiary rules, the Georgia courts excluded Moore's statement as hearsay. The Supreme Court, however, held that as a constitutional matter, the state was required to admit Moore's statement at the penalty trial. Quoting from *Chambers v. Mississippi,*[20] the Court held that "in these unique circumstances the hearsay rule may not be applied mechanistically to defeat the ends of Justice."[21]

As John Kaplan has said, *Green* and *Chambers* "are not the same. The hearsay in *Green* is a far cry both in uniqueness and in probative value from the testimony whose admissibility the Court, in *Chambers,* had held to be compelled by the due process clause."[22] In *Chambers* the declarant's hearsay statement was exceptionally probative because it related directly to the central issue in the case,[23] and it seemed uniquely reliable because it was made on four separate occasions[24] and was corroborated by other apparently reliable evidence.[25] Thus, *Green's* holding intimates that traditional evidentiary exclusionary rules that might properly be applied in an ordinary criminal case will be subjected to closer scrutiny at the penalty stage of a capital case.

On the other hand, Kaplan may be reading *Green* too broadly when he suggests that the decision is "authority for the proposition that the hearsay rule is no longer a sufficient objection on behalf of the prosecution in a capital sentencing proceeding."[26] In holding that the exclusion of Moore's statement denied Green a fair trial, the Court took pains to iterate the "substantial reasons" why the hearsay statement should be "assumed" to be reliable:

> Moore made his statement spontaneously to a close friend. The evidence corroborating the confession was ample, and indeed sufficient to procure a conviction of Moore and a capital sentence. The statement was against interest, and there was no reason to believe that Moore had any ulterior motive in making it. Perhaps most important, the State considered the testimony sufficiently reliable to use it against Moore, and to base a sentence of death upon it.[27]

Based on this analysis, several possible distinctions could be drawn between *Green* and the typical situation in which the defense offers relevant hearsay evidence at the penalty trial. The Court could limit *Green* by applying either a declaration-against-interest principle (noting that the declarant's statement was against his penal interest, a factor that would bring it within an exception to the hearsay rule in many jurisdictions)[28] or an estoppel principle (emphasizing that the government introduced the hearsay statement in an earlier proceeding). Moreover, the Court could also limit *Green* to its facts, holding that the defendant's constitutional right to admit hearsay at the penalty trial will only apply when the unique set of circumstances existing in *Green* are present. Thus, *Green's* significance is difficult to evaluate, because its holding may be read broadly or narrowly. *Green* does indicate, however, that the constitutional limitations on the trial court's power to exclude relevant evidence at the penalty trial may be stricter than those that apply in ordinary criminal cases.

Some Unresolved Evidentiary Issues

Of the innumerable unresolved evidentiary problems that are likely to arise at the penalty trial, three seem especially pertinent.

First, in view of the ambiguity of *Green* decision, it is unclear to what extent the state courts retain their traditional authority to exclude evidence that has not gained sufficient scientific acceptance to be recognized as reliable. Suppose, for example, a defendant convicted with other defendants of murdering a police officer seeks to introduce the results of a polygraph test for the purpose of showing that he was not the actual killer. The state courts would be likely to exclude this evidence on the ground that polygraph results are not recognized as reliable in the scientific community.[29]

The defendant might argue that in view of the Court's decision in *Green,* the federal courts should at least independently examine whether the particular polygraph results at issue in the defendant's case were either sufficiently reliable in themselves or viewed by the state as sufficiently reliable[30] to mandate their admission at the penalty trial. Moreover, the defendant might argue that the Court's decision in *Barefoot v. Estelle*[31] should weigh in his favor. In *Barefoot* the Court held that psychiatrists' predictions of a defendant's future dangerousness may be admitted at the penalty trial even though the relevant scientific community has judged such predictions to be wrong "most of the time."[32] The defendant could argue that since the government is permitted to introduce evidence that meets only a minimum standard of reliability, the defense should be afforded the same privilege.

The Supreme Court has not yet considered any issue of this type. If it ever does, it may be swayed as much by an awareness of its institutional limitations as it is by the merits of the opposing arguments. The Court might feel that as an institution it is ill equipped to evaluate the reliability of particular types of scientific evidence. Moreover, it would be likely to view *Barefoot* as deferring to state rules of evidence rather than establishing a standard of admissibility at the penalty trial. Thus, barring unusual circumstances, it seems likely that the state courts will be permitted to exclude scientific evidence that has not yet gained sufficient acceptance to be recognized as reliable.

A second interesting evidentiary issue arises when the capital defendant seeks to present evidence that other penalty juries have not imposed the death penalty in comparable cases. To take two examples, suppose that a defendant convicted of murdering a police officer seeks to introduce evidence first, that a codefendant convicted of the same crime has been sentenced to life imprisonment and, second, that the death penalty has been imposed in only about 20 percent of all recent cases in which defendants have been convicted of killing police officers.

In both cases, the government might argue that the evidence offered is not relevant to either the character of the offender or the circumstances of the offense. However, the first type of evidence is arguably relevant to the circumstances of the offense in the sense that it sets a standard of punishment for the particular offense committed. A reasonable juror might feel that there is an appearance of arbitrariness when two people who commit the same crime receive different punishments.

The prosecution might argue that given our present system's commitment to individualized capital sentencing, any appearance of arbitrariness is illusory. Even two capital defendants who are equally culpable may properly be given different punishments if the sentencing authority finds there are more mitigating circumstances present in one of the two situations. Moreover, the fact that two defendants are both convicted of the same crime does not mean they are equally culpable. The jury might find, for example, that the codefendant was only an accessory to the offense and the defendant was the perpetrator. Different punishments for defendants convicted of the same capital offense could be justified on a variety of theories.

But this does not rebut the claim that there is an *appearance* of arbitrariness when two defendants who are involved in the same crime receive different sentences. Even if the defendant is shown to be more culpable than the codefendant, the community's perception of the situation might be that both were shown to be responsible for the officer's death, and it is anomalous for one to receive the death sentence and the other a sentence of life imprisonment. Because we are concerned about having a system that appears to operate fairly as well as one that is fair in fact,[33] the sentencer might at least want to use the sentence imposed in the codefendant's case as a standard for comparison, contemplating that the defendant should not receive the death penalty unless there is a measurable distinction between his situation and the codefendant's. Thus, there is a strong argument in favor of allowing the defendant to introduce the fact that his codefendant was sentenced to life imprisonment at the penalty trial.

The defense might argue that the extent to which the death penalty has been applied in other police murder cases is also relevant to the circumstances of the offense in that it sets a standard of punishment for the category of offense committed. But in this situation the relevance of the standard is more tenuous. Since there are many different varieties of police murders, the penalty imposed in any one case can have relatively little bearing upon the penalty to be imposed in any other case.

Moreover, in contrast to the first example, the appearance of arbitrariness is relatively minimal. The community will recognize that there can be a real difference between two defendants convicted of the same police murder being given different sentences and two defendants convicted of different police murders being given different sentences. The community will be less likely to be aware of any disparity in the latter situation, and, if they are aware of it, more likely to recognize that the different treatment afforded to different police killers may be justified by an infinite variety of circumstances. Thus, it seems appropriate to conclude that a state court's refusal to admit this type of evidence would not violate the Constitution.

The final unresolved evidentiary issue to be considered concerns expert testimony relating to the death penalty's efficacy as a deterrent. In some cases the defense has sought to adduce testimony that the death penalty will not operate as a more effective deterrent than life imprisonment.[34] Since people often justify capital punishment on the ground that it is a more effective deterrent than any alternative punishment,[35] such testimony could provide the sentencer with a basis for imposing a sentence less than death. Moreover, the defendant may argue that the expert testimony is relevant to the circumstances of the defendant's offense because it helps the jury determine what weight should be given to particular aggravating circumstances. For example, under nearly every state death penalty statute, the fact that the victim was a police officer is identified as an aggravating circumstance.[36] The statutes do not specify, however, how much weight should be given to that circumstance when it is weighed against the mitigating circumstances established by the defense. Arguably, the deterrence expert's testimony will help the jury perform the necessary balancing process, because it will give them a better idea of the aggravating circumstance's penological significance. Presumably, the legislature's basis for making the victim's status as a police officer an aggravating circumstance is the belief that there is a special need to deter homicidal attacks on police officers. But if it appears that the death penalty is no more efficacious in deterring murder than an alternative punishment, defense counsel can argue that the victim's status as a police officer should weigh less heavily because imposing the death penalty in one police murder case will not deter people from killing police officers in the future.

Nevertheless, it is questionable whether the deterrence expert's testimony bears a sufficient relationship to the character of the offender or the circumstances of the offense. The expert's testimony would certainly be relevant to the legislature, but it does not really help the jury make an individualized sentencing determination about the defendant. If the expert could say that "executing the defendant would not deter anyone else because he is so obviously different"[37] it would be a different case, because that kind of testimony would relate to the individual defendant's particular situation. But expert testimony about the general issue of deterrence does not relate to the particular circumstances of the offense; it has to do with the legislature's judgment in providing for a death penalty and perhaps with its selection of specific aggravating circumstances. Accordingly, excluding this testimony should not be held to violate the Constitution.

Limitations on Defense Counsel's Right to Present Argument at the Penalty Trial

In arguing to save the life of a capital defendant, the great defense attorneys have successfully appealed to the emotions of the sentencer. For example, Clarence Darrow's famous argument asking the judge to spare the lives of Loeb and Leopold was said to be so moving that at its conclusion, "Darrow, the judge, and many in the audiences were crying."[38] Darrow's speech touched on a variety of themes. He painted a vivid picture of how the defendants would be executed if they were sentenced to death.[39] Drawing on deterministic theories of human behavior, he argued that the defendants were not blameworthy, because their actions were the product "of the infinite forces that conspired to form them."[40] According to one of his biographers, in the end, he took the case "far beyond the bounds of reason and logic, moving his listeners to a pity for the human race as a whole."[41]

Defense attorneys from the present era use some of those same themes, as well as others. Speaking in dramatic terms of the defendant's execution is still a very common practice:

> We are talking about whether or not Mr. Cummings is going to be destroyed, is going to be strapped in a seat in a gas chamber in San Quentin, when cyanide is dropped in sulfuric acid and he chokes because he does not want to breathe and he does. And he turns purple and his eyes . . . .[42]

Or:

> Does it add anything to society to say that some glorious day we're going to take Mike Travaglia out, and we're going to shave his head, we're going to put grease on his arms, we're going to strap him into an electric chair, and we're going to send all those volts through his body until his feet split open and his fingers split open and he dies, and he's electrocuted?[43]

Presenting the argument that defendant's actions are a product of deterministic forces beyond his control is now perhaps the most common rhetorical strategy. Weisberg recounts a particularly masterful argument of this genre:

> Donald Cummings, who at the age of three in a home of alcoholics and people who locked him and his siblings into their house when they would go downtown to drink, who wasn't fed, who wasn't clothed, who lived in dirt, who lived in filth and who lived in squalor, at the age of three when a sibling was taken from him through pneumonia, through neglect, he was present, he must have seen that. Donald Cummings, who a year later was there when, presumably was there, when his mother said to the Department of Social Services, "Take this one. I can't stand the sight of him," who a year later another sibling died of neglect in the house,

who lived in filth, who lived in squalor. "My neck hurts. My father's been squeezing my neck. I can't hear out of an ear." The
sister engaged in some sex plays with others, not toilet trained who
lived in filth, who lived in squalor, who lived in neglect, who was
locked in the house and left alone. What happened to the so
misshapen spirit on some primordial level at an age beyond control,
at an age before reason, at an age when he didn't have a choice?
Human frailty. Look at the offenses. Something happened. And it
happened then, and you know it. Human frailty. He has lived a life
that is different from the lives everyone of you have lived, has been
subjected to the influences that none of you have felt in that way,
who has seen and experienced at an age of the utmost importance
things that are unimaginable to us. "I saw bloody brains on the
sidewalk."[44]

And, as one final example,[45] an argument that is presented as a model for
defense attorney's appeals to the religious sensibilities of the jury while at
the same time emphasizing the importance of their decision:

For you, this is a decision that you are going to live with the rest
of your lives, and, possibly, beyond. I am not a particularly religious
person myself, but I cannot help thinking that one day, months,
years ahead, on some stormy night, you will awaken. You will
reflect, when Mr. Kay's cry for vengeance has long since subsided
and his voice is stilled. I pray to God that you do not think you
erred in condemning a man to his death. When memory's accusing
voice says, "Consider what happened; did you make a mistake; did
you deal too harshly with a fellow human being's life," I hope for
the salvation of all of us that the answer is "No." If you do err, if
you do make a mistake, how much kinder, how much more beau-
tiful than [sic] that mistake should be in the cause of kindness and
charity than in harshness and in vengeance. What a solace to say,
"I may have erred, but if I did, it was in order to see that a brother
didn't die."[46]

These kinds of arguments are generally presented at the penalty trial
without objection by the prosecutor.[47] But would there be an appropriate
basis for objection in some instances? And what limit, if any, does the
Constitution place on the court's right to exclude defense argument at the
penalty trial?

In some of the examples presented, the prosecutor's basis for objection would be that counsel is arguing on the basis of facts outside the
record.[48] The defense should probably not be permitted to present testimony about the actual circumstances of an execution,[49] so it is unlikely
that the record will contain testimony that a defendant in a gas chamber

"chokes because he doesn't want to breathe" and "turns purple." And, certainly, there will not be testimony in the record relating to whether the jurors will have to live with their decisions beyond the term of their lives.

Nevertheless, in most jurisdictions counsel is afforded some freedom to go beyond the record in closing argument. Generally speaking, counsel will be permitted to comment on matters outside the record when she is merely trying to provide the jury with a new perspective on evidence that has been presented. Thus, counsel may "resort to poetry, cite history, fiction, personal experiences, anecdotes, biblical stories, or tell jokes."[50] In other words, she will not be confined to matters in evidence if it appears that she is merely displaying her oratorical skills rather than seeking to present material that is outside the record.

Given this qualification, all of the examples cited should fall within the bounds of legitimate argument. It is not in the record that a defendant in the gas chamber "turns purple" before he dies, but it is a matter of common knowledge[51] that an asphyxiated person will change or lose his color. Thus, counsel's statement, if not precisely accurate, would still be appropriate. Similarly, it is a matter of common knowledge that many people believe in life after death; so counsel would be within the realm of legitimate oratory when she referred to the possibility that the jurors would have to live with their decisions beyond the terms of their lives.

Nevertheless, some defense arguments should be condemned as improper. Arguments relating to the death penalty's efficacy as a deterrent or its consistency with religious principles relate to matters that are not properly for the jury's consideration. They may be excluded on this basis, whether or not they refer to matters not in evidence. Of course, some arguments *should* be excluded on the ground that defense counsel is referring to matters not in evidence. For example, it would clearly be improper for counsel to refer to something in the defendant's past that had not been introduced into evidence. In contrast to the earlier examples cited, the reference could not be dismissed as a comment on matters within general knowledge or an exercise of rhetoric. Counsel would in effect be testifying as an unsworn witness, conveying to the jury information that was not properly introduced into the record.

Beyond this, there should be few restrictions on defense counsel's right to present argument at the penalty trial. In particular, argument that pertains to evidence in the record should not be excluded on grounds that it is overly emotional or adopts a controversial view of human behavior. *Lockett* dictates that the sentencer is required to make an individualized sentencing determination based on its perception of the defendant's personal characteristics as well as on information that is relevant to the circumstances of the offense. Under this scheme, defense counsel should be permitted to use any oratorical skills that will cause the sentencer to view the defendant's crime from a more favorable perspective. In reviewing the evidence, counsel should be permitted to adopt a deterministic view of human behavior or to suggest to the jury that they should recognize the effect of human frailty. She should be allowed to point out the immense consequences of the death penalty decision and to argue that under the circumstances of the particular case, imposing the death penalty would be an act of needless cruelty. In making these arguments, counsel should not be precluded from using any kind of eloquence that will arouse the sentencer's feelings. Under *Lockett,* the sentencer is required to act for the community in deciding whether the defendant should be executed or spared. To do so, the sentencer must rely on more than logic, and in seeking to persuade the sentencer to exercise mercy, defense counsel should be permitted to appeal to the sentencer's feelings as well as its cognitive faculties.

Conclusion

In *Lockett* and its progeny, the Supreme Court indicated that the capital defendant has a broad right to present mitigating evidence at the penalty trial. Despite its tendency to allow the states greater freedom in administering their systems of capital punishment, the Court has adhered to this principle. In fact, the Court's most recent decisions indicate that in monitoring the modern system of capital punishment, one of its principal concerns will be with restricting the government's right to exclude mitigating evidence at the penalty trial.

Nevertheless, the Court has not clearly developed the parameters of the constitutional limitations. At times, it suggests that even in the penalty trial context, the state courts will retain their authority to apply traditional rules of evidence. At other times, it indicates that the special concern for ensuring reliability in capital sentencing mandates a more permissive attitude toward the introduction of mitigating evidence.

Part of the problem stems from the fact that the type of issues to be determined at the guilt and penalty stage are quite different. At the penalty stage, the sentencer is less concerned with resolving discrete factual questions than with making a moral judgment on the basis of its total view of the defendant and the circumstances of the offense. Because the issues to be determined are less defined, the standards for excluding evidence as irrelevant or unreliable is less certain.

Nevertheless, some limits may properly be imposed on· the defendant's right to present mitigating evidence. The example of the use of polygraph results suggests that the state courts should be afforded discretion to exclude evidence that fails to meet a requisite standard of reliability. Moreover, evidence that relates to the appropriateness of the death penalty in general or its appropriateness for a particular type of offense may properly be excluded on the ground that it does not relate to the issue the penalty jury is required to decide. Under the Court's decisions, the penalty jury is not concerned with the appropriateness of capital punishment in general but only with whether the death penalty should be imposed on a particular defendant who has committed a specific offense.

The Supreme Court has not yet decided any case that concerns the restrictions that may be imposed on defense counsel's right to present argument at the penalty trial. Nevertheless, the issue is potentially an important one. The questions that might arise include: Should counsel be allowed to argue against the propriety of the death penalty in general? To what extent should counsel be permitted to comment on matters outside the record? and Should there be any limit on counsel's right to appeal to the sentencer's emotions?

I have suggested some principles that might be applied in seeking to answer these and other questions. The same principle that restricts the defense from presenting evidence about the death penalty's impropriety should preclude her from presenting argument on that subject. Moreover, although defense counsel should perhaps be allowed to exercise a certain amount of poetic license, she should not be permitted to refer to matters outside the record when the effect of this would be to convey to the jury information that neither was presented in evidence nor is a subject of general knowledge. On the other hand, so long as defense counsel is arguing about matters that are appropriate for comment,[52] she should not be restricted from presenting argument that appeals to the sentencer's emotions. Under the circumstances, emotional appeals are appropriate because the judgment to be made—whether the defendant will live or die— is one that should not be predicated on logic alone.

NOTES

1. *See* chap. 3.
2. *See, e.g.,* Commonwealth v. Beasley, 504 Pa. 485, 475 A.2d 730 (1984) (trial judge refused to allow evidence presented by defendant regarding alcoholic blackouts suffered during childhood); Dutton v. State, 674 P.2d 1134 (Okla. Crim. App. 1984) (trial judge refused to allow defendant's mother to testify at penalty trial since she had already testified at guilt trial).
3. 438 U.S. 586 (1978).
4. *Id.* at 605 (emphasis added).
5. *Id.* at 604 n.12.
6. 455 U.S. 104 (1982).
7. 106 S. Ct. 1669 (1986).
8. 455 U.S. at 109.
9. *Id.* at 114.
10. *Id.* at 115.
11. 106 S. Ct. 1669 (1986).
12. *Id.* at 1672.
13. *Id.* at 1672 n.2.
14. *Id.* at 1672.
15. *See supra* text at note 12.
16. *See supra* note 2.
17. *See, e.g.,* State v. Jenkins, 15 Ohio St. 3d 164, 473 N.E., 264 (1984) (testimony of defendant's two sisters that they didn't want to see him put to death because they love him is inadmissible at penalty trial).
18. 442 U.S. 95 (1979).
19. *See* C. McCormick, McCormick on Evidence 584 (2d ed. 1972).

20. 410 U.S. 284 (1973).
21. *Id.* at 302.
22. Kaplan, *Evidence in Capital Cases,* 11 FLA. ST. UNIV. L. REV. 369, 373 (1983) [hereinafter cited as Kaplan].
23. In *Chambers* the defendant was charged with the murder of Officer Aaron ("Sonny") Liberty. Liberty had admittedly been shot to death; the critical issue was whether he was shot by the defendant or by some other individual. The hearsay declarant, one McDonald, stated to other individuals that he had shot Liberty.
24. McDonald's out-of-court statements that he had shot Liberty included a sworn confession given to Chambers's lawyers and three other statements made in private conversations with his friends. 410 U.S. at 285.
25. A friend of McDonald's testified that he saw McDonald shoot Liberty. 410 U.S. at 287, 289.
26. Kaplan, *supra* note 22, at 374.
27. 442 U.S. at 97.
28. *See generally* C. MCCORMICK, MCCORMICK ON EVIDENCE 673–75 (2d ed. 1972).
29. Most state courts would exclude polygraph results on this ground. *See, e.g.,* State v. Royster, 57 N.J. 472, 273 A.2d 574 (1971); Commonwealth v. Jackson, 441 Pa. 237, 272 A.2d 467 (1971).
30. The latter issue might arise if polygraph results were produced as a result of a test conducted by the state. In that case, the defendant might argue that as in *Green,* the state's act of vouching for the reliability of the evidence should estop it from excluding the evidence from the penalty trial.
31. 463 U.S. 880 (1983).
32. *Id.* at 898.

33. *See, e.g.,* Gardner v. Florida, 430 U.S. 349, 358 (1977): "It is of vital importance to the defendant and the community that any decision to impose the death sentence be, and appear to be, based on reason rather than caprice or emotion."
34. *See, e.g.,* People v. Stewart, 105 Ill. 2d 22, 473 N.E.2d 840 (1984) (defense testimony on deterrent effect of death penalty properly excluded); State v. Jenkins, 15 Ohio St. 3d 164, 194, 473 N.E.2d 264, 289 (Ohio 1984) (defense testimony to effect that statistics show capital punishment is not a deterrent to murder properly excluded).
35. *See, e.g.,* Gregg v. Georgia, 428 U.S. 153, 185–86 (1976) (plurality opinion of Stewart, J.): "We may nevertheless assume safely that there are murderers, for whom the threat of death has little or no deterrent effect, but for many others the death penalty undoubtedly is a significant deterrent."
36. *See, e.g.,* 42 PA. CONS. STAT. ANN. § 9711(d)(1) (Purdon 1974) ("The victim was a fireman, peace officer or public servant who was killed in performance of his duties"); MISS. CODE ANN. § 97-3-19(2)(a) (1974) "Murder which is perpetrated by killing of a peace officer who is performing his duties is capital murder, and may elevate a sentence of life imprisonment to a sentence of death"); GA. CODE ANN. § 1210-30(b)(8) (1973). ("A murder committed against a peace officer, in performance of his duties, is an aggravating circumstance which must be weighed against any mitigating circumstances to decide whether to impose the death penalty").
37. Kaplan, *supra* note 22, at 382.

38. K. TIERNEY, DARROW: A BIOGRA-
PHY 341 (1979) [hereinafter cited
as TIERNEY].
39. TIERNEY, *supra* note 38, at 339.
40. *Id.* at 340.
41. *Id.* at 341.
42. People v. Cummings, No. 81041
(Cal. Super Ct., Santa Clara Cty.,
Jan. 10, 1983) (transcript at 2818–
19) (*quoted in* Weisberg, *Deregulating Death,* 1983 SUP. CT.
REV. 305, 382 [hereinafter cited as
Weisberg]).
43. People v. Travaglia, 402 Pa. 474,
467 A.2d 288 (1983) (transcript at
1678) (on file with author).
44. People v. Cummings, No. 81041
(Cal. Super. Ct., Santa Clara Cty.,
Jan. 10, 1983) (transcript at 2836–
37) (*quoted in* Weisberg, *supra*
note 42, at 381).
45. For other examples, *see* Weisberg,
supra note 42, at 379–83.
46. J. STEIN, CLOSING ARGUMENT 185
(1969) [hereinafter cited as STEIN].
47. Typically, the prosecutor will not
object to defense closing argument
but will claim that the defense argument gives him a right to present argument in his own closing
that would otherwise be improper.
For a discussion of the legal issues
that arise when the prosecutor responds to improper defense argument, *see* chap. 5.
48. *See, e.g.,* State v. Bradford, 219
Kan. 336, 548 P.2d 812 (1976)
(counsel is confined to remarking
only on facts within record); *see
generally* STEIN, *supra* note 46, at
28.
49. The circumstances of an execution
do not relate to the character of
the defendant or the circumstances of the offense.
50. STEIN, *supra* note 46, at 19.
51. *See, e.g.,* People v. Mendoza, 37
Cal. App. 3d 717, 112 Cal. Rptr.
565 (1974) (counsel in summation
may refer to nonevidentiary matters of common knowledge or to
illustrations drawn from common
experience, history, or literature
but may not dwell on particular
facts of unrelated cases). *See
generally* STEIN, *supra* note 46,
at 29.
52. *See generally* STEIN, *supra* note
46, at 36; Bystrom, *Oklahoma Law
on Closing Argument,* 37 OKLA. L.
REV. 463 (1984) (attack on opposing counsel's honesty, integrity,
and good faith are strongly
disfavored).

CHAPTER 5 **The Prosecutor's Closing Argument at the Penalty Trial**

A capital trial may have many vivid and exciting moments, but in terms of pure drama the high point is likely to be the closing argument, in which counsel have an opportunity to plead for or against the life of the defendant. Under our present system of capital punishment, this argument occurs at the conclusion of the penalty trial, after the defendant has been found guilty of capital murder and both sides have been afforded an opportunity to present additional evidence bearing on punishment. In most jurisdictions, defense counsel argues first and the prosecutor is permitted the final opportunity to address the jury.[1]

Any closing argument poses a splendid opportunity for a skilled advocate.[2] In the typical criminal case, counsel on both sides will use their closing arguments to try to pull the evidence together in a way that will make their positions more appealing to the jury. Defense counsel may also try to highlight some weak spot in the government's case or to put someone other than the defendant on trial. The prosecutor, on the other hand, will seek to keep the jury focused on the strong points in the government's case and, possibly, to emphasize the unsavory aspects of the defendant's character. Both sides will use a variety of forensic techniques that may range from logical discourse to blatant appeals to emotion.

At the penalty trial, the stakes involved will naturally have a considerable impact on the content of the argument. Arguing for life or death is qualitatively different from arguing about any other issue. Both sides will be affected. The defense counsel will be particularly likely to emphasize the magnitude of the stakes involved.[3] One of his primary goals will be to impress the jury with the fact that they are confronted with an awesome responsibility. He will stress that they are placed in a situation in which they have to decide whether another human being will live or die. He may dwell at some length on the ramifications of this decision, perhaps appealing to the jury's religious sensibilities, emphasizing the horror or the irrevocability of capital punishment, or simply arguing that the infliction of the death penalty is barbaric and futile.

In addition to setting the parameters of the death penalty decision, defense counsel may also try to argue the affirmative case for life.[4] Drawing on whatever mitigating evidence has been presented, he may try to minimize the seriousness of defendant's crime or at least give the jury some understanding of why he committed it. Counsel's goal will be to create a bond of empathy between the jury and defendant, to make the jury view the defendant as a fellow member of the human community. If this empathy is established, the jury will be less likely to impose a death sentence.

The prosecutor, of course, will respond to these arguments. He may seek by various means to defuse the defense's attempt to emphasize the awesome responsibility of imposing the death penalty.[5] In addition, he is likely to counter defense counsel's effort to construct an affirmative case for life by asserting an affirmative case for death. He may argue in favor of the death penalty in general, premising his argument on a penological theory like deterrence or retribution. Or he may emphasize that the death penalty is an especially appropriate punishment for the particular defendant before the jury. Frequently, these two themes will be mixed together and presented to the jury with the aid of colorful metaphors and strong emotional appeals.

Imposing limits on the prosecutor's closing penalty argument poses a particularly difficult problem for the courts. On one hand, counsel in criminal cases have traditionally been afforded substantial freedom to present closing arguments in vivid and forceful terms. The prevailing view has been that both sides should be allowed to engage in some rhetorical excess, because the jury will understand that counsel's argument is not evidence and that they need not consider it in deciding the case. The government may argue that a double standard should not apply at the penalty trial: the prosecutor, no less than defense counsel, should be allowed substantial freedom to use her forensic talents to arouse the jury's emotions. But under the modern system of capital punishment, a double standard is in fact appropriate. For reasons I will explain, in monitoring penalty trial arguments, the courts should impose more rigorous restraints on the prosecutor than on defense counsel.[6]

In *Caldwell v. Mississippi,*[7] a case decided in 1985, the Supreme Court indicated that the concern for reliability in capital sentencing gives rise to a heightened scrutiny of prosecutors' penalty trial closing arguments. In *Caldwell,* defense counsel sought to impress on the jury their awesome responsibility by saying to them, "[the defendant] has a life that rests in your hands. You can give him life or you can give him death. It's going to be your decision."[8] In response, the prosecutor asserted that this argument was "unfair," because the jury's decision was automatically reviewable by the state supreme court. Defense counsel objected to these remarks, but the trial judge overruled, stating that the jury's decision "is reviewable" and that the prosecutor could "make the full expression so that the jury will not be confused."[9] The prosecutor then reiterated his claim that defense counsel was unfair, stating to the jury, "For they know, as I know, and as Judge Baker has told you, that the decision you render is automatically reviewable by the Supreme Court. Automatically, and I think its unfair and I don't mind telling them so."[10]

In a 5-3 decision, the United States Supreme Court held that in view of the heightened need for reliability in capital sentencing demanded by the Eighth Amendment, the prosecutor's closing argument rendered the capital sentence unconstitutional. The Court's basis for this conclusion was that the prosecutor's comments did not provide the jury with an accurate picture of its role in capital sentencing. The prosecutor's remarks might easily be interpreted as suggesting that the appellate court would determine for itself whether death was the appropriate punishment; in fact, the appellate court's review of the jury's death penalty decision would be extremely limited. The state supreme court would presume that the jury's death penalty decision was correct; it would not make its own evaluation of the mitigating evidence presented by the defense nor its own determination about whether defendant's life should be spared.[11] The Court also rejected the government's claim that the defense had invited the prosecutor's comments[12] and that the comments, though improper, were not so serious as to amount to a violation of defendant's constitutional rights.[13] In response to the second argument, the Court scrutinized the effect of the prosecutor's effort to diminish the jury's sense of responsibility and concluded, "Because we cannot say that this effort had no effect on the sentencing decision, that decision does not meet the standard of reliability that the Eighth Amendment requires."[14]

Thus, in *Caldwell* the Court established several important principles: first, prosecutorial argument at the penalty trial will be subjected to heightened scrutiny; second, one focus of that scrutiny will be to examine whether the prosecutor's comments conveyed inaccurate or misleading information to the jury; third, if a death penalty was imposed after improper prosecutorial comments were made at the penalty trial, it will be reversed unless the government can establish that the improper argument had no effect on the sentencing decision.

In dealing with government closing arguments at the penalty trial, the lower courts must confront a wide range of situations. Since *Caldwell* deals only with a relatively narrow category of prosecutorial argument, it will not provide concrete guidance in the typical penalty trial case. Nevertheless, the principles established in *Caldwell* do suggest the posture lower courts should assume in dealing with specific instances of penalty trial argument.

The approach taken in some of the leading lower court cases can now be seen as improper, in light of *Caldwell*. An examination of those cases and of some specific types of prosecutorial argument will suggest strategies for dealing with some of the problems the defense encounters at the penalty trial.

Lower Court Authority

To understand the state and lower federal courts' approach to prosecutorial arguments at penalty trials, it is necessary to begin with the law relating to prosecutors' arguments in criminal cases generally. As Francis Allen recently wrote, "It does not deprecate the competence and conscientiousness of many persons performing the prosecutorial function in the United States to say that minimizing prosecutorial excess is one of the country's great unsolved problems in criminal law administration."[15] The Courts have attempted to deal with this problem. In most jurisdictions, there is a fairly well-defined set of rules intended to restrict the range of prosecutorial argument.[16] For example, in some jurisdictions the prosecutor must limit his argument to summarizing the evidence, drawing reasonable inferences from it, answering opposing counsel, and pleading for law enforcement.[17] And in most jurisdictions, there are a number of specific prohibitions. The prosecutor may not comment on the failure of the defendant to testify;[18] he may not assert facts that have not been presented in evidence;[19] he may not misstate the law applicable to the offense;[20] he may not suggest to the jury that they can disregard a defense even though it is established by the evidence;[21] and he may not express his personal belief that the defendant is guilty.[22]

But in practice these rules do not provide clear guidelines for courts or prosecutors. First, as Albert Alschuler's study of the problem[23] has demonstrated, the rules are not inclusive enough to deal with some of the major problems presented. "When it comes to what are commonly the most disruptive forms of prosecutorial misbehavior, . . . abuse and insult, inflammatory argument, and appeals to prejudice—specific judicial standards are usually lacking."[24] Moreover, even if the prosecutor flagrantly violates one of the rules, it is difficult to predict in advance whether his error will lead to reversal. In determining whether reversal is necessary, courts typically consider myriad factors, including whether the improper remarks were isolated or repeated,[25] whether defense counsel objected to them,[26] the extent to which they were provoked by a defense argument,[27] the prosecutor's intent,[28] whether the error was harmless,[29] and the effect of the judge's curative instructions,[30] if he gave any.

Most state courts have applied similar rules when dealing with prosecutorial closing argument at the penalty stage of a capital trial. While recognizing that special care must be taken in capital cases,[31] state supreme courts have allowed prosecutors to present arguments that are inflammatory in the sense that they are obviously designed to arouse the jury's emotions.[32] For example, the Georgia Supreme Court has held highly emotional arguments to be permissible. As a part of their penalty trial argument, Georgia prosecutors typically include several standard speeches, two of which may be characterized as the war analogy[33] and the prison guard scenario.[34] The war analogy is developed along the following lines:

> You know, we've had three wars in this Country just in my lifetime, World War II, war in Korea, war in Viet Nam. In each of those wars we drafted young men, take them out of civilian life, train them, equip them, sent them to fight for us, young as seventeen, perhaps some as young as sixteen years of age. And, we've sent them off to some land halfway across the world, and we've pointed them at some individual that they didn't even know, and we said, this person is the enemy, they are trying to destroy our way of life, when you see this person, kill him. . . . We've asked seventeen year olds to kill to protect our system, our home and our families. Do we ask any less of you in this situation?
> . . . Who is the enemy now? We're engaged in a war in this Country just as real as any of those, just as real, perhaps closer to home than any of those. . . . And now we are asking you to take the step to do something about this situation.[35]

The prison guard scenario, which will be discussed in detail later,[36] is designed to emphasize that defendant will pose a threat to people who work in prison if he is not given a death sentence. The Georgia Supreme Court has held that these and other standard speeches[37] are within the bounds of proper argument.[38]

The Georgia Supreme Court's permissive stance is not atypical. The Pennsylvania Supreme Court has held that it is permissible for the prosecutor to tell the jury that "[r]ight now the score is [defendants] two and society nothing"; and to go on to exhort the jury, "When will it stop? When is it going to stop? Who is going to make it stop? That's your duty."[39] And, in a Wyoming case, the state supreme court held that it was not improper for the prosecutor to tell the jury that they should impose the death penalty because they and the rest of the community have a right "to be free from fear and go to bed at night and awaken unharmed" and that "[the defendant] will kill one and all anytime" and that he should be killed "to save and defend life."[40]

The lower courts' approach to prosecutors' arguments that are admittedly improper is perhaps even more significant. In the rare instances in which improper argument is found, the state courts have evidenced a strong reluctance to overturn death penalties.[41] Even if a prosecutor's closing argument is found to be erroneous, three additional barriers usually must be surmounted before the death penalty will be reversed. Defendant must establish that the error was not "invited"[42] or "harmless"[43] and that it was properly objected to by counsel.[44] Of these three barriers, the harmless error doctrine generally is the most formidable. Typically, a state court will follow the example of the Georgia Supreme Court in *Presnell v.*

State,[45] concluding that although the prosecutor's argument was improper it "could not have inflamed the jury more than the facts of the case themselves."[46]

To date, the lower federal courts' treatment of this issue has been essentially similar. Although some federal courts have been more ready than the state courts to condemn particular arguments as improper, at least in reviewing state convictions on federal habeas corpus, they have been as reluctant as the states to reverse death penalties on the basis of this form of prosecutorial misconduct.

In *Brooks v. Kemp,*[47] for example, the Eleventh Circuit scrutinized some of the standard closing arguments delivered by Georgia prosecutors and found several of them improper. The war analogy speech[48] was ruled improper because it directed the jury's attention away from the individual characteristics of the defendant and the circumstances of the crime;[49] the prosecutor's statement that his office rarely sought the death penalty[50] was improper because it referred to facts not offered in evidence;[51] and the prosecutor's statement that the death penalty was preferable to life imprisonment because it saved the taxpayers' money[52] was improper because it injected an irrelevant issue into the case.[53] In determining whether these arguments rendered the jury's death sentence unconstitutional, however, the court applied a remarkably permissive harmless error standard. Emphasizing that the focus should be on whether the proceedings were fundamentally unfair,[54] the court concluded that the death penalty should not be reversed unless there was a "reasonable probability" that the prosecutor's improper arguments changed the outcome at the penalty trial.[55] After examining the record as a whole, the court predictably concluded that the prosecutor's misconduct had not had enough impact to mandate reversal.[56]

Critique

In view of the principles established in *Caldwell,* certain aspects of the lower courts' approach to this subject are certainly misguided. Consider first the doctrine of harmless error. *Caldwell* did not preclude the lower courts from applying a harmless error doctrine, but it did articulate a stringent test: in order for an improper penalty argument to be disregarded, it must appear that the argument "had no effect on the sentencing decision."[57] This test certainly does not permit the approach used by the Eleventh Circuit. The defendant cannot be required to show a "reasonable probability" that the death penalty would not have been imposed in the absence of the improper argument. If the record discloses even a slight probability that the prosecutor's improper argument changed the outcome, reversal is mandated, because it does not appear that the argument "had no effect on the sentencing decision."[58]

Moreover, when taken in the context of the Court's analysis, the *Caldwell* standard actually appears to direct the courts away from the traditional approach of assessing the likelihood that the prosecutor's improper remarks had an impact on the outcome. The test appears to focus on the immediate effect of the prosecutor's argument, not on whether the jury would have imposed the death penalty without it. In *Caldwell*, the Court made no attempt to assess the strength of the evidence on whether the death penalty should be imposed. In fact, the majority implicitly recognized that any such assessment would be futile, because "an appellate court . . . is wholly ill-suited to evaluate the appropriateness of death in the first instance."[59] Only the sentencing jury is in a position to evaluate the mitigating evidence presented by the defense and to determine what weight it should be afforded. Moreover, only the sentencing jury can determine how the aggravating and mitigating circumstances should be weighed against each other. Thus, in order to keep the appellate courts from engaging in futile speculation, the test must be interpreted to require an examination of the impact of the prosecutor's remarks, not an assessment of the evidence presented at the penalty trial.

Under this interpretation of the *Caldwell* test, the traditional application of the harmless error doctrine, as applied in cases like *Presnell* and *Brooks,* is improper. The lower courts may not validly uphold a death penalty on the ground that the jury would have imposed it even without the prosecutor's improper argument. The death penalty should be upheld only if the appellate court can conclude that the prosecutor's improper argument was so insignificant that its impact on the sentencing jury was only negligible. In most cases it would be difficult to infer that such an argument did not have a measurable impact on the jury. After all, the prosecutor is not likely to make closing arguments that are not calculated to influence the jury. However, if the judge gives an effective curative instruction, in certain cases it would be permissible to conclude that the jury either ignored the argument or at least was not affected by it. Barring that situation, however, state courts should not be permitted to apply the harmless error doctrine when the prosecutor has made an improper closing argument at the penalty trial.

Caldwell's analysis is also relevant to the two other doctrines frequently applied by the lower courts. The Court explicitly held that the prosecutor's improper reference to appellate review could not be treated as "invited error." The Mississippi Supreme Court had applied this doctrine, saying that even if the prosecutor's reference to appellate review was improper, it could be justified on the ground that defense counsel's closing argument improperly intimated that a sentence of life imprisonment would in fact preclude any possibility of the defendant's being released. The United States Supreme Court concluded, however, that the invited error doctrine could not properly be applied in this situation, because the prosecutor's comments were not calculated to correct the misimpression introduced by the defense.[60] If the defense improperly suggested that a defendant sentenced to life imprisonment could not possibly be released on parole, it might be permissible for the prosecutor to explain the circumstances under which that could happen. On the other hand, informing the jury that a death sentence would be reviewable does not correct the misimpression left by the defense but instead introduces a new misimpression. The Court held that an improper argument by defense counsel does not give the prosecutor license to make a different improper argument.

The Court's analysis suggests that in the context of the penalty trial, the invited error doctrine should have at most a very limited application. The prosecutor's closing argument may be justified as a response to an improper defense argument only if it is specifically designed to correct the misimpression left by the defense. The prosecution may repair specific damage done by the defense, but the prosecution may not simply inflict damage on the defense because the defense has inflicted damage on the prosecution. Moreover, implicit in this analysis is a suggestion that the prosecutor's argument should be *limited* to repairing the damage done by the defense. Thus, even if the prosecutor is specifically responding to a particular improper argument by defense counsel, his argument should not be permitted if it is likely to have an effect that goes beyond repairing the damage caused by the defense argument.

This last point needs elaboration. In many situations, defense and prosecution arguments that seem to be equivalent will not be equivalent in the eyes of the jury. To take one example, suppose that it is improper for either side to present argument concerning the deterrent effect of capital punishment.[61] Then suppose that defense counsel asserts that capital punishment does not deter murder and that the prosecutor responds by claiming that it does. On the surface, the prosecutor's argument seems calculated to do no more than neutralize the defense argument, but—especially in the penalty trial context—it is likely to have a greater impact on the jury because the jury is much more likely to be swayed by the prosecutor than the defense counsel.

In any criminal case, jurors will be likely to view the prosecutor in a more favorable light than defense counsel. As Alschuler has said, "The assistant district attorney is the representative of an elected, presumably popular public official, and the mere fact that he is a state employee may create a sense of trust and an expectation of fairness that a defense counsel would find difficult to match through the most strenuous exertion of his charm."[62] Moreover, the fact that the penalty stage jury has already found the defendant guilty of a capital crime places defense counsel at a special disadvantage. Because the jury has accepted the prosecutor's position at the guilt stage, they are especially likely to view the prosecutor as more credible than defense counsel and to give greater weight to any comments he may make during closing argument. Thus, in the context of the penalty trial, the invited error doctrine should have extremely limited application. When defense counsel makes an improper argument, in most cases the trial judge should not permit the prosecutor to respond to that argument. Instead, the prosecutor's appropriate remedy should be to object to defense counsel's comments and to have the judge issue a curative instruction.

Caldwell's analysis is also relevant to the rule that defense counsel's failure to object to improper argument will preclude her from raising that point later on. The Court did not discuss this issue, but it did repeatedly emphasize the special "need for reliability in the determination that death is the appropriate punishment in a specific case."[63] The Court's concern suggests that counsel's failure to object should be treated differently in capital and noncapital cases. In noncapital cases it may well be appropriate to hold that defense counsel's failure to object to improper argument will preclude her from raising the point later. This rule promotes the interest of finality, encourages counsel to raise objections at the appropriate time, and prevents reversals on the basis of errors that in some cases could have been eliminated by the judge's curative instructions. Nevertheless, if there is indeed a special concern for reliability in capital sentencing, it is at least arguable that in many cases that concern will outweigh these important governmental interests. At the least, defense counsel's failure to object to closing argument at the penalty trial should not absolutely preclude defendant from arguing that his death penalty should be reversed because of the prosecutor's improper argument.[64]

Establishing Guidelines for the Prosecutor

In dealing with the prosecutorial argument at the penalty trial, the state courts have tended to focus too much on the total trial record. In light of *Caldwell's* analysis, there should be more emphasis on providing guidelines for prosecutors by determining which types of arguments are permissible and impermissible. In pursuit of this objective, two general approaches might be taken: limiting the type of prosecutorial argument that is appropriate and developing rules that will alert the prosecutor to the types of arguments that are improper.

Under the first approach, the prosecutor would be directed to restrict his argument to the specific issues that are relevant to the death penalty determination. The current death penalty statutes generally provide that the jury must decide whether the death penalty will be imposed by first determining whether aggravating and mitigating circumstances are present and then weighing those circumstances to determine which preponderates.[65] Since the jury's role is shaped in this way, the prosecutor's argument should be limited to commenting on the evidence relevant to aggravating or mitigating circumstances and elaborating on the weighing process the jury must undertake. Moreover, in order to avoid distorting the jury's perception of the evidence or the weighing process, the prosecutor should confine himself to discussing the evidence in a dispassionate fashion, avoiding any deliberate appeal to the jury's emotions.

If our system is truly committed to a fair administration of capital punishment, there is much to be said for this approach. The new statutes were enacted specifically for the purpose of reducing the arbitrary imposition of capital punishment.[66] In particular, the aggravating and mitigating circumstances were designed to channel the jury's discretion so that the jury would be more likely to condemn only those capital offenders the legislature considered the most heinous. Naturally, any closing argument that diverts the jury from an objective determination and weighing of the aggravating and mitigating circumstances undermines the goal of achieving a more even-handed application of the death penalty. Thus, an approach that restricts the prosecutor to a dispassionate discussion of evidence that is relevant to the statutorily defined aggravating and mitigating circumstances is certainly consistent with the Supreme Court's goal of promoting reliability in capital sentencing.

Nevertheless, it is doubtful whether the Court would require the state courts to adopt this approach. In *Caldwell,* Justice Marshall's opinion asserts that the prosecutor's reference to appellate review was improper in part because the presence of appellate review "in itself is wholly irrelevant to the determination of an appropriate sentence."[67] Justice O'Connor's concurring opinion disagreed with this assessment, however, and suggested that a state court could properly conclude that accurate information regarding the jury's role in the capital sentencing scheme is relevant to the death penalty determination.[68] Justice O'Connor's opinion, which constitutes the fifth vote in *Caldwell,* combined with the Court's other recent decisions concerning regulation of the penalty trial,[69] suggests that the states will be afforded considerable leeway to decide what type of argument is relevant to the death penalty determination. Thus, although the states may properly require the prosecutor to limit his closing argument to matters that are relevant to the statutorily defined issues, the Supreme Court seems unlikely to require them to do so.

The second approach would seek to provide some specific prohibitions for prosecutors by drawing on principles articulated by the Supreme Court in its death penalty decisions and in other contexts. Three categories of argument seem particularly deserving of scrutiny: first, comments on the defendant's failure to testify; second, arguments for the death penalty on the basis of a penological theory; third, argument that is particularly likely to arouse the fears of the jury.

Comment on the Defendant's Failure to Testify

Estelle v. Smith[70] held that the Fifth Amendment privilege applies at the penalty stage. Moreover, in *Griffin v. California,*[71] the Court held that the privilege prohibits the prosecutor from arguing to the jury that they should draw an inference against the defendant because of his failure to testify on the issue of guilt. Since the privilege also applies at the penalty stage, *Griffin*'s holding that the prosecutor is not permitted to comment on the defendant's failure to testify should be as rigorously applied at this stage as it is at trial.

Griffin should preclude the prosecutor from making an adverse comment on a capital defendant's failure to testify at either the guilt or the penalty stage. The issue typically arises when the prosecutor tells the jury that the defendant's total silence may be considered as evidence of his lack of remorse.[72] The government might seek to distinguish *Griffin* on the ground that asking the jury to draw an inference of lack of remorse from silence does not infringe on the Fifth Amendment privilege, because the jury is not being asked to use the defendant's silence to *incriminate* him. But in the context of the penalty trial this argument is not sound. There the ultimate issue to be determined—that is, the parallel of the issue of guilt or innocence at the guilt stage—is whether the defendant deserves to die or to live. Since this is the issue, any evidence that suggests the death penalty is appropriate is incriminating. Evidence of the defendant's lack of remorse can certainly be interpreted as suggesting the death penalty is appropriate. Accordingly, asking the penalty jury to infer lack of remorse from silence is directly analogous to asking an ordinary jury to infer guilt from silence. Both arguments equally violate the Fifth Amendment privilege.

A more complex question arises when the defendant testifies for a limited purpose at the penalty trial and the prosecutor asks the jury to draw an adverse inference from his silence on other issues. When this problem arises in an ordinary criminal trial, the courts have applied what is sometimes known as the collateral issue rule, holding that when the defendant testifies only on a collateral issue not directly related to the issue of guilt, the prosecutor may not ask the jury to draw unfavorable inferences from his failure to testify to the merits of the accusation.[73] In *Calloway v. Wainwright*,[74] for example, the defendant testified only for the purpose of explaining the circumstances under which his allegedly involuntary confession was obtained. In his summation the prosecutor repeatedly referred to the defendant's failure to testify on other issues. The Fifth Circuit ruled that these comments were improper because defendant's testimony had to do with a collateral issue, not one directly related to the issue of guilt or innocence.

In the penalty trial, applying this rule is difficult because of the difficulty in determining what is a collateral issue. *Commonwealth v. Travaglia*,[75] a Pennsylvania death penalty case, illustrates the type of problem that is likely to be presented. In *Travaglia*, defendant John Lesko did not testify at the guilt stage of the capital trial and was found guilty of first-degree murder, a capital offense. At the penalty stage, Lesko testified for the limited purpose of explaining his troubled family background. In closing argument, the prosecutor commented on the defendant's failure to testify about the crime charged. He told the jury that they should "consider Lesko's arrogance" because he "didn't even have the common decency to say I'm sorry for what I did."[76]

Under the collateral issue rule, the question to be determined in this type of case is whether Lesko's testimony at the penalty trial related to a collateral issue. Since the issue to be decided at the penalty trial is whether the defendant should die, the government could argue that Lesko's explanation of his troubled childhood did not relate to a collateral issue but went directly to the merits of the ultimate issue to be decided. Therefore, the argument would go, the prosecutor should be afforded an opportunity to comment on the defendant's silence on issues relevant to the death penalty determination. If this argument were accepted, once the defendant testified to any mitigating circumstance the prosecutor would be free to comment on his failure to testify on any other issue relevant to the death penalty determination.

The difficulty with this position is that it fails to take account of the special significance of evidence that is incriminating in relation to guilt. Pursuant to the Fifth Amendment privilege, a defendant may not be forced to testify at a criminal trial, because that would place him in a cruel trilemma under which he would be forced to choose between self-incrimination, perjury, and contempt.[77] The *Griffin* rule further protects the defendant's right to remain silent by holding that a defendant who exercises his privilege not to testify may not be subject to the penalty of an adverse inference. The collateral issue rule is premised on the view that a defendant should be permitted to testify about an issue that is not material to guilt without forfeiting the protection afforded by *Griffin*. The government might argue that the rule should not apply at the penalty trial because the defendant has already been judged guilty of the crime at issue. But the Court held, in *Malloy v. Hogan*,[78] that a criminal conviction does not remove the defendant's privilege not to incriminate himself concerning the underlying criminal transaction. Therefore, since the defendant's privilege still applies at the penalty trial, the defendant should be permitted to testify about an issue collateral to guilt without affording the prosecutor an opportunity to argue that the jury may draw an adverse inference from the defendant's silence about his guilt.[79]

Thus, when the defendant testifies solely for the purpose of developing a mitigating circumstance relating to his personal history, the prosecutor should be limited to commenting on the defendant's silence about that mitigating circumstance or related mitigating circumstances. He should not be allowed to argue that an adverse inference flows from the defendant's failure to admit or deny guilt. In a case like *Travaglia*, the prosecutor should be permitted to argue that Lesko's testimony about his troubled history did not show that he was subjected to child abuse or that Lesko did not testify to anything that would suggest he was emotionally immature or mentally retarded. The prosecutor should not be permitted to comment on the fact that the defendant failed to apologize for his crime, because that would be an adverse comment on the defendant's failure to discuss his guilt or innocence.

Argument Based on Penological Theories

Prosecutorial arguments at the sentencing phase may refer explicitly or implicitly to a penological theory.[80] Typically, they refer to the general deterrent effect of the death penalty, to its particular deterrent or incapacitating effect on the prisoner who suffers it, to society's general need for retribution because of factors like the crime rate, or to society's need for specific retribution because of the particularly vile or cruel nature of the defendant's crime. Many times one closing argument contains a mixture of these.

For example, the war analogy speech[81] used by Georgia prosecutors is essentially an appeal based on the theories of both general and specific retribution. The defendant should be killed both because he is a member of the enemy and to exact vengeance for what he has done. Similarly, in *Collins v. Francis,*[82] a prosecutor mixed speculation on the deterrent effect of the death penalty with appeals to the jury to exact retribution for both the general prevalence of violent crime and the particular heinousness of the defendant's crime:

> We do not know how many criminals are deterred by capital punishment, no one can know, but what we can see every day you pick up the newspaper is that crimes of this sort . . . happen every day, that the life of a human being, lives of human beings are sacrificed every day with as little concern as the life of an animal, and that is how [the defendant] killed [the victim], like an animal.[83]

And in *Drake v. Francis,*[84] the prosecutor's argument combined appeals to the death penalty's general deterrent and incapacitating effect by directing the jury's attention to the celebrated case of Gary Gilmore who was executed in 1977: "And I submit, if your Honor please, that [capital punishment] does deter. Gary Gilmore, if your Honor please, will never kill anyone again."[85]

The United States Supreme Court has recognized deterrence and retribution as the principle justifications for legislative adoption of the death penalty.[86] It does not follow, however, that those theories are necessarily appropriate subjects for jury argument. In seeking to make capital sentencing more reliable, the Supreme Court has insisted on individualized sentencing in capital cases,[87] and in *Woodson*[88] and *Lockett*[89] the Court indicated that individualized sentencing demands that the sentencing judge or jury focus on "consideration of the character and record of the individual offender and the circumstances of the particular offense."[90]

The Court's insistence on individualized sentencing does not imply that the prosecutor is absolutely precluded from arguing about matters that do not relate to the defendant's character or the circumstances of the offense. For example, Justice O'Connor's concurring opinion in *Caldwell* suggested that the state courts could properly allow the prosecutor to give the jury an accurate description of appellate review in death penalty cases.[91] Nevertheless, some arguments based on penological theory run the risk of distorting the penalty jury's perception of its function. A prosecutor who argues in favor of general deterrence or general retribution directs the sentencing jury's attention away from its duty to give an individualized sentence. Instead of determining whether a death penalty is appropriate in light of the character of the offender and the circumstances of the offense, the jury may be diverted toward considering whether the death penalty should be imposed on the defendant because of the crimes of other defendants. In *Commonwealth v. Travaglia*,[92] for example, the prosecutor argued to the jury that "right now, the score is [defendants] two, society nothing. . . . When is it going to stop? Who is going to make it stop? That's your duty."[93] If a jury were to take this argument seriously, they would reflect on such questions as whether their imposition of the death penalty would have the effect of curbing other capital crimes or whether the death penalty should be imposed to exact vengeance on behalf of society. Obviously, they would be less likely to make their death penalty determination by focusing exclusively on the character of the defendant or the circumstances of the crime. Like the argument in *Caldwell*, arguments based on general penological theories increase the risk of inaccurate capital sentencing, because they are likely to distort the jury's perception of their role.

This analysis does not suggest that all prosecutorial references to penological theory should be barred. A prosecutor may expand on the theory of incapacitation, pointing out that the death penalty is appropriate because it is the only means by which an incorrigibly violent offender may be permanently removed from society, or she may argue in favor of specific retribution, claiming that death is the only punishment that can adequately express society's condemnation of the crime committed. Particular appeals of this type may be objectionable on other grounds,[94] but unlike the others discussed here, they do not necessarily tend to divert the jury from its proper focus on the character of the offender and the circumstances of the particular offense. Thus, appropriate guidelines for courts and prosecutors should make a distinction between arguments premised on penological theories that relate specifically to the particular defendant and broader penological arguments that are based on general deterrence or general retribution. In light of *Caldwell*'s concern for ensuring that prosecutors' arguments not mislead juries about their role in capital sentencing, the latter type of argument should be prohibited.

Appeals to Fear

Prosecutors who argue for the death penalty are especially likely to use emotional appeals that are calculated to arouse the jury's fears. In particular, they may expand on themes relating to self-defense by directly or indirectly suggesting that the death penalty needs to be imposed to protect the jury itself or other members of society. Prosecutors have displayed exceptional skill in developing these themes. Some of the most effective speeches are remarkable not only for their vivid imagery but also for the way they communicate personalized threats of danger to members of the jury themselves, people known to the jury, or hypothetical persons presented in such individualized detail that they might seem real to the jury.

Hopkinson v. State[95] is a case in which the prosecutor's articulation of threats to the jury and people known to the jury was extremely powerful. Mark Hopkinson was on trial for four murders. Three of the killings occurred when a hit man hired by Hopkinson threw a bomb into the house of an attorney who had opposed him in several civil matters. Later, while Hopkinson was in prison, he arranged for the contract killing of the fourth victim, a man who was to testify against him in a grand jury proceeding. The case was prosecuted by the well-known Wyoming attorney Gerry Spence. Spence used the circumstances of the crimes to fully exploit the persuasive possibilities of the self-defense appeal. He laid the groundwork for his appeal by telling the jury that he was not speaking to them as an advocate but "to let you know how I feel as a person."[96] He further told the jury that he was opposed to the death penalty both as retribution and as deterrent.[97] The core of Spence's appeal was a personalized, forceful argument that the jury's imposition of the death penalty was necessary to protect Spence, his staff, the witnesses, and the jurors themselves from Hopkinson's revenge:

> We have been in fear, my family and I. . . .
> . . . And I never experienced what that was like . . . before this case. And it has something to do with waking up and wondering and worrying, being concerned, being afraid, little children having difficulty to sleep, nightmares in the night. For the first time an issue came that I have never thought about before as an attorney or as a person and that is the issue of survival. It was the same issue of survival for old Mr. J. R. Goo and for all the people in this case that have in one way or another drug up their courage sufficiently to testify from this witness stand and they have been frightened people. . . . Whether it's a dandelion that hugs the ground to get the warmth of the ground and to save itself from the fall frost so that it can bloom, or whether it is a rabbit running from a coyote or whether it's you or me, the right to survive is an inate [sic], God given natural right that all of us, have. . . .

Now we haven't been free, none of us. I haven't been free nor my family. We have been captives and we have a right to be free. I have been a captive along with my staff and my family, their families, of fear. We have a right to go places without guards, go to the movies, live our lives, to go to the grocery store, to go to the office, to go to bed. Those are rights that belong to us. We have been deprived of those rights. You [the jury] have similar rights.[98]

Defense counsel objected to this argument on the ground that counsel was referring to matters outside the record, since there was no evidence that Hopkinson had threatened Spence, his family, or anyone connected with the case.[99] This objection was overruled, however, and the Wyoming Supreme Court held that Spence's closing argument was proper.

The *Hopkinson* case is extraordinary in that the nature of the defendant's alleged crimes naturally suggested that people connected with the case might be in danger. In cases not involving these unique circumstances the prosecutor will often seek to communicate danger to future victims by bringing a hypothetical person to life. One version of the prison guard scenario is a particularly skillful example of this genre. In *Tucker v. Francis*,[100] the prosecutor argued to the jury as follows:

You're afraid of putting this man to death? Let the next victim of Richard Tucker be on your conscience. Let some prison guard, fifty-five years old, been working for twenty years at Reidsville—let some poor prison guard down there who can't carry a weapon because these people down there will grab it and use his weapon against him—let some prison guard down there who is right now on the job thinking about his pension, thinking about retiring in a few years.[101]

The Georgia Supreme Court has held that this argument is proper; and in a recent retreat from its decision in *Tucker,* the Eleventh Circuit Court of Appeals agreed.[102] The federal court held that this kind of speech is a permissible comment on the defendant's future dangerousness.[103]

Developing workable guidelines in this area is particularly difficult because of the competing interests at stake. On the one hand, our adversary system demands that the prosecutor be permitted considerable freedom to express the implications of the defendant's conduct in terms that will be meaningful to the jury. If the prosecutor has a dramatic flair and an ability to communicate effectively, he should not be precluded from using those talents simply because the exercise of his rhetorical skills results in arousing the jury's fear. On the other hand, there is a need for special sensitivity because of the potential impact of these appeals. Research in the field of social psychology indicates that appeals to fear,[104] especially those made by prestigious, attractive figures,[105] are particularly likely to persuade. The *Caldwell* decision is premised on the view that closing arguments that distort the jury's perception of their proper role in capital sentencing are constitutionally impermissible. Although appeals to fear will not directly mislead the jury about their function, there is some risk that they will divert the jury from their proper role of determining whether the death sentence should be imposed on the basis of the relevant evidence relating to the character of the offender and the circumstances of the crime.

The arguments in cases like *Hopkinson* and *Tucker* seem to pose special risks to the Court's goal of ensuring reliability in capital sentencing. The problem stems from the prosecutor's personalization of a future victim. The prison guard scenario is a typical example of the kind of dangers presented. Under the Court's decisions,[106] evidence relating to the defendant's future dangerousness may properly be relevant to the death penalty decision. Thus, if a government psychiatrist has testified that the defendant is a sociopathic personality who will be likely to kill again if given a chance,[107] the prosecutor should be allowed to emphasize that in his closing penalty argument. Nevertheless, when the prosecutor vividly brings a future hypothetical victim to life and sets him before the jury, the danger that the jury will be deflected from an assessment of the defendant and his crime becomes acute. In a case like *Tucker* the jury is likely to focus on the fifty-five-year-old prison guard and consider whether the death penalty should be imposed to protect that fictionalized person's life. In view of the Court's concern that the jury not be diverted from its proper role in capital sentencing, arguments of this sort should be improper.

The argument in *Hopkinson* presents an issue that is harder in one way and easier in another. The defendant's murder of an attorney and a witness legitimized some comment on his dangerousness to people involved in litigation with him. The prosecutor should have been permitted to remark on the reprehensible quality of the defendant's acts and point out their implications. He could have been allowed to say, for example, that the victims in the case had taken valid legal action against the defendant, that they were now dead, and that the defendant's course of conduct demonstrated that he could be a continuing threat to other people who might take valid legal action against him. Of course, the jury might have drawn from such comments (or from the defendant's acts themselves) the inference that the defendant posed a danger to people connected with the prosecution of the present case or even to themselves. Their evaluation of these possibilities would have inevitably played a part in their sentencing determination. But the argument actually made in *Hopkinson* very likely had a much greater impact on the jury. Gerry Spence's dramatic exposition of "the issue of survival" surely tended to deflect their attention away from evaluating the defendant's character or future dangerousness and toward considering whether the death penalty should be imposed to protect Spence and his family and protect themselves. In view of the Court's concern for ensuring that the jury not be misled about its role in capital sentencing, the risk that a speech of this kind would divert the jury from its proper role in capital sentencing is simply too great to be tolerated.

The problem of arguments that appeal to fear is a complicated one that requires much more consideration. As a beginning, however, although the prosecutor should not necessarily be precluded from using vivid language or from discussing the defendant's possible future danger to society, he should not be allowed to focus the jury's attention on either hypothetical or real future victims. He should be allowed to say that the defendant is a danger to society. He should not be allowed to say that the defendant is a danger to the witnesses in the case or to a hypothetical prison guard.

Conclusion

The principles articulated in the *Caldwell* case suggest some specific guidelines for evaluating prosecutors' closing penalty trial arguments. For example, the prosecutor should not be permitted to present arguments based on broad penological theories like general deterrence or general retribution; and in arguments designed to arouse the jury's fears, the prosecutor should not be permitted to focus the jury's attention on either hypothetical or real future victims. Although the prosecutor should be afforded fairly wide freedom to make case-specific arguments that are based on the evidence, he should not be permitted to make either legislative arguments that suggest the death penalty should be imposed because it will have a generally beneficial effect on society or security arguments that suggest the death penalty is needed to protect some particular victim.

In some respects, then, the standard for evaluating prosecutorial closing argument should be different from the standard for evaluating defense closing argument. Some restrictions should be imposed on defense closing argument, but the defense should be permitted a broad opportunity to elicit the jury's sympathy for the defendant and to argue that under the circumstances of the particular case the imposition of the death penalty would be an act of needless cruelty.[108] Thus, under my scheme, defense counsel would be allowed to argue that the jury should not impose the death penalty because of their recognition that the defendant is a fellow human being, but the prosecutor would not be permitted to argue that the death penalty should be imposed to protect some future victim from the defendant. Similarly, the defense attorney would be permitted to argue that the infliction of the death penalty would be an act of needless cruelty, but the prosecutor would not be allowed to argue that the death penalty should be imposed to strike a blow in the war against crime. How may this double standard be justified?

The double standard applies because of the nature of the modern capital sentencing statutes. As I have emphasized, the modern statutes are designed to strike a balance between channeling the sentencer's exercise of discretion and providing for individualized sentencing based on a full presentation of evidence relating to the circumstances of the crime or the character of the offender. Because *Lockett v. Ohio*[109] guarantees the defendant a broad right to present mitigating evidence, defense counsel should be afforded at least an equally broad opportunity to argue that the defendant's life should be spared. Some limitations may be appropriate, but in general counsel should be allowed to present any argument that relates specifically to the question whether the particular defendant before the jury should be put to death.

On the other hand, the modern capital punishment statutes are *not* intended to provide the prosecutor with total discretion to present any evidence that might dispose the jury toward imposing a death sentence. Indeed, if the prosecutor were afforded this freedom, the primary purpose of the new statutes would be largely defeated. Their carefully defined aggravating circumstances were intended to channel the jury's exercise of discretion, thereby reducing the likelihood that the death penalty will be arbitrarily imposed. Under the new statutes, the jury's role is to determine whether aggravating circumstances are present and to weigh them against the mitigating circumstances established by the defense. If the prosecutor is allowed to make arguments that will divert the jury from performing this function, the new statutes' intended curb on arbitrariness will obviously be undermined.

Thus, an approach that imposes different restrictions on the prosecutor and defense counsel during the closing penalty trial argument is justified by the different role that each is intended to fulfill under our modern scheme of capital punishment. As under the old system, the defense attorney's role is essentially to argue for mercy. Thus, she should be allowed wide freedom to present emotional arguments so long as they bear in some way on the question whether the particular defendant before the jury should be spared. Since the prosecutor's role is more limited, however, he should be curbed from presenting any penalty trial argument that will divert the jury from evaluating and weighing the relevant aggravating and mitigating circumstances. If these differing restrictions are enforced, the Court's goal of maintaining a proper balance between individualized sentencing and a nonarbitrary imposition of the death penalty can be more nearly achieved.

NOTES

1. *See, e.g.,* 42 PA. CONS. STAT. ANN. § 9711(2)(3) (Purdon 1982) (argument by counsel may be presented at the penalty trial); PA. R. CRIM. PROC. 1116 (prosecutor's argument shall be presented last). In some states the prosecutor is allowed to give the first and last

closing argument. *See, e.g.,* CAL. PENAL CODE § 1093 (West Supp. 1983–84).

2. For trial manuals discussing techniques utilized in criminal closing arguments, *see generally* A. AMSTERDAM, TRIAL MANUAL FOR THE DEFENSE OF CRIMINAL CASES §§ 444–48 (4th ed. 1984); J. STEIN, CLOSING ARGUMENT: THE ART AND THE LAW (2d ed. 1982); H. ROTHBLATT, SUCCESSFUL TECHNIQUES IN THE TRIAL OF CRIMINAL CASES 173–79 (1961).

3. For an example of a defense argument that skillfully exploits this issue, *see* chap. 4.

4. *See generally* Goodpaster, *The Trial for Life: Effective Assistance of Counsel in Death Penalty Cases,* 58 N.Y.U. L. REV. 299 (1983).

5. As Weisberg has explained, one approach that the prosecutor may use is to tell the jury that they are not required to make a moral judgment whether the death penalty should be imposed; rather, under the new statutes their role is simply to engage in a kind of legal arithmetic in which they carefully weigh the statutorily defined aggravating circumstances against the mitigating circumstances. *See* Weisberg, *Deregulating Death,* 1983 SUP. CT. REV. 305, 375–79. Of course, another approach is to seek to defuse the jury's sense of responsibility by suggesting that they are not the only body involved in the death penalty decision.

6. For a discussion of the limits that should be imposed on defense counsel's right to present closing argument at the penalty trial, *see* chap. 4.

7. 105 S. Ct. 2633 (1985).

8. *Id.* at 2637.

9. *Id.* at 2638.

10. *Id.*

11. *Id.* at 2640–41.

12. *Id.* at 2643–44.

13. *Id.* at 2644–46.

14. *Id.* at 2646.

15. Allen, *A Serendipitous Trek Through the Advance-Sheet Jungle: Criminal Justice in the Courts of Review,* 70 IOWA L. REV. 311, 335 [hereinafter cited as Allen].

16. *See generally* Crump, *The Function and the Limits of Prosecution Jury Argument,* 28 SW. L.J. 505 (1974) [hereinafter cited as Crump]; Alschuler, *Courtroom Misconduct by Prosecutors and Trial Judges,* 50 TEX. L. REV. 629 (1972) [hereinafter cited as Alschuler].

17. *See, e.g.,* Rhodes v. State, 450 S.W.2d 329, 331–32 (Tex. Crim. App.), *cert. denied,* 400 U.S. 927 (1970); *see generally* Alschuler, *supra* note 16, at 636 n.32.

18. *See, e.g.,* Griffin v. California, 380 U.S. 609 (1965); *see generally* Alschuler, *supra* note 16, at 634.

19. *See, e.g.,* Kemph v. State, 464 S.W.2d 112 (Tex. Crim. App. 1971); *see generally* Alschuler, *supra* note 16, at 634.

20. *See, e.g.,* Cadenhead v. State, 369 S.W.2d 44 (Tex. Crim. App. 1963); *see generally* Crump, *supra* note 16, at 512–13.

21. *See, e.g.,* Rodgers v. State, 111 Tex. Crim. 419, 13 S.W.2d 116 (1926); *see generally* Alschuler, *supra* note 16, at 640.

22. *See, e.g.,* United States v. Grunberger, 431 F.2d 1062, 1068 (2d Cir. 1970); *see generally* Alschuler, *supra* note 16, at 634 n.22.

23. *See* Alschuler, *supra* note 16.

24. Alschuler, *supra* note 16, at 634.

25. *See, e.g.,* Donnely v. DeChristoforo, 416 U.S. 637 (1974).

26. *See, e.g.,* United States v. Socony

Vaccume Ore Co., 310 U.S. 150 (1940); see generally Alschuler, supra note 16, at 648–56.

27. See, e.g., United States v. Young, 105 S. Ct. 1038 (1985).

28. See, e.g., United States v. Eiland, 741 F.2d 738 (5th Cir. 1984) (prosecutor's comment on defendant's silence will be reversible error when it is shown that prosecutor's intent was to comment on defendant's failure to testify).

29. See, e.g., Baker v. United States, 115 F.2d 533, 543 (8th Cir. 1940), cert. denied, 312 U.S. 692 (1941) (district attorney's conduct "although reprehensible and improper, could not have been prejudicial"); see generally Allen, supra note 15, at 329–30; Alschuler, supra note 16, at 658–66.

30. See, e.g., Yett v. State, 110 Tex. Crim. 23, 24, 7 S.W.2d 94, 94 (1928) (admonition and instruction to disregard held sufficient to cure racially oriented argument); see generally Alschuler, supra note 16, at 639, 652–55.

31. See, e.g., State v. Kirkley, 308 N.C. 196, 205, 302 S.E.2d 144, 152 (1983) (in capital cases, appellate court may review prosecutor's argument for gross impropriety not objected to at trial).

32. See, e.g., Connor v. State, 251 Ga. 113, 121, 303 S.E.2d 266, 275 (1983) (appeals to passion permissible so long as there is no appeal to prejudice, particularly racial prejudice).

33. See, e.g., Hance v. Zant, 696 F.2d 940, 952 (11th Cir. 1983), cert. denied, 103 S. Ct. 3544 (1983); Brooks v. Francis, 716 F.2d 780, 788–89 (11th Cir. 1983).

34. See, e.g., Hance, 696 F.2d at 952; Tucker v. Francis, 723 F.2d 1504, 1507 (11th Cir. 1984).

35. See Hance, 696 F.2d at 952.

36. See infra text at notes 100–107.

37. For other standard speeches given by Georgia prosecutors see infra notes 100, 101, and accompanying text.

38. See generally Connor v. State, 251 Ga. 113, 303 S.E.2d 266 (1983) (permitting broad prosecutorial latitude); see, e.g., Hance v. State, 245 Ga. 856, 268 S.E.2d 339 (1980); Brooks v. State, 244 Ga. 574, 261 S.E.2d 379 (1979).

39. See Commonwealth v. Travaglia, 502 Pa. 474, 502, 476 A.2d 288, 302 (1983).

40. See Hopkinson v. State, 632 P.2d 79, 161–66 (Wyo. 1981).

41. See infra text at notes 42–56.

42. See supra note 27 and accompanying text.

43. See supra note 29 and accompanying text.

44. See supra note 26 and accompanying text.

45. 241 Ga. 49, 243 S.E.2d 496 (1978).

46. Id. at 60, 243 S.E.2d at 507.

47. 762 F.2d 1383 (11th Cir. 1985).

48. Id. at 1396. For a similar war analogy speech in another case, see supra text at note 35.

49. 762 F.2d at 1413.

50. Id. at 1395.

51. Id. at 1410.

52. Id. at 1396.

53. Id. at 1412.

54. Id. at 1398–1403.

55. Id. at 1413.

56. Id. at 1416.

57. 105 S. Ct. at 2646.

58. Id.

59. Id. at 2640.

60. Id. at 2644.

61. For a discussion of this issue, see infra text at notes 78–92.

62. Alschuler, supra note 16, at 632.

63. See, e.g., Caldwell, 105 S. Ct. at 2640.

64. In determining the significance of counsel's failure to object to closing argument, the possible effect of curative instructions should be a significant factor. If the improper effect of the prosecutor's argument could have been eliminated by an appropriate instruction from the judge, the defendant should perhaps be bound by counsel's failure to object, because counsel's inaction prevented the possibility of eliminating the error. On the other hand, if the prosecutor's error could not have been corrected by a curative instruction, reversing the death penalty on the basis of the improper argument does not prejudice the government, because exactly the same result would have been necessary if defense counsel had made an appropriate objection at trial.
65. *See* chap. 1.
66. *See id.*
67. 105 S. Ct. at 2643.
68. *Id.* at 2646 (concurring opinion of O'Connor, J.).
69. *See* chap. 1.
70. 451 U.S. 454, 462–63 (1981).
71. 380 U.S. 609 (1965).
72. *See, e.g.,* People v. Ramirez, 98 Ill. 2d 439, 445, 457 N.E.2d 31, 37 (1983).
73. *See, e.g.,* McGaher v. Massey, 667 F.2d 1357 (11th Cir. 1982); Calloway v. Wainwright, 409 F.2d 59, 64–66 (5th Cir. 1969), *cert. denied,* 395 U.S. 909 (1969); *see generally* C. McCORMICK, McCORMICK ON EVIDENCE §§ 131, 132 (E. Cleary ed. 1984).
74. 409 F.2d 59, 64–66 (5th Cir. 1969), *cert. denied,* 395 U.S. 909 (1969).
75. 502 Pa. 474, 467 A.2d 288 (1983).
76. *Id.* at 498, 467 A.2d at 300.
77. *See, e.g.,* United States v. Scully,

225 F.2d 113, 116 (2d Cir. 1955) (dicta). For an excellent account of the historical evolution of the Fifth Amendment privilege, *see* L. LEVY, ORIGINS OF THE FIFTH AMENDMENT: THE RIGHT AGAINST SELF-INCRIMINATION (1968).
78. 380 U.S. 609 (1965).
79. In this case that rule is especially appropriate, because the defendant's conviction might be reversed on appeal and any incriminating testimony given at the penalty trial might be used against him at a subsequent retrial.
80. Theories of punishment include: (1) prevention or particular deterrence (deterrence of the criminal as an individual by giving him an unpleasant experience he will not want to endure again); (2) restraint or incapacitation (protection of society by isolating or executing individuals dangerous to it); (3) rehabilitation (giving the criminal appropriate treatment so he will return to society without the need or desire to commit further crimes); (4) deterrence or general prevention (imposing suffering on the criminal so that others will be deterred from committing crimes lest they suffer the same fate); (5) education of the public concerning what conduct is good and bad; and (6) retribution or revenge (imposition of suffering on a criminal because it is considered fair that one who has imposed suffering on others should himself endure suffering). *See generally* W. LaFAVE & A. SCOTT, CRIMINAL LAW § 5 (1972).
81. *See supra* text at note 35.
82. 728 F.2d 1322 (11th Cir. 1984).
83. *Id.* at 1341.
84. 727 F.2d 990 (11th Cir. 1984).
85. *Id.* at 996.

86. See Gregg v. Georgia, 428 U.S. 153, 182–87 (1976) (plurality opinion of Stewart, J.).

87. See Lockett v. Ohio, 438 U.S. 586, 605 (1978) (plurality opinion of Burger, C.J.); Woodson v. North Carolina, 428 U.S. 280, 304 (1976) (plurality opinion of Stewart, J.).

88. Woodson, 428 U.S. 280.

89. Lockett, 438 U.S. 586.

90. 438 U.S. at 604; 428 U.S. at 304.

91. See 105 S. Ct. at 2646–47 (concurring opinion of O'Connor, J.).

92. 502 Pa. 474, 467 A.2d 288 (1983).

93. Id. at 502–3, 467 A.2d at 302.

94. See, e.g., infra text at notes 95–107.

95. 632 P.2d 79 (Wyo. 1981).

96. Id. at 161.

97. Id. at 162–64.

98. Id. at 161–62.

99. Id. at 162. This objection raises an interesting question. The government could argue that the prosecutor's statement does not refer to matters outside the record but merely draws a legitimate inference from facts in evidence. Spence was not suggesting that he and his family lived in fear because of threats made by the defendant; he was merely making the logical inference that the defendant's past conduct indicated that he was a danger to people who pursued legal action against him. That is a legitimate argument. On the other hand, in determining whether the prosecutor's argument improperly refers to matters outside the record, the focus should be on whether the jury would be likely to understand the prosecutor's argument as referring to facts that were not presented in evidence during the capital trial. In this case, it certainly appears likely that the jury would have interpreted Spence's remarks to mean that he and his family had been threatened by people associated with the defendant. Therefore, the defendant's objection should have been sustained.

100. 723 F.2d 1504 (11th Cir. 1984).

101. Id. at 1507.

102. See Brooks v. Kemp, 762 F.2d 1383 (11th Cir. 1985).

103. Id. at 1411–12.

104. See generally, W. J. McGuire, The Nature of Attitudes and Attitude Change, in 3 THE HANDBOOK OF SOCIAL PSYCHOLOGY 136, 203–5 (G. Lindsey ed. 1968).

105. See generally, e.g., R. G. Hass, Effects of Source Characteristics on Cognitive Responses and Persuasion, in COGNITIVE RESPONSES IN PERSUASION 141 (R. Petty, T. Ostrom & T. Brock ed. 1981).

106. See, e.g., Barefoot v. Estelle, 463 U.S. 880 (1983); Jurek v. Texas, 428 U.S. 262 (1976).

107. This kind of testimony appears in a number of Texas death penalty cases. See, e.g., Barefoot, 463 U.S. at 899–901 n.7; Estelle v. Smith, 451 U.S. 454, 459–60 (1981).

108. See chap. 4.

109. 438 U.S. 586 (1978).

CHAPTER 6

Discrimination

On July 7, 1986, the United States Supreme Court granted certiorari in *McCleskey v. Kemp*,[1] a case in which the defendant is claiming that the Georgia death penalty is discriminatorily applied against killers of white victims. Thus, some time in 1987 the Court will for the first time decide a case that directly deals with the issue of racial discrimination in capital sentencing.

The Court has obliquely dealt with this issue before. In *Furman v. Georgia*,[2] Justices Douglas and Marshall, two of the five concurring justices, indicated that the existence of racial discrimination in capital sentencing was a factor that contributed to their decision to hold the then existing system of capital punishment unconstitutional.[3] In addition, Justice Stewart indicated that in his view, the issues of arbitrariness and racial discrimination were inextricably intertwined. In finding that the death penalty was arbitrarily imposed, he emphasized that the only discernible basis for separating the few who had been sentenced to death from the many others who were guilty of equally culpable offenses was the "constitutionally impermissible basis of race."[4]

Furman, of course, does not provide much of a benchmark. The opinions of individual justices do not establish that *Furman* prohibited any particular level of racial discrimination in capital sentencing. At most, it can be said that *Furman* invalidated a system of capital punishment that produced arbitrary results. Nevertheless, in view of the concerns expressed by the concurring justices in *Furman*, the modern interpretation has been that racial discrimination is an element of the arbitrariness that "was condemned in *Furman*, and one of the evils that the post-*Furman* capital-sentencing reforms were designed to cure."[5] In *McCleskey* the Court will almost certainly assess the extent to which the post-*Furman* reforms have achieved this goal. In this chapter, I will do the same.

The changes effected by the post-*Furman* reforms, and their impact, can be analyzed by means of both soft and hard data. The observations of knowledgeable observers, particularly defense attorneys who specialize in capital cases, illuminate some of the areas in which race continues to play a part in the administration of capital punishment. This soft methodology does not allow a precise measurement of the changes between the pre-

and post-*Furman* eras, but by providing a clearer picture of the sources of racism in capital sentencing it creates a framework within which the strengths and limitations of the post-*Furman* reforms may be assessed more realistically. Some of the hard data and the lower court's reaction to it in *McCleskey* will sharpen the focus and lead to some general observations concerning the extent to which race continues to play a role in capital sentencing and the implications that this has for society.

Pre-*Furman* Discrimination

To most people, racial discrimination in capital sentencing means that a capital defendant is more likely to receive the death penalty because he belongs to a particular race. At the time *Furman* was decided, that type of discrimination had been clearly established only in rape cases; the empirical evidence indicated that certain southern states clung to the historical practice of reserving the death penalty in rape cases almost exclusively for instances in which a black man raped a white woman.[6] In murder cases, there was evidence that race made a difference, but there was no conclusive evidence that black capital defendants suffered a disadvantage because of race.

Before *Furman*, the most striking racial pattern in capital sentencing was the disproportionate number of black executions. The disparity was extraordinarily great in rape cases,[7] but it was also present in homicide cases. Between 1930 and 1967 approximately 49 percent (1,630 out of 3,334) of those executed for murder were black.[8] Although dramatic, this statistic did not in itself prove discrimination. During the same period, the black homicide rate was several times higher than the white homicide rate. Thus, the disparity in executions could merely have reflected the disparity in homicides.

In several pre-*Furman* studies, social scientists sought to determine scientifically whether racial discrimination affected capital sentencing in homicide cases. That was difficult to do, however, because of the myriad factors that might play a part in capital sentencing. Merely showing that black defendants were executed disproportionately often would not establish racial discrimination in capital sentencing, because the disproportionate executions might be attributable to some nonracial factor. For example, suppose that, other things being equal, a felony-murderer is more likely to be executed than an ordinary murderer. In that case, if it could be shown that black murderers were disproportionately likely to commit felony-murder, that fact and not race itself would explain the disproportionate number of black executions.

Naturally, there are many nonracial factors that might affect capital sentencing. Although a study's value (and the reliability of its results) is closely related to the number of relevant factors considered, even a relatively unsophisticated study can have some value. During the pre-*Furman* era, a number of such relatively unsophisticated studies did attempt to measure the extent of racial discrimination in capital sentencing for homicide.

The results of the studies are summarized by Gary Kleck.[9] In general, they conclude that the death penalty was applied discriminatorily against blacks in certain southern states, particularly in the early part of the century.[10] Outside the South, the data indicate that black defendants have been less likely to receive the death penalty than white defendants.[11] This may be explained, however, by the fact that black defendants are more likely to kill black victims, and in homicide cases the death penalty is less likely to be imposed in black victim cases than in white victim ones.[12] Indeed, the strongest trend that emerges from the pre-*Furman* studies is that the killer of a white victim, whatever his race, is far more likely to receive the death penalty than the killer of a black victim.[13]

The Effect of the Post-*Furman* Procedural Reforms

The sentencing guidelines provided in the post-*Furman* statutes were designed to reduce the possibility of discrimination in capital sentencing. For example, by requiring the sentencing jury to make the death penalty determination by finding specific aggravating and mitigating circumstances and then balancing them against each other, the new statutes theoretically made it less likely that the jury would be swayed by racial considerations. Instead of making a totally discretionary death penalty determination, the jury would be required to reach its determination on the basis of specific objective criteria. Focusing on specific findings would, it was hoped, keep the jury from letting their prejudices affect the death penalty decision.

In fact, however, most knowledgeable observers agree that the switch to the post-*Furman* statutes has had only a minimal effect on racial discrimination in capital sentencing. Perhaps the most significant reason for this is that racial prejudice is a powerful force that may not be easily extirpated by statutory or verbal formulas. Even if the new statutes in fact required the sentencer to rest its death penalty determination solely on specific findings, racial prejudice could still distort the sentencer's judgment by coloring its view of the relevant facts. Moreover, for the most part, the new statutes do not require the sentencer to act as simply a fact finder. Some of the findings required—for example, whether the murder was committed by torture[14] or whether the defendant is likely to present a future danger to the community[15]—involve guidelines that are so vague that they restrain the sentencer's exercise of discretion only slightly. Furthermore, most of the post-*Furman* statutes require the sentencer to make the ultimate death penalty decision by weighing the aggravating factors or circumstances against the mitigating ones,[16] leaving it to the sentencer to decide exactly what weight each factor should be given. Thus, despite the guidelines, the sentencing authority still has vast discretion to make what is essentially a moral judgment. The new statutes have simply not altered the sentencer's role in a way that would be expected to curb the effect of racial prejudice.

Other changes in our system of capital punishment probably have had more impact than the explicit statutory revisions. First, observers have noted that some prosecutors, sensitive to the concerns about racism expressed in the wake of *Furman,* have bent over backwards to avoid any appearance of acting in a racist fashion. In his study of capital prosecutions in Florida, Hans Zeisel even found one case in which the prosecutor explicitly stated that the death penalty should be imposed on white defendants so as to demonstrate that the system does not discriminate against blacks. In arguing that white defendants convicted of killing a black victim should be given the death penalty, the prosecutor told the jury, "Our founding fathers talked about equal justice and today you have a chance to say we have equal justice. . . . The case is crying out for justice to be done."[17]

Similarly, Kevin McNally, a public defender in Kentucky, said that for some time after the *Furman* decision, a Kentucky defense attorney could almost expect more favorable treatment from the prosecutor when representing a black capital defendant than when representing a white one. In plea bargaining or discussing other issues that might affect the likelihood of a death sentence, prosecutors were sensitive to possible charges of racism. Moreover, if a black defendant went to trial on a capital charge, McNally said that at least if defense counsel "waved the flag" a little, the prosecutor would be likely to allow some blacks on the jury so as to avoid the imputation of racism that might arise if the death penalty were imposed by an all-white jury.

But the change of attitude that occurred at the beginning of the post-*Furman* era may have run its course. McNally also reported that in the last few years Kentucky prosecutors have not shown the same sensitivity to charges of racism and that the system is beginning to operate pretty much as it did in the past. Other defense counsel agreed. In fact, some suggested that the prosecutors' tendency to deal with white victim cases more severely than black victim cases may be even more marked in 1986 than it was in 1972. Thus, the heightened racial consciousness that occurred in the wake of the *Furman* decision seems to have been fleeting, a temporary phase that is not likely to have a lasting impact on our system of capital punishment.

Two other changes also had a significant impact on the post-*Furman* capital punishment system. First, in 1977 the Supreme Court held that death as a punishment for rape of an adult woman violated the Eighth Amendment.[18] As noted above,[19] when *Furman* was decided, the evidence of racial discrimination in the application of the death penalty was far more striking in rape cases than it was in homicide cases. Thus, by removing rape charges from the reach of capital punishment, the Court effectively removed the category of cases that had historically carried the greatest potential for racial discrimination.

Changes in our system of jury selection may also have reduced the discriminatory application of the death penalty. Even at the time of the *Furman* decision, Chief Justice Burger noted that jury selection in many parts of the country had changed from what it had been "when Negroes were systematically excluded from jury service and when racial segregation was the official policy in many states."[20] Since *Furman,* the courts have taken further steps to make sure that blacks will be fairly represented on juries.[21] As a result of these changes, a black capital defendant tried in a community that has a substantial black population will have a greater likelihood than in pre-*Furman* times of being tried by a jury that has one or more black members. That gives black capital defendants protection in at least two ways, according to defense counsel. First, the presence of the black juror or jurors may have a salutary effect on the jury deliberations, reducing the extent to which white jurors openly make judgments on the basis of racial stereotypes or a prejudiced perspective. Second, and more important, black jurors are much more likely to empathize with a black defendant, and the more a juror empathizes with a capital defendant, the less likely she is to vote in favor of a death sentence.

Nevertheless, the extent to which the change in our system of jury selection has affected racial discrimination in capital sentencing is difficult to assess without more information relating to the dynamics of capital sentencing. For example, what other factors besides race will play a part in determining whether a particular juror has empathy for a capital defendant? How often will the prosecutor choose to (and be able to) eliminate prospective black jurors by using peremptory challenges?[22] And how often will black jurors who are initially opposed to the death penalty be persuaded by the majority to change their minds?[23]

Obviously, precise answers to such questions are not possible. An account of one recent capital case, however, will illustrate some of the ways in which racial prejudice still has an impact on capital sentencing. The case is not necessarily a typical one, but it is not radically different from other capital cases either. It illustrates that at least in certain situations, the powerful factors that have historically operated to produce a racist system of capital punishment have not been stifled.

The Roosevelt Green Case[24]

Roosevelt Green, a young, attractive-looking black man, was charged with a capital offense as a result of his participation in crimes committed against Teresa Allen, an eighteen-year-old white college student. Allen was abducted on December 12, 1976, while she was working as a part-time cashier in a convenience store in Cochran, Georgia. Two days later, her body was found on a rural dirt road in Monroe County, Georgia; she had apparently been shot twice at close range with a high-powered rifle. In addition, tests showed that she had been raped before she was murdered.

Subsequently, the police arrested two suspects: Carzell Moore, an older black man who lived with his mother on the far side of a pasture directly behind the convenience store where Allen had worked, and Green, an Alabama native, who had never been in Cochran, Georgia, until he came to visit Moore there on the day before the crime. Green and Moore had previously known each other at prison and, according to people who knew them there, Moore was the dominant figure in the relationship, Green the follower.

Shortly after the crime, police obtained a statement from Moore's friend Thomas Pasby. According to Pasby, Moore confessed that he and Green had abducted the victim and that he alone had killed her. Pasby testified that Moore confessed that he took the victim to a deserted scene, "told [Green] to get some gas and then [after Green was gone] he shot her once and then he shot her again." Moore told Pasby that he decided to kill the victim to keep her from identifying him. He added that Green "didn't know he [Moore] was going to shoot her." According to Pasby, Moore also said that before the shooting occurred, both he and Green had raped Allen. The tests conducted by the government, however, show that Allen had been raped by a man with blood type A. Moore had blood type A and Green blood type B.

Green and Moore were tried in Monroe County, Georgia, a rural community that is about 60 percent white.[25] For the most part, the white and black people live in separate parts of the county and do not know each other. According to Green's lawyers, his case was the first interracial death penalty case to be tried in the county in five years. The last previous one took place when the wife of a prominent white man in the county was raped and killed by a black man. A black man from one of the isolated parts of Monroe County was charged with the crime. The white people on the jury wanted the death penalty for the defendant, but the black jurors were not willing to vote for death because they were not even sure the defendant was guilty. A compromise was reached under which the defendant was convicted but not given the death penalty. This compromise was not satisfactory to the white community, and according to sources in the black community, some of the white community felt that imposing the death penalty on Moore and Green would rectify the earlier injustice.

In any event, the Allen case generated extremely intense feelings against the defendants within the white community. This feeling was reflected in the voir dire during jury selections. Every prospective juror had heard about the case, most had formed an opinion about it, and many admitted that their feelings about the case would prevent them from giving one or the other of the defendants a fair trial.

Carzell Moore was brought to trial first. He was convicted of murder and given the death sentence. A key part of the state's sentencing case against him was his statement to his friend Pasby, admitting his central role in the murder. The state entered Pasby's testimony into evidence and argued to Moore's jury that it justified a death sentence. In a separate trial, Green was also convicted of murder. During the penalty phase, Green's defense sought to introduce Moore's confession to Pasby for the purpose of showing that Green had not killed the victim and was not aware that she was going to be shot. The state successfully moved to exclude Pasby's testimony from Green's penalty trial on the ground that it was hearsay. Green was given the death sentence. The Georgia Supreme Court affirmed Green's conviction and death sentence. Subsequently, however, the United States Supreme Court reversed his death sentence and remanded for a new penalty trial on the ground that Moore's statement exonerating Green should not have been excluded from the penalty trial.[26]

Green's second penalty trial was held in November, 1979, almost three years after the time of the killing. Despite the lapse of time, the media continued to focus attention on the case. For example, in a front-page article following the Supreme Court's reversal of the original death sentence, Sheriff Ed Coley was quoted as saying, "I think it's ridiculous. I think they ought to electrocute him." Moreover, during the voir dire, every prospective juror again acknowledged familiarity with the case; most remembered hearing people in the community talk about it. The recollection of prospective juror Fannie Watts was typical: "I did hear talk that Green was one of the accused and when I heard it, first thing I heard was that he would get the electric chair." Moreover, according to Green's lawyers, during each of the six days of Green's second penalty trial, the courtroom was filled to overflowing, mostly with hostile white spectators.

In Green's second penalty trial one of the hotly contested issues was whether Green had raped the victim before she was shot. In some ways it was surprising that this was even an issue. At his first trial, Green had been convicted of murder on the theory that he was Moore's accomplice, but the jury had declined to find him guilty of rape. The defense claimed that it would violate Green's rights under the double jeopardy clause[27] to allow the prosecutor at the second trial to present proof that Green was guilty of rape. Nevertheless, the prosecution was able to introduce Thomas Pasby's testimony to the effect that Moore had stated to him that he and Green had both raped Teresa Allen after they had abducted her and taken her away in her automobile. The state also presented evidence of other aggravating circumstances, including the fact that Green had a prior felony conviction. As mitigating evidence, the defense presented Pasby's testimony exonerating Green from the actual shooting, as well as two character witnesses, Green's mother and his sister.

The racial composition of Green's penalty jury was ten whites and two blacks. In addition, one of the alternate jurors who later replaced a regular jury member was also black. The penalty jury began deliberating on Saturday, November 10, 1979. At about 5:00 P.M., after about three hours of deliberations, the jury returned to the courtroom, and Martha McGee, the foreperson, asked the judge whether the defendant could be given a sentence of "life in prison without parole." After some consideration, the judge responded that he could not answer that question. After another brief question and answer, the jury began to withdraw to resume its deliberations. At this point, one of the two black jurors, Dorothy Mae Ponder Todd, fell to the floor in the hallway outside the courtroom and, according to some witnesses, repeatedly cried, "I can't do it."

The trial record is unclear about exactly what happened next, but shortly thereafter, the trial judge briefly questioned the foreperson of the jury about Todd's condition. No attempt was made to seek expert medical advice on the extent of Todd's disability (if any), to determine whether she might recover after a short respite, or even to question the juror before discharging her. Instead, the trial judge directed that Todd be removed from the jury and replaced by an alternate.

Soon after, the jury returned with a sentence of death. After some hesitation, Green's counsel, Richard Milam, requested that the jury be polled. During the polling, Samuel Mobley, the second black member of the jury, responded to the judge's questions as follows:

BY THE COURT: Mr. Mobley, Samuel Mobley. You have heard the verdict read, Mr. Mobley, was this your verdict in the jury room?

BY JUROR MOBLEY: Yes, it was, your honor.

BY THE COURT: Is this your verdict now?

BY JUROR MOBLEY: No, it's not, your honor. I cannot do it.

At this point, according to Green's lawyers, the large white crowd in the courtroom became extremely hostile. Nevertheless, the jury returned to the jury room. Subsequently, the judge examined the bailiff, who reported that after returning to the jury room, Mobley stated that he "didn't know what polling the jury was," and that "[s]omehow he got the idea that the [judge's] question was directed to him as a person, 'Did you do this?'" The trial judge then recalled the jury and proceeded to poll them again by saying to each juror, "You have heard the verdict published. Is this your verdict?" All of the jurors responded affirmatively.

In subsequent proceedings, Green's lawyers attacked his death sentence on several grounds, two of which are particularly pertinent to the issue of racial discrimination. First, they asserted that Green's trial counsel, Milam, had failed to conduct an adequate investigation to locate witnesses who might be able to offer mitigating evidence at the penalty trial. At the second penalty trial, Milam did not attempt to present witnesses who would develop Green's life story[28] but merely presented Green's mother and brother, who offered very brief and perfunctory evidence as character witnesses.

After Green's second death penalty sentence, his habeas lawyers asked a black investigator to interview Green and people who knew him in greater depth. The black investigator found that Green had originally lived in Minter, Alabama, a small town near Selma. He was a victim of child abuse. At the age of four, he was abandoned by his mother, and he went to live with his grandmother, who was working for a white man, E. W. Greene, the richest man in the county. The understanding was that the employer would save part of the grandmother's salary and at her death would pay it to Roosevelt Green. When Roosevelt Green was about ten years old, his grandmother died. He asked Greene for the money that had been accumulated on his behalf, but Greene refused to give him any money and told him to get off the land. Bitter and angry, Roosevelt Green left Minter and went north for five years. At the age of fifteen, he returned to Greene's land in another attempt to regain his inheritance. He and a friend broke into Greene's house while he and his family were away. While Roosevelt Green was inside the house, Greene and his wife returned from town and confronted him there. When Roosevelt Green tried to leave, Greene shot him in the back. As a result of this episode, fifteen-year-old Roosevelt Green was convicted of a felony and given a fifteen-year prison sentence.

Testimony about those events would have been helpful to a jury trying to understand why Roosevelt Green became involved in the episode involving Teresa Allen. In addition, there was further evidence that might have given the jury greater insight into Green's behavior. While at prison, Green had a generally good record until he came in close contact with Carzell Moore. A black probation officer who knew both Green and Moore at prison said that Green was "a very likeable kid" and that he could not "see him as a murderer." The probation officer added, however, that Moore was a much more hardened criminal who was easily capable of murder. He also said that Green was a follower and that while in prison he was under Moore's domination.

Testimony of that kind would have provided information useful to the jurors in evaluating Green's conduct. In relation to the crime itself, they might have seen Green as a victim of circumstances rather than a willing accomplice. Moreover, their understanding of Green's background might have enabled them to empathize with him and understand the motivation for his involvement in an interracial crime. The state and federal courts decided, however, that Milam's failure to find this testimony did not amount to ineffective assistance of counsel.

This result is certainly understandable. In many respects Milam's representation of Green was exemplary. He made extraordinary efforts to investigate the facts of the case and to establish a rapport with the jury. At the first trial, he pursued a reasonable trial strategy, emphasizing that Green was not the actual killer and was certainly less culpable than Carzell Moore. Moreover, when the first trial resulted in a death sentence, he was able, with the help of other attorneys, to get that sentence reversed by the United States Supreme Court. At Green's second penalty trial, he pursued the same strategy he had used at the earlier trial. As the Eleventh Circuit Court of Appeals said, he "conducted a spirited defense and was quite successful in extracting testimony from the state's witnesses in support of his argument that [Green] was less culpable than his co-accused."[29] Under all the circumstances, it might seem almost churlish to claim that Milam was ineffective because he failed to interview black witnesses who would be able to develop his client's life story. After all, a lawyer has limited time and resources. He cannot be expected to do everything that could possibly be done for his client.

Nevertheless, Milam's failure to unearth favorable black witnesses does suggest one reason black defendants may be at a disadvantage in certain cases. Most lawyers who represent capital defendants are white. In many communities the segregated racial backgrounds and the atmosphere of suspicion or distrust that pervades black and white relations makes it difficult for white lawyers to establish a close rapport with black clients. As a result, a black defendant may be very reluctant to reveal his personal history to his attorney. In the *Green* case, the black woman who interviewed Green after his second death sentence was able to uncover the favorable mitigating evidence in about thirty-six hours; Milam had no hint that such evidence existed despite the fact that he had represented Green for over two years and had met with him on many occasions. This does not show that Milam was ineffective; rather, it indicates that white attorneys who represent black defendants may often have less access to favorable mitigating evidence than they would when representing white defendants. As a result, black defendants as a group will be disadvantaged at the penalty trial.

Green also attacked his death penalty on the ground that the trial judge improperly excluded Dorothy Mae Ponder Todd, the black juror, from the jury. This attack precipitated a series of further hearings that explored the exact circumstances of Todd's removal. Todd herself filed an affidavit and later testified that shortly before her collapse, the jury had taken a vote on whether the death penalty should be imposed. The vote had been 10-2 in favor of the death penalty and she had been one of the two opposed. Todd also stated in her affidavit, "I don't remember ever making any statements to anyone asking to be taken off the jury. . . . [T]he judge never asked me personally whether I could continue. I was capable of continuing to serve as a juror and I'm sure that I would have standed [sic] firm with my convictions."[30]

At the hearing in federal court, one of the critical questions concerned whether the trial judge had an adequate basis for removing Todd from the jury. On the record, the judge's decision appeared to be based on the following colloquy with Martha McGee, the foreperson:

> BY THE COURT: Mrs. McGee, I understand that the Juror, Dorothy Mae Ponder Todd a few minutes ago upon leaving the Courtroom fainted in the corridor, is that correct?
>
> BY FOREPERSON McGEE: Yes, sir.
>
> BY THE COURT: And you have stated to me that upon returning to the jury room, this juror is in your opinion incapable of continuing deliberation in this case because of the fact that she is physically and emotionally unable to continue and participate in the deliberation of this jury, is that true?
>
> BY FOREPERSON McGEE: Yes, sir, it is.
>
> BY THE COURT: And has this person requested of you that she be released from further service?
>
> BY FOREPERSON McGEE: Yes, sir.
>
> BY THE COURT: In your opinion, from having examined her, is she in this condition?
>
> BY FOREPERSON McGEE: Yes, sir, she is.

The judge then immediately ordered that Dorothy Todd be removed from the jury and replaced by an alternate.

The judge's decision to remove Todd solely on the basis of this exchange seems questionable on its face. McGee was not shown to have any special qualifications that would enable her to form an opinion about another juror's physical or emotional condition. Moreover, she did not tell the judge either the basis for her opinion about Todd's condition or the circumstances under which Todd had requested release from jury service. The judge's decision to remove a juror on the basis of such a meager showing seems especially surprising in view of the fact that Georgia trial judges do not traditionally replace regular jurors with alternates without a strong showing that the regular juror is incapable of serving.[31] For example, during the guilt phase of Roosevelt Green's trial, a juror was permitted to continue to serve despite the fact that he suffered an epileptic seizure during the jury deliberations.

At the hearing in federal court, the parties explored both the basis for McGee's report to the judge and the circumstances surrounding the colloquy between the judge and McGee. McGee's statement that Todd had asked to be released from jury service seemed contrary to the other evidence. Todd testified that she didn't remember saying to anyone that she wanted to be released from jury service. Moreover, other jurors who were crowded together in a hallway when she collapsed testified to the circumstances of her collapse without mentioning that she made any request for release from service. McGee testified that after she heard someone fall, she turned around and

> I see Mrs. Todd on the floor; and at that point, she was in a state of emotion that she's jerking and her head is going from side to side, and her eyes—I could almost see the whites of her eyes, and she was not totally flat on her back, but she was sort of on the side, lying with her right side to me. She was muttering, and she was in a terrible state; and at that point, I knelt down and touched her on her shoulder, which would have been her right shoulder, and I hear her say, "I can't go on," and I touched her on her shoulder and looked at her, and she looked at me, and I said, "Do you want to be replaced," and her answer to me at that time, and her head is still going and moving, and she is still trembling terribly bad, and her answer is, "Uh-huh, uh-huh, uh-huh" and at that point, we were all shoved into an elevator and sent upstairs.

McGee further testified that Todd's statement was not "loud enough for any of the jurors that were standing around her, not kneeling over her, to hear it."

This testimony would explain why McGee was the only one who knew of Todd's desire to be replaced. But not one of the other jurors recalled McGee's act of bending over the fallen juror. It also seems striking that although several witnesses testified that Todd had said in a loud voice, "I can't do it," McGee testified that Todd spoke in a voice that only McGee could hear and that her words were "I can't go on." Moreover, under the circumstances, it seems unusual that McGee's first question to Todd was, "Do you want to be replaced?" McGee was rendering aid to a stricken woman who had collapsed on the floor. Even if the woman's words were "I can't go on," most people would probably be more likely to ask her what was wrong with her or to try to determine what she needed than to focus immediately on whether she wanted to remain on the jury.

McGee's account of the circumstances surrounding her colloquy with the trial judge was even more extraordinary. The in-court questioning by the judge obviously reflects some prior knowledge that Todd had requested that she be released from further service and that McGee had formed the opinion that Todd was not fit to continue:

> BY THE COURT: And you have stated to me that upon returning to the jury room, this juror is in your opinion incapable of continuing deliberation in this case because of the fact that she is physically and emotionally unable to continue and participate in the deliberation of this jury, is that true?
>
> BY FOREPERSON McGEE: Yes, sir, it is.
>
> BY THE COURT: And has this person requested of you that she be released from further service?
>
> BY FOREPERSON McGEE: Yes, sir.

The judge's questions must have been predicated on some kind of off-the-record communication between McGee and himself. Yet in her testimony in federal court, McGee insisted that that was not the case:

> Q [BY MR. BOGER]: Did you convey to anyone the information about the exchange between yourself and Mrs. Todd or your opinion of her physical condition at any point outside the courtroom?
>
> A [BY MRS. McGEE]: Outside the courtroom? No.
>
> Q. Inside the courtroom, did you convey that opinion at any point except in the jury box with the Court Reporter there when the testimony was being given?
>
> A. The only thing, the conversation I had, was in answer to the question that Judge [Whalen] asked me at that point.

In response to further questions, McGee reiterated that before entering the courtroom, she had not communicated with the bailiff or with other jurors and that she had no idea how the judge learned of her opinion of Todd's condition or of Todd's request that she be released from the jury.

If McGee's testimony is credited, then some of the questions the judge asked during the colloquy are inexplicable. He might conceivably have surmised from the hallway clamor that Todd had become unfit to continue, but if he had received no prior communication from McGee, he could have had no basis for believing that McGee had formed the same opinion. Moreover, he certainly had no way of knowing whether Todd had requested release from jury service. According to McGee, nobody else heard Todd's statements to her, and she did not recount these statements to anyone before testifying in court.

If the implications of McGee's testimony are accepted, the judge was suggesting certain facts to McGee even though he had no basis for doing so. Why would the judge do this? One possible explanation is that he wanted to have Todd removed from the jury, because he believed she was opposed to the death penalty.[32] Accordingly, he might have suggested facts to McGee because he wanted to establish a basis for removing Todd from the jury as quickly and expeditiously as possible. If this theory is accepted, then it is certainly plausible to believe that McGee's answers to the judge were prompted by the way he framed the questions. Thus, she said that Todd had requested release from jury service because the judge suggested that in his question to her. Afterward, of course, she had to justify her response to the judge, and thus she gave her somewhat remarkable testimony relating to her conversation with Todd.

This suggests, of course, that the trial judge acted improperly and that the foreperson of the jury perjured herself. Given the strong feelings generated by the case, the suggestion is hardly shocking. Most of the white community was strongly in favor of the death penalty. Todd, by her vote in the jury room and her statement in the hallway, seemed to represent the most immediate impediment to a sentence of death. Under the circumstances, it is not surprising that the white trial judge would take the initiative in seeking to establish some basis for removing Todd or that the white foreperson of the jury would comply with the judge's suggestions and shape her later testimony in a way that would protect the death penalty's validity.

Other interpretations of the record are possible, of course. It could be that McGee did communicate with the judge (either directly or through a court officer) before she responded to his questions in court and simply forgot about it. Or it could be that McGee testified truthfully at both the colloquy and the federal court hearing and it was merely coincidental that the judge correctly anticipated her testimony at the colloquy.

After considering all the testimony, the federal courts concluded that the trial judge had not acted improperly in removing Todd from the jury.[33] Even if this conclusion is accepted, the case still shows that the switch to a jury selection system in which blacks are more adequately represented may not completely protect black capital defendants from the effects of racism. Roosevelt Green did receive some benefit from having two blacks on his jury. Both of them apparently viewed the case from a different perspective than the white members of the jury did; one of them strongly opposed the verdict of death and the other initially repudiated his vote for the death penalty. Nevertheless, neither of these jurors was ultimately able to prevent the imposition of the death sentence. It is not clear exactly why that was true, but it certainly seems likely that the strong pro–death penalty feeling in the white community played a part in bringing about the changed response of one juror and the collapse and removal of the other one. Thus, it appears that at least in certain cases, if the white community is strongly in favor of imposing the death penalty on a black defendant, the pressures generated by that feeling may minimize the extent to which black representation on the jury will protect the rights of the defendant.

The final stage of the Green case illustrates another dimension of the problem. In a last effort to save Green from the death penalty, Green's lawyers appealed for clemency to the Georgia Board of Pardons and Parole. In a Georgia clemency hearing, the defendant may offer any evidence or argument that he wishes to present, and the board has total discretion to decide whether the death penalty will be commuted. Jack Boger, one of Green's attorneys, recalls that the commutation hearing was rather unstructured. Each of Green's attorneys in turn presented some facet of the case. When Boger's turn came, he stressed Green's minor role in the killing. He argued that the state's own evidence showed that at most, Green participated in the kidnapping of Teresa Allen and that he was not present when she was killed. Boger recalls that at this point, one influential member of the board of pardons responded to him by saying, "The evidence is clear that he raped the girl and that's good enough for me." Boger responded that the Supreme Court held in 1977 that death was a constitutionally excessive punishment for the crime of rape. The board member then said, "You're not at the legal stage now." Ultimately, the board of pardons denied Green's appeal for clemency, and he was executed.

The board member's comment shows that *Coker v. Georgia*,[34] the case in which the Supreme Court ruled death an unconstitutional punishment for rape, has not completely eliminated the discriminatory application of the death penalty in rape cases. If Green had been a white defendant or Teresa Allen a black victim, it seems unlikely that anyone would have felt that the defendant should be executed because he raped the victim. Moreover, the evidence that Green in fact raped the victim was not strong. He was never convicted of rape. Indeed, the scientific evidence suggested that he was not guilty of that crime. The only evidence that pointed to a contrary conclusion was a hearsay statement by a confederate who was admittedly guilty of rape and murder. Yet, since Green was black and the victim white, this evidence was apparently enough for one member of the Georgia Board of Pardons, even though Green's involvement in the killing of the victim was admittedly slight. Thus, where the law allows it, the historic pattern of discriminating against black defendants involved in interracial sex crimes will continue to play a part in the administration of capital punishment.

Cases like *Green* provide an explanation, in microcosm, of the statistical patterns of racial discrimination that have been detected by most researchers who have examined the post-*Furman* sentencing schemes in macrocosm. A study of individual cases cannot, however, determine whether racial discrimination in capital sentencing is sufficiently pervasive to render any of the post-*Furman* death penalty statutes unconstitutional. This issue can be determined only if two other questions are first considered. First, to what extent do factors relating to race play a part in determining which capital defendants will be sentenced to death? Second, what degree of racial bias in the system will be constitutionally tolerable? A recent study attempts to answer the first question, and the Eleventh Circuit's decision in *McCleskey v. Kemp*[35] addresses the second one.

The Baldus Study

As I suggested at the outset,[36] empirical studies designed to assess racial discrimination in capital sentencing can never be complete, because they cannot take into account every conceivable factor that could possibly bear on whether a capital sentence will be imposed. The best studies, however, try to consider as many potentially significant factors as possible. Then, if there seems to be a correlation between the race of the victim or the defendant and the imposition of the death penalty, there is a good basis for determining whether the correlation occurs because the imposition of the death penalty is in fact related to race or whether it may be attributed to some other factor. So the more exhaustive the study, the sounder the basis for reaching conclusions about discrimination in capital sentencing.

In 1983, David Baldus and two colleagues completed the most exhaustive study of racial discrimination in capital sentencing that has ever been conducted.[37] The study was actually composed of two parts. For the first part, the researchers compiled information on over two hundred variables for each of 594 defendants tried and sentenced for murder in Georgia from March, 1973, through July, 1978. Though this study was more comprehensive than any previously conducted, it still lacked data on the strength of the government's case against the defendants; moreover, since it was restricted to murder convictions, it did not examine the possibility of pretrial discrimination in charging and plea bargaining. These gaps were filled in the second part of the study, which covered 1,066 Georgia homicide prosecutions from 1973 through 1980—manslaughter convictions and guilty pleas as well as murder convictions—and included data relating to about five hundred variables.[38]

The results of the Baldus study were striking in several respects. First, the researchers found that in contrast to the strong antiblack bias that appeared in their pre-*Furman* data, a statewide examination of their post-*Furman* data revealed "no evidence of discrimination against black defendants because of their race."[39] The post-*Furman* data did show that "in rural areas black defendants with white victims still received some-what more severe treatment,"[40] but in urban areas the "discrimination was against white defendants."[41] Thus, the lack of discrimination on a statewide basis was explained by the fact that "the discrimination against black defendants in rural areas and the discrimination against white de-fendants in urban areas cancelled each other out."[42]

On the other hand, the data did reveal strong evidence of discrimina-tion against killers of white victims. Overall, it appeared that the killer of a white victim was 4.3 times more likely to receive the death penalty than the killer of a black victim.[43] Not surprisingly, the researchers also found that the discrimination against killers of white victims was greatest in the middle range of cases (cases that were neither the most routine nor the most heinous), in which the imposition of the death penalty was neither very unlikely nor a virtual certainty. Put in statistical terms, the re-searchers' conclusions were that "on average a white victim crime is 6 percent more likely to result in the [death] sentence than a comparable black victim crime,"[44] but for the middle range of cases (defined as those in which the overall death sentence rate was 10 to 80 percent), the dif-ference between death sentence rates for white and black victim crimes increased to 20 percent.[45]

As Samuel Gross has observed,[46] conclusions stated in the terms of percentages without further explanation are not very meaningful and may even be misleading. For example, a difference in the death penalty sen-tencing rate of .06 may sound fairly insignificant. However, Gross points out that since the overall death sentencing rate is about .05, a .06 dif-ference is highly significant. In fact, as Gross shows,[47] Baldus's overall differential of 6 percent reflects a finding that the death sentencing rate was approximately 9 percent in white victim cases and 3 percent in black victim cases. The bottom line, then, is that even when all other relevant factors are held constant, killers of whites are several times more likely to receive the death penalty than killers of blacks, and the disparity becomes particularly evident in cases where there is a reasonable probability but not a certainty that the death penalty will be imposed.[48]

The *McCleskey* Case

In several cases, litigators have presented the Baldus data in support of a claim that the Georgia capital punishment statute is unconstitutional as applied.[49] But in *McCleskey v. Kemp*,[50] the Eleventh Circuit Court of Ap-peals held that even if the findings of the Baldus study are valid, they are insufficient to establish that the Georgia death penalty is being applied in violation of the Constitution.[51]

The court's statement of the test to be applied presaged its result. The majority held that the defendant could not establish a claim unless that disparate impact is so great that it compels a conclusion that the system is unprincipled, irrational, arbitrary and capricious such that purposeful discrimination—i.e., race is intentionally being used as a factor in sentencing—can be presumed to permeate the system.[52]

Both the standard of proof and the substantive test suggest the difficulty of the defendant's burden. In most cases a party is required to establish his case by a preponderance of the evidence; here the defendant could not prevail by meeting either that standard or even the more stringent one of proof beyond a reasonable doubt. Instead, the defendant's proof would have to "compel a conclusion"—presumably a very difficult standard to meet.

Moreover, the defendant is required to prove not merely that there is a correlation between race and capital sentencing but rather that "race is intentionally being used as a factor in sentencing."[53] Given the difficulty of proving intentional discrimination on the basis of statistical evidence,[54] the defendant's task would be virtually impossible.

Predictably, the majority held that the 6 percent disparity revealed by the Baldus study was not enough to establish a constitutional violation.[55] In arriving at this conclusion, they made two additional observations that are of particular interest. First, disregarding its initial concession that the Baldus results would be presumed to be valid, the court said that despite the comprehensive list of factors considered by the Baldus study, it was incomplete because it

not only ignores quantitative differences in cases: looks, age, personality, education, profession, job, clothing, demeanor, and remorse, just to name a few, but it is incapable of measuring qualitative differences of such things as aggravating and mitigating factors. There are, in fact, no exact duplicates in capital crimes and capital defendants.[56]

Obviously, some if not all of the factors mentioned by the court simply cannot be measured. Thus, the court's remarks imply that no statistical study could ever be complete enough to show that race operates as a factor in capital sentencing.

The court's final statement made a different point, however. The court said that assuming the statistical evidence is valid, it "confirms rather than condemns the system."[57] The court based this conclusion in part on the fact that the "Baldus study revealed an essentially rational system, in which high aggravation cases were more likely to result in the death sentence than low aggravation cases."[58] The court interpreted the Baldus data as showing that at least in Georgia, the post-*Furman* system of capital punishment is more rational and less discriminatory than the pre-*Furman* one:

> In a state where past discrimination is well documented, the study showed no discrimination as to the race of the defendant. The marginal disparity based on the race of the victim tends to support the state's contention that the system is working far differently from the one which *Furman* condemned.[59]

The court concluded by observing that the fact that in "a small percentage of cases" it is not easy to explain why some defendants got the death penalty and some did not is "no reason to declare the entire system unconstitutional."[60]

Analysis

The final portion of *McCleskey* is interesting especially because the majority's two somewhat conflicting attempts to come to grips with the implications of the Baldus data seem in a sense to symbolize the current judicial reaction to the problem of racism in capital sentencing. In one breath, the majority intimates that the Baldus study cannot be accepted as valid because it fails to consider a long list of factors, including looks, age, personality, and demeanor; in its next breath, it says that the study in any event "confirms rather than condemns the system," because it shows that the death penalty is being imposed less arbitrarily and discriminatorily than it was in the pre-*Furman* era. In both statements, the majority seems to be straining to erect barriers against any imputation that the capital punishment system is tainted by racism. If a study shows that race plays a part in capital sentencing, the study isn't good enough to be accepted as valid; if the study is accepted as valid, it shows that the system is not really operating in a racist fashion. The study was not destined to prevent the majority from adopting an optimistic view of our present system.

The majority's first statement seems especially strained. As Gross points out,[61] the Baldus study did in fact consider some of the factors iterated by the court, including age, employment, and expressions of remorse.[62] Moreover, some of the other factors, such as looks, are, as one of the dissents said, "often used to mask . . . racial prejudice."[63] For example, a juror who is racially prejudiced will be very likely to prefer a white person's looks over a black person's looks. In this regard, the questions asked by Gross are pertinent: "Why should 'looks' justify racial disparities in capital sentencing? And what aspects of looks have this power-attractiveness? hair style? complexion?"[64] In retrospect, the majority's litany of the relevant factors not considered in the study seems superficial and unconvincing.

But in fact the majority's conclusion does not depend on Baldus's failure to include any particular factor. Rather, its central point—which echoes statements made in past opinions[65]—is that in this area no statistical study can ever be accepted as valid because "[t]here are, in fact, no exact duplicates in capital crimes and capital defendants."[66] Of course, if that conclusion is correct, it casts doubt on nearly every statistical study that is offered to establish a relationship in the real world. For example, studies that explore the relationship between smoking and heart disease[67] control for a number of variables that might explain the relationship—age, blood pressure, diabetes, and obesity, for example—but inevitably they do not consider every factor that could possibly influence the health of each particular person. If the *McCleskey* majority's analysis is valid, these kinds of studies would also be futile, because there are "no exact duplicates" in individuals' personal or medical history.

In short, the majority's first conclusion proves too much. If accepted, it would require us not only to reject any future statistical studies relating to the administration of capital punishment but also to reject a multitude of other studies that are routinely used to inform our decision making.

In its final statement, the court asserts that the Baldus data show that "the system is working far differently from the one which *Furman* condemned." From one perspective, this assertion is defensible. The studies showed that during the pre-*Furman* era, there was more racial discrimination in capital sentencing for rape cases than exists in any form of capital sentencing today. For example, one pre-*Furman* study showed that in southern states black defendants who were convicted of raping white victims were eighteen times more likely to receive death sentences than all other convicted rapists.[68] If this kind of benchmark is used, Baldus's data show that our system has improved considerably. The Baldus study found that killing a white victim rather than a black one increased the odds of a death sentence by a factor of about 4. That is a substantially reduced ratio; more important, it reflects a less virulent form of racism—one that is directed only toward victims, not victims and defendants.

But this comparison seems inappropriate. The Baldus data pertain to homicide cases. To determine whether there has been a significant change in the application of the death penalty pre- and post-*Furman*, the relevant comparison should be between the Baldus data and pre-*Furman* data relating to homicide cases. Baldus and his collaborators did make that comparison. It showed that statewide, discrimination against black defendants took place in the pre-*Furman* era but not in the post-*Furman* era. However, closer examination of the data showed that discrimination based on the race of the defendant does continue to exist. It merely does not appear statewide, because discrimination against black defendants in the rural areas is counterbalanced by discrimination against white defendants in the urban areas, where the black population is higher and blacks have more political influence. So the comparison does not show that the system is working "far differently"; rather, it shows that the system is working about the same, but the results are different because in certain Georgia cities blacks are more likely to participate in the criminal justice system (and be on juries) now than they were in the pre-*Furman* era.

Moreover, commentators who have extensively examined the pre- and post-*Furman* data on the death penalty's application in homicide cases would strongly disagree with the court's conclusion. Gross's analysis of the data led him to conclude that "the comparisons that can be made show little or no change since *Furman*."[69]

Gross holds that the studies indicate that a black defendant's risk of receiving the death penalty is about the same or slightly higher now than it was in the pre-*Furman* era.[70] As for the data on race-of-victim discrimination, he emphasizes that the post-*Furman* studies are not only methodologically superior but also much more consistent in finding discrimination by race of victim. He concludes that "the evidence of widespread discrimination by race of victim in post-*Furman* capital sentencing is stronger than *any* evidence of racial discrimination in capital sentencing for homicide that was available in 1972."[71]

In view of this conclusion, one portion of the Eleventh Circuit's concluding statement seems especially out of place. In supporting its claim that the Baldus data show that the capital punishment system is working relatively well, the court refers to the study's finding of a "marginal disparity" based on the race of the victim.[72] The phrase *marginal disparity* connotes a small or insignificant difference. It does not seem appropriate in the present context. Gross intimates that the court's use of the term *marginal* may stem from its misunderstanding of the significance of the 6 percent disparity found by Baldus.[73] That is possible. But if so, the majority was unusually obtuse. After all, the court recognized that Baldus found that the selection of a white rather than a black victim makes the death penalty four times more likely.[74] How could that kind of a difference be dismissed as "marginal"?

Perhaps the best explanation is that at that point in its opinion, the majority was less interested in presenting an accurate picture of the studies than it was in asserting as strongly as possible that race plays a less important role in the administration of capital punishment now than it did in the pre-*Furman* era. Judge Roney, who wrote the majority opinion in *McCleskey,* is certainly not the first judge to make that kind of claim. In recent cases, members of the Supreme Court (and, to a lesser extent, the Court itself)[75] have also asserted that the switch to the post-*Furman* system of capital punishment has drastically changed the extent to which the death penalty is arbitrarily and discriminatorily applied. For example, Justice Powell, joined by three other justices in a dissent from a stay of execution, contrasted the two systems as follows:

> Surely, no contention can be made that the entire Georgia judicial system, at all levels, operates to discriminate in all cases. Arguments to this effect have been directed to the type of statutes addressed in *Furman v. Georgia.* . . . As our subsequent cases make clear, such arguments cannot be taken seriously under statutes approved in *Gregg.*[76]

As I have already pointed out,[77] this remarkable assertion can be made only so long as one is willing to avoid or discount the available evidence. Moreover, like the Eleventh Circuit's concluding statement, it was not necessary to support Justice Powell's position.[78] Why, then, do courts and justices make these strong statements about the post-*Furman* system?

Gross suggests that the Eleventh Circuit made its assertion because it wants to believe that the system now works in the way it says it does. I have a more cynical explanation. The Eleventh Circuit (and other courts) want to make it *appear* that the capital punishment system is operating in a less discriminatory fashion than it was previously, and they believe that making strong declarations about the way the system works will, to some degree at least, shape people's view of reality.

Why should any court seek to alter our perception of the capital punishment system by making statements that are contrary to the evidence? After all, the Eleventh Circuit could have decided *McCleskey* as it did without suggesting that racial discrimination no longer taints the application of the Georgia death penalty statute. The court could have admitted that the Baldus study shows that in Georgia the death penalty is imposed disproportionately often upon killers of white victims; and (taking the classic view of Supreme Court capital punishment decisions),[79] it also could have held that that defect, while unfortunate, did not render the Georgia statute unconstitutional under *Furman* or any other Supreme Court decision. If it had wanted to end with a rhetorical flourish, the court could have concluded its opinion by saying something like this: We live in a tragic world in which difficult choices are necessary; if we want to have a death penalty, we may have to accept that race will continue to be a factor in determining who will be selected to receive that punishment; the fact that capital punishment carries with it this cost is not, however, a basis for concluding that capital punishment is unconstitutional.

Of course, it is understandable that a court would be reluctant to write this kind of opinion. The *Furman* decision, although it was not based on any explicit constitutional theory, does seem to condemn a system of punishment that allows the death penalty to be applied discriminatorily. The Supreme Court has not overruled *Furman;* in fact, it has repeatedly indicated that the decision is now a part of our constitutional fabric. Thus, a decision finding that race continues to be an important factor in determining who gets the death penalty would inevitably suggest that measured against the *Furman* standard, the present system of capital punishment rests on a brittle foundation. It can be distinguished from the pre-*Furman* system only by the difference in the procedures used, not by the results obtained. Obviously, no court would want to be placed in a position of having to defend that kind of distinction. On the other hand, given the present political and moral climate, no court is likely to hold that the death penalty (or even a state death penalty statute) is unconstitutional because of the way it is applied. Therefore, the courts' reluctance to come to grips with the implications of the present relationship between race and the imposition of the death penalty is understandable.

The Implications of the Relationship

From an objective standpoint, what are the implications of a system that imposes the death penalty much more frequently on killers of white victims than on killers of black ones? In comparison to a system that discriminates on the basis of the race of the defendant, this kind of racial disparity may seem relatively benign. Black defendants are not placed at a disadvantage, and the fact that both black and white defendants will be more likely to be executed if they kill a white rather than a black victim may seem more like a harmless anomaly than like something that taints the operation of the system.

Yet the disparity does highlight an aspect of racism in our society. The fact that killing a white rather than a black victim increases the odds of a death sentence by a factor of about four says that society places a higher value on a white life than on a black one. Of course, even if there were no death penalty, punishing killers of whites more severely than killers of blacks would communicate the same message. But the death penalty places the message in a clearer and starker perspective. Society recognizes that death is different in kind from all other punishments. The fact that the death penalty is reserved primarily for killers of white victims, tells us that in our society the loss of a white life provokes a fundamentally different level of concern than the loss of a black one.

The relationship between race of victim and the death penalty also bears on the question of arbitrariness. The death penalty is arbitrarily imposed if it is imposed on the basis of factors that have no relationship to either the crime committed or the character of the offender. The race of the victim is certainly such a factor. It has no more relevance to the nature of the crime or the character of the offender than the color of the defendant's eyes or the day of the week on which the crime was committed. Thus, the fact that there is a substantial relationship between the race of the victim and the imposition of the death penalty shows that the death penalty continues to be arbitrarily applied.

Can this arbitrariness be corrected? It seems doubtful. The courts have tried to effect reforms that reduce the extent to which race will play a part in capital sentencing. But as my account of the Roosevelt Green case indicates,[80] some of the forces that create racism in capital sentencing are simply too powerful to be swept away by procedural tinkering. This means that if we come to recognize the effect of race on our system of capital punishment, we will have to choose between retaining a capital punishment system that operates arbitrarily or abandoning the death penalty entirely.

NOTES

1. 106 S. Ct. 3331 (1986).
2. 408 U.S. 238 (1972).
3. See id. at 364–65 (Marshall, J., concurring), 256–57 (Douglas, J., concurring).
4. Id. at 310 (Stewart, J., concurring).
5. Gross, Race and Death: The Judicial Evaluation of Evidence of Discrimination in Capital Sentencing, 18 U.C.D. L. REV. 1275, 1279 (1985) [hereinafter cited as Gross].
6. See Maxwell v. Bishop, 257 F. Supp. 710 (E.D. Ark. 1966), aff'd, 398 F.2d 138 (8th Cir. 1968); see generally Wolfgang & Riedel, Rape, Race, and the Death Penalty in Georgia, 45 AM. J. ORTHOPSYCHIATRY 658 (1975) [hereinafter cited as Wolfgang & Riedel]; Wolfgang & Riedel, Race, Judicial Discrimination and the Death Penalty, 407 ANNALS 119 (1973).
7. See infra text at note 68.
8. Gross & Mauro, Patterns of Death: An Analysis of Racial Disparities in Capital Sentencing and Homicide Victimization, 37 STAN. L. REV. 27, 38 (1984) [hereinafter cited as Gross & Mauro].
9. See Kleck, Racial Discrimination in Criminal Sentencing: A Critical Evaluation of the Evidence with Additional Evidence on the Death Penalty, 46 AM. SOCIOLOGICAL REV. 783 (1981) [hereinafter cited

as Kleck]; See also Gross & Mauro, supra note 8, at 38–42.
10. See Gross & Mauro, supra note 8, at 40.
11. See Kleck, supra note 9, at 799.
12. Id. at 800.
13. Id.
14. See, e.g., GA. CODE ANN. § 17-10-30 (1982); 42 PA. CONS. STAT. ANN. § 9711 (Purdon 1982).
15. See, e.g., VA. CODE § 19.2-264.2 (1983); TEX. CRIM. PROC. CODE ANN. § 7.071 (Vernon Supp. 1986).
16. See, e.g., GA. CODE ANN. § 17-10-31 (1982); 42 PA. CONS. STAT. ANN. § 9711 (Purdon 1982).
17. See Zeisel, Race Bias in the Administration of the Death Penalty: The Florida Experience, 95 HARV. L. REV. 456, 465–66 (1981).
18. See Coker v. Georgia, 433 U.S. 584 (1977).
19. See supra text at note 6.
20. 408 U.S. at 391 n.12 (dissenting opinion of Burger, C.J.).
21. See, e.g., Batson v. Kentucky, 106 S. Ct. 1712 (1986) (prosecutors not permitted to exercise peremptory challenges to strike black prospective jurors because of race); Castineda v. Partida, 430 U.S. 482 (1977) (applying fairly lenient standard for proof of racial discrimination in selection of jury venires).
22. Although Batson precludes the

prosecutor from peremptorily striking blacks from the jury because they are black, the prosecutor will be permitted to strike blacks from the jury if he can show that he had a "neutral" reason for removing them. 106 S. Ct. at 1723.

23. In most jurisdictions the jury must be unanimous before it can impose a penalty of death. *See, e.g.,* CAL. PENAL CODE § 190.4(b) (West 1978).

24. The following account is drawn from the transcripts of Green's trial and hearings in federal courts, the Fifth Circuit opinion, and interviews with Green's attorneys. I have provided references only to the Fifth Circuit opinion.

25. In 1980 Monroe County was 37.82 percent black. *See* BUREAU OF THE CENSUS, U.S. DEP'T OF COMMERCE, COUNTY AND CITY DATA BOOK (10th ed. 1983).

26. Green v. Georgia, 442 U.S. 95 (1979).

27. The double jeopardy clause provides that no person shall be "twice put in jeopardy of life or limb" for "the same offense." In Bullington v. Missouri, 451 U.S. 430 (1981), the Supreme Court held that this clause applies at the penalty phase of a capital trial.

28. For the importance of presenting the defendant's life story at the penalty stage, see chap. 3.

29. Green v. Zant, 738 F.2d 1529, 1538 (Fifth Cir. 1984).

30. *Id.* at 1532 n.1.

31. The Georgia statute provides that a juror may be replaced by an alternate only if the court finds that the juror is "unable to perform his duty." GA. CODE ANN. § 15-12-172 (1985).

32. The judge did know that at the time of her collapse, Todd had made the statement "I can't do it."

33. *See* 738 F.2d at 1533.

34. 433 U.S. 584 (1977).

35. 753 F.2d 877 (11th Cir. 1985), *cert. granted,* 106 S. Ct. 3331 (1986).

36. *See supra* text following note 8.

37. For some of the results of the Baldus study, see Baldus, Woodworth & Pulaski, *Monitoring and Evaluating Contemporary Death Sentencing Systems: Lessons from Georgia,* 18 U.C.D. L. REV. 1375 (1985) [hereinafter cited as Baldus et al.]. Baldus, Pulaski & Woodworth, *Comparative Review of Death Sentences: An Empirical Study of the Georgia Experience,* 74 J. CRIM. L. & CRIMINOLOGY 661 (1983).

38. *See* McCleskey v. Zant, 580 F. Supp. 353–55 (N.D. Ga. 1984); *see generally* Gross, *supra* note 5, at 1281.

39. Baldus et al., *supra* note 37, at 1404.

40. *Id.* at 1406.

41. *Id.*

42. *Id.*

43. *Id.* at 1401.

44. Gross, *supra* note 5, at 1296.

45. *See* Gross, *supra* note 5, at 1296.

46. *Id.* at 1303–4.

47. *Id.* at 1302.

48. In the middle range of cases the killer of a white victim is more than five times as likely to receive the death penalty as the killer of a black victim.

49. *See, e.g.,* Ross v. Hopper, 716 F.2d 1528, 1539 (11th Cir. 1983); Spencer v. Zant, 715 F.2d 1583 (11th Cir. 1983), *vacated for reh'g en banc,* 715 F.2d 1583 (11th Cir. 1983).

50. 753 F.2d 877 (11th Cir. 1985).

51. The court considered whether the Georgia death penalty statute was applied in violation of the equal protection clause of the Fourteenth Amendment, the due process

clause of the Fourteenth Amendment, or the cruel and unusual punishment clause of the Eighth Amendment. It decided that there is "little difference in the proof that might be required to prevail under any of the three theories," *id.* at 890, and that the Baldus data were insufficient to establish a violation of any of them.

52. *Id.* at 892.
53. This allocation of the burden of proof seemed inconsistent with rules set forth in recent Supreme Court cases, such as Batson v. Kentucky, 106 S. Ct. 1712 (1986). In *Batson* the Court said that although the defendant in an equal protection case has the burden of proving purposeful discrimination, *[The defendant] may make out a prima facie case of purposeful discrimination by showing that the totality of relevant facts gives rise to an inference of discriminatory purpose. . . . Once the defendant makes the requisite showing, the burden shifts to the State to explain adequately the racial exclusion. . . . The State cannot meet this burden by mere general assertions that its officials did not discriminate or that they properly performed their duties. Rather the State must demonstrate that "permissible racially neutral selection criteria and procedures have produced the . . . result."* *Id.* at 1719–20.
54. *See, e.g.,* Maxwell v. Bishop, 398 F.2d 138, 148 (8th Cir. 1968) (dicta).
55. The court rejected Baldus's finding of a 20 percent disparity in the middle range of cases because it was "unpersuaded that there is a rationally classified, well-defined class of cases in which it can be demonstrated that a race-of-the-victim effect in operating with a magnitude approximating 20%." 753 F.2d at 898.
56. *Id.* at 899.
57. *Id.*
58. *Id.* at 896.
59. *Id.* at 899.
60. *Id.*
61. Gross, *supra* note 5, at 1309.
62. *See* McCleskey, 580 F. Supp. at 357–58.
63. 753 F.2d at 925 n.24 (dissenting opinion of Clark, J.).
64. Gross, *supra* note 5, at 1309.
65. *See, e.g.,* Maxwell v. Bishop, 398 F.2d 138, 146–48 (8th Cir. 1968), *vacated and remanded on other grounds*, 398 U.S. 262 (1970).
66. 753 F.2d at 899.
67. *See, e.g.,* Doyle, Dawber, Kanmel, Kinch & Kahn, *The Relationship of Cigarette Smoking to Coronary Heart Disease*, 190 J.A.M.A. 886 (1964).
68. *See* Wolfgang & Riedel, *supra* note 6.
69. Gross, *supra* note 5, at 1321.
70. *Id.* at 1317–18; *see also* Kleck, *supra* note 9, at 798 Table 6.
71. Gross, *supra* note 5, at 1319.
72. 753 F.2d at 899.
73. Gross, *supra* note 5, at 1298.
74. 753 F.2d at 897.
75. *See* Pulley v. Harris, 104 S. Ct. 871, 881 (1984); Gregg v. Georgia, 428 U.S. 153, 206–7 (1976) (plurality opinion); *see generally* Gross, *supra* note 5, at 1314.
76. 104 S. Ct. 562, 564 n.2 (1984) (Powell, J., dissenting) (citations omitted).
77. *See supra* text at notes 69–71.
78. In determining whether the defendant's stay of execution should be granted, the issue before the Court was whether the federal district court properly exercised its discretion in finding that the defendant

abused the writ of habeas corpus. The Court could have decided this issue without considering the merits of the defendant's claim. As Justice Powell said, the inquiry should have been directed to "petitioner's reasons for not having raised the claim in his first habeas proceeding." 104 S. Ct. at 563 (Powell, J., dissenting).

79. For a discussion of the classic view of the Supreme Court death penalty decisions, see Weisberg, *Deregulating Death*, 1983 SUP. CT. REV. 305, 318–28.

80. *See supra* text at notes 24–36.

CHAPTER 7

Defendants Who Elect Execution

Some defendants actually choose to be executed; of these, Gary Gilmore is the most famous. On two successive nights in July, 1976, he robbed and killed a service station attendant in Orem, Utah, and a motel night clerk in Provo, Utah.[1] Less than twelve weeks later, he was convicted and sentenced to death for the Provo murder.[2] After that, Gilmore said he was willing to accept the death penalty and adamantly resisted efforts by his attorneys and family to oppose it. In fact, Gilmore fired his attorneys for appealing his case to the Utah Supreme Court;[3] he refused to authorize any other effort to attack his conviction and death sentence;[4] and when his mother, Bessie Gilmore, who claimed to be acting as his next friend, sought a stay of his execution in the United States Supreme Court, Gilmore, through his attorneys, filed a response "challenging the standing of Bessie Gilmore to initiate any proceedings on his behalf."[5] In his concurring opinion upholding Gilmore's position, Chief Justice Burger noted that Gilmore's "only complaint against Utah or its judicial process . . . has been with respect to the delay on the part of the State in carrying out the [death] sentence."[6]

In retrospect, Gilmore's complaints about delay seem unfounded. In a 5-4 decision the Supreme Court rejected Bessie Gilmore's application for a stay,[7] and on January 17, 1977, only three and one-half months after his conviction, Gilmore became the first person to be executed in the United States in almost ten years.

The phenomenon of a defendant who elects execution is by no means uncommon. G. Richard Strafer has documented the fact that "at one point or another," five of the first eight men to be executed during the modern era of capital punishment "not only 'chose' to forgo further efforts to contest their executions, but vigorously, and in the end successfully, opposed efforts by third parties to continue the battles in their stead."[8]

At least one of these defendants was even more adamant than Gilmore in expressing his desire for execution. Steven Judy was convicted of raping and killing a young woman and then drowning her three children, ages two, four, and five.[9] Once convicted of the four murders, Judy instructed his attorneys not to present any evidence of mitigating circumstances during the sentencing hearing and not to argue against the death penalty. During the penalty trial, Judy testified and told the jury that they should give him the death penalty because "he had no doubt that he would kill again if he had an opportunity, and some of the people he might kill in the future might be members of the jury."[10] After hearing this testimony, the jury took his advice and returned the death sentence.

In contrast to Gilmore and Judy, some of the "volunteers" for execution have vacillated between vigorously pursuing their appeals and resisting all efforts to prevent their executions. For example, John Louis Evans, who was executed on April 22, 1983, pled guilty to murder, and at his penalty trial demanded the death sentence, threatening to kill again if it was not imposed.[11] After the jury imposed the death penalty, Evans initially opposed all appeals on his behalf.[12] Subsequently, however, he changed his mind, and "[h]aving originally demanded execution from his trial jury and from various appellate courts, near the end of his six years on death row he sought aggressively but unsuccessfully to have his conviction and sentence overturned by the courts."[13]

Because of defendants who vacillate between seeking execution and opposing it, it is difficult to estimate what proportion of the defendants now on death row may be properly characterized as electing execution. If electing execution is defined as expressing a clear preference for the death penalty over life imprisonment, then probably a majority of those on death row have at some point elected execution. Indeed, one experienced defense counsel said that nearly every capital defendant he represented at one time or another expressed this preference. Most defendants eventually change their minds and resist the death penalty. Nevertheless, under any definition the proportion of capital defendants who elect execution is significant.[14] In considering the modern scheme of capital punishment, it is important to consider some of the issues that arise when defendants make that choice.

The Dilemma for Defense Attorneys

The defendant who volunteers to be executed poses a special dilemma for defense attorneys who specialize in representing capital defendants. Most such attorneys have chosen to represent capital defendants in part at least because they are personally opposed to capital punishment. Thus, if a defendant says that he would prefer to be executed rather than to be sentenced to life imprisonment, an attorney may be confronted with a conflict: he must choose between his own interest in opposing the death penalty and his possible obligation to pursue his client's choice to accept a death sentence.[15]

The conflict is complicated by the fact that the attorney's ethical obligation is by no means clear. The attorney-client relationship is a joint enterprise in which the goals to be achieved by the representation usually are mutually agreed upon. In most instances, the criminal defense attorney must show considerable respect for his client's autonomy. For example, the ABA Code dictates that a lawyer must not "[f]ail to seek the lawful objectives of his client through reasonably available means."[16] And the lawyer's obligation to carry out the client's objectives is elaborated in an ethical consideration[17] that provides that "the lawyer should always remember that the decision whether to forgo legally available objectives or methods because of non-legal factors is ultimately for the client and not for himself."[18] On the other hand, in allocating decision-making responsibility between criminal defendants and defense attorneys, the ethical guidelines do not specifically identify the decision whether to oppose the death penalty as one of those in which the defendant has ultimate authority.[19] Moreover, the ethical guidelines recognize that the attorney may assume greater decision-making responsibility when his client's mental capacities are impaired.[20] The cases that have dealt with the ethical dimension of this problem are split.[21]

Surprisingly, many capital defense attorneys do not see the conflict. Most of the attorneys I talked to said that they had encountered situations in which a client said that he would prefer death to life imprisonment, but almost all of the attorneys also said that in their view the defendant's expression of this sentiment posed an obstacle to effective representation rather than an ethical dilemma. For example, Bob Ravitz of Oklahoma said, "When a defendant says that he wants to die, I generally don't worry too much about it because I'm confident that I can persuade him to change his mind."

Ravitz and other attorneys said that the reason they are generally successful in changing the defendant's mind is that in the course of representing him they will develop a close rapport with him. As a result, the defendant will not only listen to the attorney's advice but may be loath to take any action that will eliminate his relationship with the attorney. It may sound incredible to say that a defendant would reverse a decision to elect execution in order to continue a relationship with his attorney, but defense attorneys insist that the defendant's relationship with his attorney is at least a psychological factor that often plays a critical part in influencing the defendant's decision making. Perhaps this indicates that some decisions to elect execution spring from despair and loneliness rather than from reason.

When a defendant persists in his decision to accept execution, some capital defense attorneys place few limits on the arguments they use to induce a change of heart. For example, David Wymart of Colorado said that if the defendant has a family, he will point out the effect the execution might have on family members. He might refer to the fact that the defendant wants to be a good father and say, "What will it be like for your kids when the other kids read in the paper about you being executed? Your kids will be taunted; they'll be abused; they'll have to suffer because of your selfishness in refusing to fight."

Other attorneys say that in some situations they persuade the defendant by appealing to his immediate interest in avoiding incarceration on death row. They point out that even if he abandons all efforts to save his life, he will be held there for months and perhaps years. On the other hand, if the defendant is able to avoid the death sentence, he will be incarcerated in the general prison population. Defense attorneys can usually make the point by merely stating that fact. Most prisoners are well aware of the advantages of serving time in the general prison population rather than on death row.[22] When more persuasion is needed, however, attorneys explain the advantages. Some recall cases in which they have told capital defendants that confinement in the general prison population offers a better chance to escape.

In other cases, attorneys have explained to their clients why confinement in the general prison population will help them deal with some specific problem. For example, a Pennsylvania attorney recalls a case in which the defendant was an alcoholic who was unable to get a drink while confined on death row. After receiving a death sentence, the defendant insisted that he preferred death to life imprisonment and that no further efforts should be made to save his life; he changed his mind, however, when his attorney pointed out that the immediate effect of vacating his death sentence would be to allow him access to alcohol, which can be obtained through illegal sources in the general prison population, but is not available at all on death row.

Defense attorneys who exert strong pressures on capital defendants to continue the fight for life often say that they believe they are acting in the defendants' best interests. They support this position in a variety of ways. They often say that few if any capital defendants are able to make a rational judgment about whether they want to be executed. They point out that many have severe mental problems and seem incapable of making firm decisions about anything. Moreover, according to defense attorneys, conditions on death row may be so debilitating as to impede the decision-making capacity of defendants who originally were rational. Drawing on an illuminating article by Strafer, some attorneys argue that "death row inmates cannot be considered to be acting voluntarily when they demand their swift executions."[23]

Other capital defense attorneys argue that in representing a capital defendant they have obligations that extend beyond protecting the defendant's self-interest. For example, some attorneys insist that they have obligations to members of the defendant's family, including his children, who will suffer if he is executed, and that they have an obligation to society to make sure that the death penalty is not imposed improperly.

These justifications may sound somewhat contrived, and at least one defense attorney admits that for him they are essentially make-weights. Bruce Ledewitz, a Pennsylvania law school professor who represents many capital defendants, says that when one of his clients indicates that he wants to elect execution, Ledewitz's unyielding opposition to any form of killing leads him to use whatever means he can to dissuade the defendant. He is well aware that a criminal defense attorney ordinarily has an obligation to respect the goals selected by his client. He says that ordinarily if a client told him to drop an appeal or not to present a particular defense, he would feel bound by his client's wishes. In explaining why the issue of self-execution is different, Ledewitz says that in this situation there is an overriding principle that outweighs the client's interests. According to Ledewitz, "The state's goal of killing someone is immoral." He concludes that his paramount objective is to prevent the state from realizing its immoral goal. Ledewitz says that in comparison with that objective the defendant's "desire to be killed is not important to me."

Ledewitz says that nearly every client he has represented has at some point indicated a desire not to oppose the death penalty and that they have generally taken this position most strongly before he has had an opportunity to develop a close relationship with them. He believes that the client's desire to be executed influences plea bargaining, because a client who expresses a preference for the death penalty will almost never agree to a plea bargain under which the sentence will be life imprisonment or a long prison term. Like other attorneys, Ledewitz will often strongly pressure defendants to accept such bargains.[24] But when the defendant adamantly maintains his preference for execution, Ledewitz's efforts will be frustrated.

Aside from plea bargaining, Ledewitz says that to date his conduct in trying a capital case has not been affected by a client's expressed desire for execution. When a client tells him before trial that he does not want mitigating evidence presented at the penalty trial because he prefers the death sentence to a sentence of life imprisonment, Ledewitz responds by telling the defendant that under Pennsylvania law he has no choice but to present the strongest case in opposition to the death penalty that he can. Similarly, if the defendant tells him that he does not want to appeal the sentence of death, Ledewitz responds by saying that under Pennsylvania law he (as the defendant's attorney) has an obligation to take an appeal and to raise every legitimate issue relating to the validity of the death penalty. Ledewitz admits that Pennsylvania law on these issues is unclear.[25] He is not certain whether his representations to his clients are strictly correct. He adds, however, that because of his commitment to opposing the death penalty he will continue to make these statements as long as he doesn't "know that they are in fact untrue."[26]

Ledewitz says that most of the defendants who express a desire to volunteer for execution are either not very firm in their resolve or, because of their mental problems, do not have a full understanding of the situation confronting them. He says that in most cases it would be easy for any attorney to rationalize a decision not to treat his client's desire to be executed seriously. Ledewitz is involved in at least one case, however, in which a client who is of above average intelligence and seems to be in full control of his mental faculties has expressed a clear and unequivocal wish to receive the death penalty rather than a sentence of life imprisonment. Even in this case, Ledewitz has not hesitated to oppose the death penalty to the utmost of his ability. He admits that the client's desire for execution may be rational. From the client's perspective, a lifetime in prison may indeed be a fate worse than death. Ledewitz adds that he likes the client and would ordinarily want to accommodate his desires. Nevertheless, because of his overriding opposition to capital punishment, Ledewitz will not yield to his client's wishes. He says, "[W]hen I represent a capital defendant, I'm not there to let him kill himself. He can discharge me as his attorney if he wants to. But as long as I'm in the case, I will continue to oppose the death penalty by every available legal means."

Other capital defense attorneys are not as outspoken as Ledewitz, and when pressed, some of them acknowledge the ethical problems inherent in opposing a client's wishes. Nevertheless, of the attorneys with whom I spoke, not one indicated that he could imagine a case in which he would voluntarily allow a capital defendant to submit to execution.[27] Thus, for these attorneys, the bottom line is that the goal of preventing the government from killing a human being outweighs a defense attorney's normal obligation to respect his client's autonomy.

The Legal Issues

When a convicted capital defendant elects execution, courts must decide whether to consider some or all of the issues that bear on the validity of his death sentence. The Supreme Court dealt with certain aspects of this question in *Gilmore v. Utah*,[28] but as the opinions in that case suggest, some of the most basic issues remain unresolved.

In *Gilmore* Justice White in dissent posed the basic question. He asserted that "the consent of a criminal defendant in a criminal case does not privilege a state to impose a punishment otherwise forbidden by the Eighth Amendment."[29] The Court attempted to sidestep this question, however. Referring to Justice White's suggestion that Gilmore was " 'unable' as a matter of law to waive the right to state appellate review," Chief Justice Burger, in his concurring opinion, wrote,

[W]hatever may be said to the merits of this suggestion, the question is simply not before us. Gilmore, duly found to be competent by the Utah courts, has had available meaningful access to this court and has declined expressly to assert any claim here other than his explicit repudiation of Bessie Gilmore's effort to speak for him as next friend.[30]

Thus, the chief justice's position was that the Supreme Court could not decide whether Gilmore should be permitted to waive his right to state appellate review. Neither Gilmore's mother nor any other third party had standing to present this issue so long as Gilmore was competent. The effect of this analysis is that at least as far as the Supreme Court is concerned,[31] a competent capital defendant may waive his right to state appellate review.

The Court's position raises subsidiary questions relating to the issue of competency. When will a hearing to evaluate the defendant's competency be required? And what will be the criteria for determining whether a capital defendant is competent to waive his rights?

The *Gilmore* decision seems to indicate that a hearing to evaluate the defendant's competency to waive his rights will not be required unless evidence apart from the defendant's desire for execution suggests that he is incompetent. In *Gilmore* the Court concluded that the state court's "determinations of [Gilmore's] competence knowingly and intelligently to waive [his] rights were firmly grounded."[32] The Court's conclusion was apparently predicated on the fact that three of the five court-appointed psychiatrists who examined Gilmore before trial "found no evidence of mental illness or insanity."[33] Of course, it could be argued that especially in view of Gilmore's erratic behavior following his conviction and sentence,[34] the state-appointed psychiatrists' determination that he was competent for certain purposes prior to trial should not have been sufficient to establish that he was competent for a different purpose several months later. Nevertheless, the Court's conclusion in *Gilmore* indicates that a further hearing to determine a capital defendant's competence to waive his appellate rights will not be necessary simply because the defendant has attempted the waiver.

If an adequate preliminary showing of the capital defendant's inability to waive his rights has been made, a court must hold a hearing to determine his competency. Pursuant to the Supreme Court's decision in *Rees v. Peyton*,[35] the standard for evaluating a capital defendant's competency to waive his rights seems roughly equivalent to the standard used to determine competency to stand trial: the defendant will be competent unless he lacks sufficient "capacity to appreciate his position and make a rational choice with respect to continuing or abandoning further litigation."[36] Based on the cases dealing with competency to stand trial,[37] this would appear to be a relatively low standard. A defendant with quite serious mental problems is held competent to stand trial so long as it appears that he has "a rational as well as a factual understanding of the proceedings against him."[38] Similarly, under the *Rees* standard, capital defendants with serious mental problems will be held competent to waive their rights so long as it appears that they have an adequate understanding of the choice that confronts them.

Analysis

Some of the issues that arise as a result of defendants who elect execution relate to the capital defendant's freedom of choice. Should a capital defendant be permitted to volunteer for execution? If so, at what point in the process? What standard of competency should he be required to meet? And what, if any, safeguards should be imposed to prevent an attorney (or others) from interfering with his choice?

Clearly, an individual who has not been convicted of a criminal offense has no right to demand that he be executed by the state. Even a criminal defendant who has been convicted of a capital offense has no right to dictate to the government which of the two authorized penalties should be imposed. In all cases, the sentencing authority should decide on the appropriate penalty based on the criteria set forth in the sentencing statute. The question remains, however, whether a convicted capital defendant who prefers a death sentence should be allowed to take action that will make the imposition of that sentence more likely.

In considering this issue, it is difficult to find a helpful analogy. The defendant's preference for death over life imprisonment is not the same as a preference for one institution over another or even for prison over probation. Because the punishment of death is different in kind from all others, society's interest in ensuring an appropriate sentence is arguably greater in the death penalty situation than it is when other sentencing decisions are involved. Moreover, under our modern system, the death penalty determination is in some respects more analogous to the guilt determination than to other sentencing decisions. It is made in the context of an adversary proceeding in which the sentencer's decision depends to some extent on findings of fact.[39] If the guilt trial is viewed as the appropriate model, then society's interest in maintaining the integrity of the fact-finding process may provide an additional basis for curtailing the defendant's right to seek his own execution.

On the other hand, protecting a capital defendant's individual autonomy is also an important consideration. The Supreme Court has afforded that interest substantial weight even at the guilt stage. For example, society's interest in maintaining the integrity of the fact-finding process does not outweigh the individual's right of self-representation. A criminal defendant who can demonstrate a minimal level of competence will be allowed to act as his own attorney[40] even though that will generally mean that his representation will suffer.[41] Similarly, a competent defendant who wishes to plead guilty is at most required to demonstrate that there is a factual basis for his plea.[42] This means that so long as the defendant can show that he *may* be guilty,[43] he will be allowed to bypass the fact-finding system and in effect elect a guilty verdict. Thus, even if the guilt determination is the appropriate analogy, there is a substantial basis for arguing that the capital defendant should not be precluded from using the system of justice "as an instrument of self-destruction."[44]

Moreover, the major arguments in favor of circumscribing the capital defendant's autonomy may not be able to withstand analysis. First, the analogy between the guilt and penalty determination is flawed, after all. Even though the penalty trial has the trappings of the adversary system, the death penalty determination is fundamentally different from the guilt determination. The guilt determination is concerned with findings of fact; the penalty determination is a discretionary judgment whether the defendant should be sentenced to life imprisonment or death. Since the penalty decision is not ultimately based on specific findings of fact, at that stage there is less reason to be concerned about protecting the integrity of a fact-finding process.

Second and more important, the argument that society has an especially strong interest in ensuring appropriate death penalty decisions should be subject to some qualifications when a competent defendant indicates that he prefers death over a sentence of life imprisonment. The Court's conclusion that death is different in kind from other punishments stems primarily from a perception that that the death penalty is uniquely harsh.[45] If the defendant does not share that perception, there is less basis for holding that extraordinary safeguards should apply. Moreover, a defendant should be able to waive protections that exist for his benefit.

Public interests are also at stake when the death penalty is involved. Because every execution is in some sense a public spectacle, society has a special interest in making sure that death sentences are imposed only in accordance with the rule of law. Moreover, in view of the concerns expressed in *Furman,* there is a public interest in making sure that the death penalty is not imposed arbitrarily. But the system can protect these interests without requiring every capital defendant to oppose the imposition of the death penalty.

Determining when a death sentence is imposed in accordance with a rule of law may be difficult in some instances. But ordinarily, the legality of any decision should be judged on the basis of the evidence that the parties choose to present. The courts can judge the legality of a death sentence without requiring a capital defendant to present evidence that may bear on the sentence's validity. And the system can adequately protect the legal validity of individual death sentences without requiring that capital defendants who prefer execution present legal arguments against the death penalty. If the courts need help in considering the appropriate legal issues, a third party who is not associated with the defendant may be appointed to present the issues to them.[46]

The issue of arbitrariness poses greater problems. If capital defendants are permitted to seek their own executions, the system will inevitably be less effective in selecting only the most heinous offenders for execution. Nevertheless, the force of this point is dissipated by recent developments in Eighth Amendment doctrine. As Stephen Gillers has said, "Arbitrariness mainly operates at the definition stage of capital punishment law, but after *Lockett v. Ohio,* it plays a minor role at the selection stage."[47] In most jurisdictions, the primary safeguard against arbitrariness is the rule that the capital defendant will not be eligible for the death penalty unless the prosecution establishes at least one aggravating circumstance. *Lockett* dictates that after the prosecution establishes that the death penalty is appropriate, the sentencer must make a discretionary decision based on a consideration of all evidence relevant to the "defendant's character, record, or any circumstances of his offense."[48] Determining whether an aggravating circumstance is present is generally quite simple, so in most cases the defense's advocacy of the death penalty will not prevent the sentencer from making an accurate determination on that issue. Thus, under our modern system, allowing the defendant to seek the death penalty at the penalty stage will not greatly affect the extent to which the penalty is arbitrarily applied.

This analysis shows that the capital defendant should be free to pursue his own goals at the penalty stage. It might seem appropriate, therefore, to hold that a defendant who prefers execution may, with his attorney's help, present relevant evidence (such as his own testimony) that argues in favor of the death penalty and may preclude his attorney from presenting relevant mitigating evidence. But two complicating factors militate against that solution: the capital defendant's competency to choose between execution and life imprisonment; and the irrevocability of the death penalty.

The issue of competency is a troubling one. The present standard for competency to elect execution is roughly equivalent to the test for competency to stand trial.[49] But the decisions involved in the two situations are entirely different. When competency to stand trial is at issue, the court is required to determine whether the defendant understands the charges against him and has the capacity to communicate effectively with his attorney.[50] When competency to elect execution is involved, the issue is whether the defendant has the capacity to choose between life and death. The focus should be on not only the defendant's ability to understand the basic issue but also his ability to resolve it knowingly and voluntarily. Defense attorneys who specialize in capital cases claim that many capital defendants who have an adequate understanding of the charges against them and are fully competent to communicate with counsel should nevertheless be barred from electing execution, because they lack either the judgment or the emotional stability to make a firm and stable decision, much less an informed one.

The irrevocability of the death penalty further complicates the process. If a defendant has mental or emotional problems that preclude him from making a firm choice about anything, it may be especially inappropriate to allow him to make an irrevocable choice not to live. And the irrevocable consequences may occur rather swiftly. As the *Gilmore* case indicates, a defendant who elects execution may in fact be executed quickly.[51] Even if the defendant does change his mind, making a choice at the initial penalty trial means that the chance of successfully attacking the death penalty at a subsequent stage will be very slim. For example, a defendant like John Louis Evans, who changed his mind after initially telling the penalty jury that they should execute him, is likely to find that he has no legal basis for attacking the death penalty.[52]

Perhaps these problems could be dealt with by subjecting the capital defendant's decision to elect execution to greater scrutiny. For example, all defendants who choose the death penalty could be given a competency examination and required to meet an exceptionally high standard of competency.[53] But this approach would inevitably raise questions of infringement on the defendant's autonomy. Given the conditions at prison and on death row, the mere fact that a capital defendant prefers execution to life imprisonment should not be prima facie evidence of incompetency.[54] And even if the defendant does view matters from a perspective that is different from ours, why should that deprive him of an opportunity to make a fundamental choice about his own destiny? In his brief to the Supreme Court in the Gilmore case, William Barrett of the Utah attorney general's office put the matter eloquently:

> Historical, religious, and existential treatises suggest that for some persons at some times, it is rational not to avoid physical death at all costs. Indeed the spark of humanity can maximize its essence by choosing an alternative that preserves the greatest dignity and some tranquility of mind.[55]

If a capital defendant is required to meet an extraordinarily high standard of competency before being allowed to elect execution, his autonomy will be seriously compromised. Indeed, the defendant might end up in a kind of no-man's-land in which he is held competent to go to trial but not competent to elect execution. The defendant could be forced to sit by and watch his attorney press for a sentence of life imprisonment even though that sentence would be contrary to his wishes.

The point is that the system should take into account some measure of respect for the capital defendant's autonomy. Otherwise, as Judge Sneed has said, there is some danger that the government will "incarcerate the [defendant's] spirit—the one thing that remains free and which the state need not and should not imprison."[56] If a reasonably competent defendant asserts that he would prefer to be executed rather than spend the rest of his life in prison, why shouldn't he be permitted to make that choice? Indeed, shouldn't the defendant's attorney be obligated to assist the defendant in pursuing this goal rather than, as is often the case, letting his own opposition to the death penalty take precedence over his client's wishes?

Given the conflicting interests at stake, the problem has the elements of a tragic choice.[57] If we seek too vigorously to guard against irrational decisions to elect execution, we inevitably infringe on individual autonomy. On the other hand, if we attempt to preserve the individual's right to decide whether to seek a punishment of life imprisonment or death, we may create an ironic situation in which defendants who are allowed to elect their own executions are ultimately executed against their own wishes.

Waiver of the Right to Appeal

When a competent defendant who has been sentenced to death decides to volunteer for execution, the issue posed by Justice White in *Gilmore* is presented. Will the defendant be permitted to relinquish his right to attack his death sentence on appeal? In most criminal cases, this issue does not arise. If a defendant has been convicted and sentenced in a court of competent jurisdiction, the sentence imposed is presumed to be valid unless the defendant attacks it in another court of competent jurisdiction. If the defendant fails to appeal his sentence, he will be held to have waived his right of appeal and will be required to serve the sentence.

In cases where the defendant's sentence is the death penalty, there is some justification for deviating from this traditional doctrine. Hornbook law states that a defendant can waive rights personal to himself but not those in which the government maintains an interest.[58] Certainly the government has a substantial interest in preventing the "illegal execution of a citizen."[59]

To take one example, suppose that in 1975 Gary Gilmore had been sentenced to death under a statute providing that anyone convicted of first-degree murder would automatically be sentenced to death. A year later, in 1976, the Supreme Court held in *Woodson v. North Carolina*[60] that that sort of statute was unconstitutional. Yet if capital defendants were allowed to waive their right to appeal and no next friend were allowed to intervene, Gilmore could have been executed under the statute in 1977, even though by that time it would have been apparent that his sentence violated the Eighth Amendment. In certain contexts the defendant's preference for death rather than life imprisonment should perhaps be respected. But the interest in preserving the legality of the system of capital punishment should be afforded a higher priority. Clearly, this interest is significantly impaired when a defendant is executed pursuant to a patently unconstitutional statute.

If a defendant may not preclude review of his death sentence, a number of subsidiary issues arise. For example, if the defendant declines to challenge his death penalty himself, who should be appointed to present the appropriate issues to the court?[61] Which issues should the court be required to consider?[62] And which courts should be required to consider them?[63] These issues would of course be avoided if a capital defendant could waive his right to appeal (or otherwise attack) his death sentence. Nevertheless, given the significant governmental interests involved, it seems appropriate to reject that solution and to hold that regardless of a particular capital defendant's wishes, every death sentence must be given at least limited review by state and/or federal courts.

The Psychological Factors

Why is it that a substantial proportion of the death row population would prefer execution to a sentence of life imprisonment? Several commentators have suggested that one reason may be the dehumanizing conditions on death row. According to the available studies, death row inmates are subject to extraordinary deprivations:[64] they are separated from the general prison population, they have no access to rehabilitative programs, they have little or no opportunity to exercise, they are isolated in their cells for extremely long periods. When those barren conditions are combined with the psychological stress that results from being forced to live with "the spasmodic certainty and uncertainty of being sentenced to die,"[65] it is not surprising that many prisoners find existence on death row intolerable. Indeed, several inmates have stated that those conditions gave rise to their preference for the death penalty. For example, one prisoner on death row said, "If they could fry me tomorrow, that would be preferable to spending the rest of my life here. This isn't living. It's just existing."[66]

Nevertheless, the barren conditions on death row provide only part of the explanation. When it comes to a choice between life and death, most people would subscribe to the view expressed by Claudio in Shakespeare's *Measure for Measure:*

The weariest and most loathèd worldly life
That age, ache, penury, and imprisonment
Can lay on nature is a paradise
To what we fear of death.[67]

Indeed, people who have been subjected to conditions far more stressful and dehumanizing than life on death row have not voluntarily accepted death but have struggled to survive.[68] And most of the inmates who have volunteered for execution have made their choices before being subjected to the debilitating conditions of death row. The phenomenon of defendants volunteering for execution must be attributed at least in part to the psychological makeup of the volunteers rather than to the external conditions surrounding their choice. In other words, defendants who volunteer for execution do so because they are different from the rest of us, not merely because they are subjected to a more stressful and dehumanizing experience.

Two psychological factors may bear particularly on a capital defendant's willingness to volunteer for execution. The more superficial of the two relates to the capital defendant's macho perception of himself. Nearly every defense attorney I talked to said that most capital defendants are concerned about maintaining their tough, indifferent images. That leads some of them to demand the death penalty in order to show they are not afraid of it. Gary Gilmore's statements seemed to reflect this attitude of defiance. In a statement made shortly after his death sentence Gilmore said, "You sentenced me to die. Unless it's a joke or something, I want to go ahead and do it."[69] Gilmore's final words reiterated his position. When the warden asked him if he had anything to say, Gilmore replied, simply, "Let's do it."[70] One interpretation of these statements is that they reveal an attitude of bravado. Gilmore was in effect daring the state of Utah to give him the death penalty. By asserting his willingness to accept the worst that the state could inflict on him, he was demonstrating his manhood.[71]

Gilmore's statements could also be interpreted as evidencing a deeper psychological urge. On some level, perhaps, Gilmore genuinely wanted the state to execute him. According to Norman Mailer's account of his case, when Gilmore explained his decision to accept execution to his attorneys, he asked if he didn't have "the right to die" and intimated that he needed to be executed to atone for a crime he had committed during an earlier life in eighteenth-century England.[72] Moreover, when a federal judge issued a stay, temporarily postponing the execution, Gilmore exhibited genuine rage.[73] One observer said he had never seen him so angry.[74] It appears, then, that at some point in the process Gilmore became convinced that he wanted to be executed.

Gilmore himself said that he chose to be executed because he preferred death to confinement in prison for life.[75] But some observers have argued that he actually opted for execution long before he was confronted with the choice between life imprisonment and the death sentence. Gilmore had served more than half of his life behind bars, including eighteen of his last twenty-one years. When he was released from prison in Oregon, he chose to be paroled in Utah, "the one place in the nation where blood atonement, in the form of a firing squad, may be used to administer the death penalty for murder."[76] After a few months of freedom in Utah, Gilmore on two successive nights committed two execution-style felony-murders, though he did not need the money they brought him. John Woods, chief of forensic psychiatry at Utah State Hospital and one of the psychiatrists who examined Gilmore before trial to determine his sanity, concluded that Gilmore's own impulse toward self-destruction was in fact the primary motivation for the killings. According to Woods, Gilmore

> went out of his way to get the death penalty; that's why he pulled two execution style murders he was bound to get caught for. I think it's a legitimate question, based on this evidence and our knowledge of the individual, to ask if Gilmore would have killed if there was not a death penalty in Utah.[77]

Perhaps the deeper psychological explanation for much of Gilmore's conduct was his strong urge for self-destruction together with his concomitant desire to "turn the job of his destruction over to someone else."[78]

Psychiatrists have long recognized that some killers' motivation for killing is to bring about their own executions.[79] In cases like Gilmore's, the motivation may be unconscious and impossible to establish with a scientific certainty. In others, however, the killer's desire to be executed may be conscious. Psychiatrists have documented cases in which killers have openly stated that their reason for killing was to have the state execute them.[80]

The *French* Case

Consider the case of James French.[81] In 1958, French killed a motorist who picked him up while he was hitchhiking through Oklahoma. After being charged with murder, French entered a guilty plea and requested the death penalty. Much to his chagrin, however, he was sentenced to life imprisonment, apparently because of a deal entered into between the prosecutor and his court-appointed public defender. French wrote repeated letters to the governor demanding execution or a new trial. The letters were ignored.

Three years later, in the Oklahoma State Penitentiary at McAlester, French strangled his cellmate. French frankly admitted that his only motive for this killing was "to get himself executed."[82] French further solicited this sentence "in well-organized, literate epistles to the courts, and in provocative, taunting challenges to judges and jurors."[83] During a 1965 psychiatric examination, French admitted

> that he had seriously attempted suicide several times in the past but always "chickened out" at the last minute. His basic (and obviously abnormal) motive in murdering his inoffensive cellmate was to force the state to deliver to him the electrocution to which he felt entitled and which he deeply desired.[84]

After three trials, French got his wish. He was sentenced to death and executed. He was the only person executed in the United States during the year 1966. Writing about the case in 1975, the examining psychiatrist concluded that "[i]f Oklahoma had *not* had the death penalty, it is likely that both of the men murdered by James French would still be alive."[85]

The Policy Implications

The phenomenon of capital defendants who elect execution bears particularly upon the issue of deterrence. The vast empirical literature relating to the question whether the death penalty deters the commission of capital crimes has generally been judged inconclusive. As Charles Black has said, "The general problem that blocks knowledge here is that no adequately controlled experiment or observation is possible or (so far as we can see) ever will be possible."[86] We do not know and may never be able to know whether in this context "the threat of death is . . . [a] greater deterrent than the threat of long imprisonment."[87]

Nevertheless, proponents of the death penalty have argued that the death penalty should be employed so long as there is some possibility that it will deter capital crimes. In an argument that has been characterized as "possibly the most ingenious retentionist statement ever made,"[88] Ernest van den Haag has argued that the problem is one of properly allocating the risk. Van den Haag begins by accepting the assumption that we do not know whether capital punishment deters murder more effectively than an alternative punishment. His argument then proceeds as follows: If the death penalty is not in fact a more effective deterrent and we nevertheless execute a murderer for the purpose of deterring others, the murderer loses his life for no good purpose. If, on the other hand, capital punishment does deter more effectively and we refrain from executing the murderer, the innocent victims of those who might have been deterred will lose their lives. After posing this choice, van den Haag concludes that the death penalty is justified on deterrent grounds because "I'd rather execute a man convicted of having murdered others than . . . put the lives of innocents at risk."[89]

In posing his choice, van den Haag does not allow for the possibility that the death penalty may be a *less* effective deterrent than life imprisonment. He assumes that either the death penalty is a more effective deterrent (and thus capital punishment will save innocent lives) or the two penalties are equally effective deterrents (and therefore capital punishment will not save or lose innocent lives). But if the death penalty is a less effective deterrent than life imprisonment, capital punishment actually will result in a net loss of innocent lives. That a substantial number of defendants elect execution suggests that the third possibility should at least be considered. If so many capital defendants prefer execution over life imprisonment, it is not implausible to believe that a system of punishment that does not include the death penalty may in fact be a more effective deterrent than one that does.

Retentionists who claim that the death penalty will deter murder more effectively than life imprisonment generally support their position by arguing that most people perceive the death penalty as a more severe punishment than life imprisonment.[90] But if the issue is deterrence, the general population's perception of the death penalty is not critical. The inquiry should focus on the perceptions of the class of people who are likely to commit murder. The fact that many if not most capital defendants at one time or another say that they will opt for execution over life imprisonment[91] provides some indication that potential murderers as a group do not view the death penalty in the way the general populace does. Because of their experience with prison life, some potential murders may have made a rational judgment that death is preferable to life imprisonment.[92] If it is assumed that potential murderers take into account possible punishments before deciding whether to commit murder, for them a system of punishment that includes the death penalty will be a less effective deterrent than one that does not.

Ultimately, this line of analysis may not be very rewarding. Criminologists doubt that many murderers actually do consider the possible penalties in deciding whether to commit murder.[93] In addition, the fact that a convicted murderer says that he would prefer the death penalty does not necessarily mean that he preferred that penalty before he committed the crime in question. Moreover, we have no idea of the numbers of people involved. Even if we could estimate the number of murderers who were less deterred by the threat of the death penalty than by the threat of life imprisonment before they committed their crimes, we could not know how many potential murderers refrained from crime because they feared the death penalty more than life imprisonment. Thus we are brought back to our starting point, with one addition. We do not know and may never be able to know whether a system of punishment that includes the death penalty is a more effective or a *less effective* deterrent for murder than a system of punishment that does not.

But van den Haag's analysis suggests that the problem might be viewed from a different perspective. Unless the reports of reputable psychiatrists are to be discounted, the case histories of defendants like French and Gilmore demonstrate that some defendants kill so that society will execute them. On the other hand, to the best of my knowledge, there are no documented cases of people who decided to kill because they sought a sentence of life imprisonment.

Perhaps the appropriate question then is whether the number of innocent lives that may be saved as a result of the death penalty's purported superior efficacy as a deterrent will be sufficient to counterbalance the number of innocent lives that may be lost as a result of the death penalty's role in precipitating murders that would not have otherwise occurred. Given the imponderables involved in measuring the death penalty's efficacy as a deterrent and the near certainty that it will in fact precipitate killings that would not have otherwise occurred, I for one would be reluctant to make this judgment.

NOTES

1. Newsweek, Nov. 29, 1976, at 26.
2. *See* Gilmore v. Utah, 429 U.S. 1012 (1976).
3. *Id.* at 1015 n.4 (Burger, C.J., concurring).
4. *Id.*
5. *Id.* at 1014.
6. *Id.* at 1013 n.1.
7. *Gilmore,* 429 U.S. 1012.
8. Strafer, *Volunteering for Execution: Competency, Voluntariness and the Propriety of Third Party Intervention,* 74 J. Crim. Law & Criminology 860, 861 (1983) [hereinafter cited as Strafer].
9. Judy v. State, 416 N.E.2d 95, 98 (1983).
10. *Id.* at 100; *see generally* Streib, *Executions Under the Post-Furman Capital Punishment Statutes: The Halting Progression from "Let's Do It" to "Hey, There Ain't No Point in Pulling So Tight,"* 15 Rutgers L. Rev. 399 (1984) [hereinafter cited as Streib].
11. *See* Evans v. State, 361 So. 2d 654, 660–61 (Ala. 1977), *cert. denied,* 440 U.S. 930 (1979).
12. *See* Streib, *supra* note 10, at 462.
13. Streib, *supra* note 10, at 463.
14. According to *Death Row, U.S.A.,* nine of the sixty-two defendants executed as of August 1, 1986, voluntarily elected execution. *See* Death Row, U.S.A., August 1, 1986, at 4.
15. The dilemma experienced by these attorneys is not a new one. In his absorbing account of the NAACP Legal Defense Fund's efforts to bring a halt to capital punishment, Michael Meltsner discusses the dilemma in the context of the case of Robert Lee Massie, a prisoner on death row who demanded execution in 1967. *See* M. Meltsner, Cruel and Unusual: The Supreme Court and Capital Punishment 144–48 (1973). As Meltsner indicates, the dilemma for defense attorneys may have been even more acute in 1967 than it is now, because "Massie's death would have affected every other death-row inmate by breaking the moratorium, which was then over two years old." *Id.* at 147.
16. Model Code of Professional Responsibility DR 7-101(A)(1) (1977).
17. "The Ethical Considerations are aspirational in character and represent the objectives toward which every member of the profession should strive . . . The Disciplinary Rules, unlike the Ethical Considerations, are mandatory in character." Model Code of Professional Responsibility Preliminary Statement (1977).
18. Model Code of Professional Responsibility EC 7-8 (1977).
19. Model Rules of Professional Conduct Rule 1.2(a) comment (1983).
20. Model Code of Professional Responsibility EC 7-12 (1977).

21. *Compare, e.g.,* Martin v. Maggio, 711 F.2d 1273, 1280 (5th Cir. 1983) (capital defendant's instruction to lawyer to obtain an acquittal or death sentence did not justify lawyer's failure to investigate for evidence that might reduce degree of crime or be mitigating at penalty trial) *with* Evans v. State, 361 So. 2d 654, 661–62 (Ala. Crim. App. 1977) (commending counsel for excellent representation even though he elicited defendant's penalty trial testimony that he wanted death penalty and would be likely to "come after" jurors if it were not imposed).

22. For an elaboration of the differences between the general prison population and death row, see *infra* text at notes 64–66.

23. Strafer, *supra* note 8, at 892.

24. *See* chap. 2.

25. In Commonwealth v. McKenna, 476 Pa. 228, 383 A.2d 174 (1978), the Pennsylvania Supreme Court held that regardless of the capital defendant's wishes, the court must decide whether the sentencing statute under which defendant's death penalty was imposed was in violation of the federal Constitution. The court did not decide, however, what other issues relating to the death sentence's validity must be considered on appeal or at trial.

26. Ledewitz adds that in making these statements he does not intend to deceive his clients and that in his opinion the statements are consistent with his obligation to act as an officer of the court. Indeed, Ledewitz says that on more than one occasion he has made these statements in open court and has not been corrected or challenged by the prosecutor or the judge.

27. Some attorneys did say that they would not seek to prolong a capital defendant's agony when there appeared to be no hope of saving him from execution. Thus, several said that they would willingly acquiesce in a defendant's decision to forgo further attacks on a death sentence when the chances of success appeared to be nil.

28. 429 U.S. 1012 (1976).

29. *Id.* at 1018 (White, J., dissenting).

30. *Id.* at 1017 (Burger, C.J., concurring).

31. Particular states have held that as a matter of state law, a capital defendant will not be permitted to waive his right to appellate review. *See, e.g.,* Commonwealth v. McKenna, 476 Pa. 228, 383 A.2d 174 (1974); *See generally* Strafer, *supra* note 8, at 882–83 nn.80–81.

32. 429 U.S. at 1013.

33. *Id.* at 1015 n.5 (Burger, C.J., concurring).

34. In particular, Gilmore attempted suicide while in prison. *See* 429 U.S. at 1019 (Marshall, J., dissenting).

35. 384 U.S. 312 (1966) (per curiam).

36. *Id.* at 314.

37. *See, e.g.,* Dusky v. United States, 362 U.S. 402 (1960) (per curiam); United States v. Dunn, 594 F.2d 1367 (10th Cir. 1979), *cert. denied,* 444 U.S. 852 (1979).

38. 362 U.S. at 402.

39. *See* chap. 3.

40. *See* Faretta v. California, 422 U.S. 806 (1975).

41. In *Faretta* the majority did not dispute Chief Justice Burger's statement concerning the effect of allowing criminal defendants to represent themselves: "[I]n all but an extraordinarily small number of

cases an accused will lose whatever defense he may have if he undertakes to conduct the trial himself." 422 U.S. at 838 (dissenting opinion of Burger, C.J.).

42. *See, e.g.,* North Carolina v. Alford, 400 U.S. 25, 38 (1970) ("[i]n view of the strong factual basis" for defendant's guilty plea to a crime he denied committing, judge did not commit constitutional error in accepting plea).

43. Under the Federal Rules of Criminal Procedure, the factual basis for a guilty plea may be established if the defendant admits guilt and the court satisfies itself "that the conduct which the defendant admits constitutes the offense charged." FED. R. CRIM. P. 11(f) Advisory Committee Note.

44. *Faretta,* 422 U.S. at 840 (Burger, C.J., dissenting).

45. *See, e.g.,* Gregg v. Georgia, 428 U.S. 153, 187 (1976) (plurality opinion of Stewart, Powell, and Stevens, JJ.): "There is no question that death as a punishment is unique in its severity and irrevocability."

46. For further discussion of this issue, *see infra* notes 61–63 and accompanying text.

47. Gillers, *Deciding Who Dies,* 129 U. PA. L. REV. 1, 25 (1980).

48. Lockett v. Ohio, 438 U.S. 586, 607 (1978).

49. *See supra* text at notes 35–38.

50. *See* Dusky v. United States, 362 U.S. 402 (1960) (per curiam).

51. *See supra* text following note 7.

52. If the defendant at the penalty trial presented evidence that favored the imposition of the death penalty, mounting a successful attack on the death penalty at some later stage of the proceedings would obviously be more difficult,

because there would be less basis for attacking the evidence in support of the jury's penalty decision.

53. Strafer favors this approach. *See* Strafer, *supra* note 8, at 879–85.

54. *Cf.* Drope v. Missouri, 420 U.S. 162, 181 (1975) ("a suicide attempt need not always signal 'an inability to perceive reality accurately' ").

55. N. MAILER, THE EXECUTIONER'S SONG 706 (1979) [hereinafter cited as MAILER].

56. Lenhard *ex rel.* Bishop v. Wolff, 603 F.2d 91, 94 (9th Cir. 1979) (Sneed, J., concurring), *stay of execution denied,* 444 U.S. 807 (1979) (mem.).

57. *See generally* G. CALABRESI & R. BOBBITT, TRAGIC CHOICES (1978).

58. *See* 21A AM. JUR. 2D, *Criminal Law* § 633 (1981).

59. Commonwealth v. McKenna, 476 Pa. 428, 441, 383 A.2d 174, 181 (1978).

60. 428 U.S. 280 (1976).

61. Strafer discusses the related issue of what parties have standing to intervene when a capital defendant declines to attack his own death sentence. *See* Strafer, *supra* note 8, at 910–11. But affording parties other than the defendant standing to attack the defendant's death sentence does not necessarily ensure that an appellate court will examine the legality of every death sentence. It is quite possible that no interested party would choose to contest the defendant's death sentence. But if we decide that a defendant should not be executed pursuant to an illegal sentence, there should be some procedure under which an appellate court will consider the legality of the defendant's death sentence in every case. Of course, an appellate court

could merely review the legality of the death sentence on its own without having a party present the appropriate issues to it, but that would not be sufficient to provide the detailed scrutiny that is generally mandated by our adversary system. Cf. Anders v. California, 386 U.S. 738 (1967) (indigent defendants entitled to have issues considered on appeal must be represented by counsel so that issues are adequately presented to court). Accordingly, in cases where neither the capital defendant nor anyone with standing to act on his behalf desires to attack the death sentence, a lawyer should be appointed to present the appropriate issues to the court.

62. Various lines could be drawn. At one extreme, it might be claimed that execution pursuant to any illegal death sentence is in violation of the public interest. Under this view, the attorney challenging the death penalty should be required to pursue every possible attack. From another perspective, however, it might be claimed that the public interest in preventing an illegal execution is not seriously infringed unless the system of capital punishment under which the death sentence was imposed is unconstitutional. If this view were accepted, the reviewing court would only be required to consider attacks on the sentencing statute.

63. For example, it could be held that review of defendant's death penalty by the state supreme court would be sufficient. On the other hand, in order to vindicate the federal interest at stake, it might be held that any claim that the defendant's death penalty violates the federal Constitution should be reviewed by at least one federal court.

64. *See generally* R. JOHNSON, CONDEMNED TO DIE: UNDER SENTENCE OF DEATH (1981); B. JACKSON & D. CHRISTIAN, DEATH ROW (1980); Gallemore & Panton, *Inmate Responses to Lengthy Death Row Confinement, reprinted in* CAPITAL PUNISHMENT IN THE UNITED STATES 527–34 (H. Bedau & C. Pierce eds. 1976); Strafer, *supra* note 8, at 869–75; Johnson, *Warehousing for Death, Observations on the Human Environment of Death Row,* 26 CRIME & DELING. 545 (1980).

65. Strafer, *supra* note 8, at 867.

66. Robert Lee Massie, another prisoner on death row, expressed the same views even more forcefully. According to Strafer, "Massie stated that he did *not* want to be executed, nor did he object to spending the rest of his life incarcerated. Given, however, the 'choice' of execution or life on death row, he preferred execution." *Id.* at 874.

67. W. SHAKESPEARE, MEASURE FOR MEASURE, act 3, sc. 1, lines 129–33.

68. For example, the great majority of prisoners incarcerated at Auschwitz and the other death camps struggled to stay alive despite the fact that they were forced to live in intolerable circumstances where the possibility of survival seemed almost nonexistent. *See* L. Eitinger, *On Being a Psychiatrist and a Survivor, reprinted in* CONFRONTING THE HOLOCAUST: THE IMPACT OF ELIE WIESEL 196–97 (A. Rosenfeld & I. Greenberg, eds. 1978).

69. Deseret News, Nov. 1, 1976 (published in Provo, Utah).

70. NEWSWEEK, Jan. 31, 1977, at 32.

71. Gilmore's statement to his Uncle Vern on the day before his execu-

tion reflects a similar attitude. In Norman Mailer's account of Gilmore's last days, he says that Gilmore told Vern he wanted him to witness his execution. When Vern asked why, Gilmore explained, "'Well, Vern,' Gary said, 'I want to show you. I've already shown you how I live'—he gave his most mocking smile—'and I'd like to show you how I can die.'" MAILER, *supra* note 55, at 984.

72. *See id. supra* note 55 at 490.

73. *Id. supra* note 55 at 938.

74. *Id. supra* note 55 at 939.

75. *Id. supra* note 55 at 489.

76. H. BEĐAU, THE COURTS, THE CONSTITUTION, AND CAPITAL PUNISHMENT 121–23 (1977)

77. *See* Strafer, *supra* note 8, at 866.

78. *See id.,* quoting Woods.

79. *See generally* Solomon, *Capital Punishment as Suicide and as Murder, reprinted in* CAPITAL PUNISHMENT IN THE UNITED STATES 432–44 (H. Bedau & C. Pierce eds. 1976) [hereinafter cited as Solomon]; West, *Psychiatric Reflections on the Death Penalty, reprinted in* CAPITAL PUNISHMENT IN THE UNITED STATES 426–31 (H. Bedau & C. Pierce eds. 1976) [hereinafter cited as West].

80. *See generally* Solomon, *supra* note 79; West, *supra* note 79; I. WERTHAM, THE SHOW OF VIOLENCE (1949); Strafer, *supra* note 8, at 864–66.

81. *See* West, *supra* note 79, at 426–27.

82. *Id. supra* note 79 at 426.

83. *Id. supra* note 79 at 427.

84. *Id.*

85. *Id.*

86. C. BLACK, CAPITAL PUNISHMENT: THE INEVITABILITY OF CAPRICE AND MISTAKE 25 (1974).

87. *Id.* For a discussion of the most recent empirical data relating to the issue of the death penalty's efficacy as a deterrent, see Lempert, *Desert and Deterrence: An Assessment of the Moral Bases for Capital Punishment,* 69 MICH. L. REV. 1177 (1981).

88. Gorecki, *Capital Punishment: For or Against,* 83 MICH. L. REV. 1180, 1183 (1985).

89. E. VAN DEN HAAG & J. CONRAD, THE DEATH PENALTY—A DEBATE 69 (1983).

90. *See, e.g.,* E. VAN DEN HAAG, PUNISHING CRIMINALS 207 (1975): "Most people believe that death is a more serious punishment than the usual alternative, life imprisonment."

91. *See supra* text following note 13.

92. The noted social critic Jacques Barzun indicated that he would make the same choice. *See* Barzun, *In Favor of Capital Punishment,* 31 AM. SCHOLAR 181, 188–89 (1962).

93. *See* R. BARRETT & J. HAGEL III, ASSESSING THE CRIMINAL 140–41 (1977).

CHAPTER 8

The Supreme Court and the
Death-Qualified Jury

The most important capital punishment decision of
1986 involved a case in which the defendant was not sentenced to
death. In *Lockhart v. McCree*,[1] the Supreme Court rejected a challenge—brought by Ardia McCree, who had been convicted of murder and
sentenced to life imprisonment after his trial in an Arkansas state court—
to the current practice of death qualifying a jury in capital cases before
the guilt phase of the trial. The Court held that death qualification does
not violate a capital defendant's Sixth Amendment right to trial before an
impartial jury. In reaching this result, the Court rejected a procedural claim that had been raised by several hundred death row inmates.[2]

To understand the claim rejected by the Court in *McCree*, it is helpful
to divide prospective jurors into four groups based upon their attitudes
toward capital punishment. The groups would consist of (1) those who
favor or are neutral toward the death penalty; (2) those who oppose the
death penalty but are willing to vote for it in some cases (the "scrupled"
jurors); (3) those who will never vote for the death penalty but could be
fair in deciding the guilt or innocence of a defendant in a capital case (the
automatic life imprisonment group, or the "*Witherspoon* excludables");
(4) those whose opposition to capital punishment is so strong that it would
prevent them from making an impartial determination about the defendant's guilt (the "nullifiers"). In capital cases, the prosecutor and defense
counsel are permitted to ask prospective jurors about their attitudes toward capital punishment during the voir dire.[3] Under the Court's decision
in *Witherspoon v. Illinois*,[4] the prosecutor is permitted to remove from a
jury that will decide a capital defendant's *penalty* all prospective jurors
who state either (1) that they would automatically vote against the death
penalty (*i.e.*, *Witherspoon* excludables) or (2) that their attitude toward
capital punishment would prevent them from making an impartial decision as to the defendant's guilt[5] (*i.e.*, the nullifiers). In *Lockhart* the defendant claimed that the removal of the automatic life imprisonment

group at the guilt phase violated his right to an impartial jury on the issue of guilt or innocence. More specifically, the defendant claimed that the removal for cause of the *Witherspoon* excludables violated his right to a jury selected from a cross-section of the community and his right to an impartial jury.

The claim that death qualifying the jury deprives a capital defendant of a fair trial on the issue of guilt is not a new one. Walter Oberer presented the basic argument more than twenty-five years ago: "A jury qualified on the death penalty is one more apt to *convict*," and therefore, "a defendant tried before such a jury is denied a fair trial on the *basic issue of guilt or innocence*."[6] Oberer's argument is fascinating from both an empirical and a legal perspective.

Empirically, the question is how a court should determine whether a death-qualified jury is in fact more likely to convict. Should the court simply rely on its own intuition or should it require proof? If the latter, what type of evidence will be sufficient to establish the truth of the proposition at issue?

Legally, there is the fundamental problem of defining what constitutes a fair trial. Supposing that it is established that a death-qualified jury is more likely to convict than a non-death-qualified one, why does it follow that the defendant is deprived of a fair trial? The government has often claimed that so long as the jury actually selected is not biased against the defendant, the defendant has no right to a selection process that is likely to result in a more favorable jury. Should that claim be accepted? And if not, what should be the criteria for determining whether a conviction-prone jury is not impartial within the meaning of the Sixth Amendment?

The claim that a death-qualified jury denies the capital defendant a fair trial on the determination of guilt is often referred to as the prosecution proneness issue.[7] The two Supreme Court cases that deal with it were decided eighteen years apart, in different eras of capital punishment. *Witherspoon v. Illinois*,[8] was decided in 1968, in the pre-*Furman* era of capital punishment, when the sentencing jury had absolute discretion as to whether the death penalty would be imposed. *Witherspoon*, in fact, was the first case in which the Supreme Court considered the constitutionality of a procedure employed in capital cases. *Lockhart v. McCree*,[9] on the other hand, was decided in 1986, ten years into the modern era of capital punishment. In the years between *Witherspoon* and *McCree*, the Court decided more than twenty significant cases relating to the constitutionality of procedures employed in capital cases.[10]

Comparing the Court's treatment of the prosecution proneness issue in *Witherspoon* and in *McCree* will not only shed light on the specific legal and empirical issues presented in those cases but also (and more importantly) make clear what the decisions mean in the context of the Court's effort to regulate our system of capital punishment.

Witherspoon

In *Witherspoon v. Illinois,*[11] the defendant was on trial for the capital charge of murder in an Illinois state court. Consistent with the law in most American jurisdictions,[12] the prosecutor was permitted to death qualify the jury. Pursuant to an Illinois statute, he was allowed to challenge for cause any venireman who stated during the voir dire that he had "conscientious scruples against capital punishment or that he [was] opposed to the same."[13] Thus, the issue was different from the one presented in *Lockhart,* because the prosecutor was permitted to challenge prospective jurors whose views on the death penalty placed them in the scrupled jurors' group as well as those in groups three (the automatic life imprisonment group) and four (the nullifiers).

Early in the voir dire, the trial judge set the tone for the death-qualification process. He said, "Let's get these conscientious objectors out of the way, without wasting any time on them."[14] Then, in rapid succession, forty-seven out of the ninety-five veniremen examined were successfully challenged for cause because of their attitudes toward the death penalty.[15]

The defendant claimed that a jury selected in this fashion was constitutionally biased with respect to the determination of guilt because it was more likely to convict than a non-death-qualified jury. As I have already suggested,[16] in making this claim the defendant was asserting two propositions, one empirical and one legal. The empirical proposition was that death-qualified juries are more likely to convict than non-death-qualified juries, and the legal proposition was that requiring a capital defendant to be tried before a jury that is more likely to convict than an ordinary jury violates the Constitution. The Court's response to both of the assertions was interesting.

The Empirical Question

Empirical questions should be distinguished from ordinary factual questions. Some examples of ordinary factual questions are: Was the light green when the plaintiff was hit by the truck? Did the defendant kill the victim? What was his state of mind at the time of the killing? Factual questions of this nature are at issue in nearly every lawsuit. They are resolved by juries and courts on the basis of evidence that is introduced by the parties and made a part of the record of the case.

Empirical questions pertain to phenomena or relationships that extend beyond the events of a particular lawsuit. Some examples of empirical questions are: Will black students be psychologically damaged if they are required to attend racially segregated schools? Is the death penalty applied arbitrarily? Are there numerous mistaken identifications? In asserting that death-qualified juries are more likely to convict than non-death-qualified juries, the *Witherspoon* defendant was answering an empirical question. He was not making a claim that pertained to his particular case; rather, he was asserting that a certain phenomenon exists in the world at large.

The Supreme Court's response to the defendant's empirical assertion was very unusual. When an empirical question is potentially relevant to a constitutional issue, the Court generally takes one of two approaches. It either resolves the empirical question itself[17] or it defines the constitutional issue so that the empirical question will not be relevant to the issue to be decided. In *Witherspoon,* however, the Court adopted neither of these approaches. Instead, it said that it was unable to decide the empirical question because there was a lack of proof: "The data adduced by the petitioner . . . are too tentative and fragmentary to establish that jurors not opposed to the death penalty tend to favor the prosecution in the determination of guilt."[18] In fact, the defendant had adduced very little evidence that would bear on the empirical question at issue. No evidence at all was presented at trial. In his brief to the Supreme Court, the defendant cited unpublished studies involving experiments with college students, and in his petition for certiorari he cited a preliminary unpublished summary of the results of Hans Zeisel's interviews with 1,248 jurors in New York and Chicago. Since the studies were neither published nor presented into evidence, the Court felt that it could "only speculate . . . as to the precise meaning of the terms used, . . . the accuracy of the techniques employed, and the validity of the generalizations made."[19] Based on the record, then, the Court's conclusion that the defendant had presented insufficient proof was not surprising.

What was surprising was the Court's suggestion that the defendant was required to supply such proof. Recognizing that parties to a particular lawsuit are unlikely to have any special access to information that is relevant to an empirical question, courts have traditionally decided empirical questions for themselves, either on the basis of their own intuition[20] or with the aid of evidence gleaned from the social sciences.[21]

In *Witherspoon,* however, the Court concluded that it could not resolve the present empirical question "either on the basis of the record now before us or as a matter of judicial notice."[22] It emphasized, however, that the empirical question remained open. In footnote 18 of the opinion, the Court said a defendant convicted by a death-qualified jury "in some future case might still attempt to establish that the jury was less than neutral with respect to guilt."[23] The Court went on to say that if the defendant were successful in that attempt, certain legal issues would have to be considered.[24]

The *Witherspoon* case was unusual, then, in that it identified an empirical question as potentially relevant to a constitutional issue and yet failed to resolve it. The Court stated the question in various ways, and the precise terms of the question to be answered were not entirely clear. Was the question simply whether a death-qualified jury is more likely to convict than a non-death-qualified one? Or was the defendant required to establish that death qualifying the jury "results in an unrepresentative jury on the issue of guilt or substantially increases the risk of conviction?"[25] Moreover, the Court offered no guidelines for the type of proof that would be sufficient to establish the empirical proposition. Nevertheless, the Court's analysis made it clear that the prosecution proneness issue identified by Oberer remained open and that data relating to the differences, if any, between death-qualified and non-death-qualified juries would have some bearing on the final resolution of that issue.

The Legal Issues Left Open

In footnote 18, the Court sketchily defined the legal issues that would arise if some future defendant were able to resolve the empirical question in his favor:

> If he were to succeed in that effort, the question would then arise whether the State's interest in submitting the penalty issue to a jury capable of imposing capital punishment may be vindicated at the expense of the defendant's interest in a completely fair determination of guilt or innocence—given the possibility of accommodating both interests by means of a bifurcated trial, using one jury to decide guilt and another to fix punishment.[26]

This language was particularly significant because it seemed to accept the premise that trial before a prosecution-prone jury would not be "completely fair." By accepting this premise, the Court implicitly rejected the argument that a conviction-prone jury could still be impartial so long as no member of the jury was actually biased against the defendant. Instead, the Court indicated that a sufficient showing that death-qualified juries are prosecution prone would trigger a balancing process under which the defendant's interest in a fair guilt determination would have to be weighed against the government's interest in death qualifying the jury before the guilt stage. The Court did not establish, however, either what showing of prosecution proneness would be sufficient to precipitate this balancing process or the parameters of the balancing process itself.

The Legal Issue Decided

The *Witherspoon* defendant did not come away empty handed. The Court vacated his death sentence on the ground that removing from the penalty jury all those who were opposed to the death penalty or had conscientious scruples against imposing it had deprived the defendant of an impartial jury on the issue of sentence. The Court indicated that in contrast to the prosecution proneness issue, this issue presented little difficulty. It asserted that "it is self-evident that, in its role as arbiter of the punishment to be imposed, [the defendant's] jury fell woefully short of that impartiality to which [he] was entitled under the Sixth and Fourteenth Amendments."[27] The Court's rationale was that with respect to the penalty determination, it was impermissible to "stack the deck against the [defendant]" by removing all prospective jurors whose views on the death penalty placed them in either the scrupled or the automatic life imprisonment group. Nevertheless, in delineating the scope of its holding, the Court made it clear that the prosecution could continue to challenge for cause prospective jurors who fell within the automatic life imprisonment group or were nullifiers. The Court said that nothing in its decision barred the state from excluding

> veniremen . . . who made it unmistakably clear (1) that they would
> automatically vote against the imposition of capital punishment
> without regard to any evidence that might be developed at the trial
> of the case before them, or (2) that their attitude toward the death
> penalty would prevent them from making an impartial decision as
> to the defendant's *guilt*.[28]

Thus, *Witherspoon* produced the system of death qualification that was challenged in *McCree*. In addition, by holding that a jury that was more likely to favor the prosecution with respect to the determination of sentence was not impartial, *Witherspoon* provided an important precedent for the Court to deal with in *McCree*.

McCree

Social scientists perceived *Witherspoon*'s footnote 18 as an invitation to produce data relevant to the prosecution proneness issue. As Michael Finch and Mark Ferraro have said, "The response of the social science community to the perceived invitation . . . has been exceptional."[29] In 1968 there were only three unpublished studies relating to the empirical question defined by the Court; by 1986 there were at least sixteen published studies that were relevant to the prosecution proneness question. Moreover, the later studies used more sophisticated methodologies[30] and explored a wider range of relevant issues than the earlier ones.[31]

The new empirical data, like the older data, were entirely consistent with Oberer's thesis. All the evidence supported the view that a death-qualified jury differs from a non-death-qualified jury in that its attitudes are more favorable to the prosecution and that it is in fact more likely to convict a criminal defendant. In addition, a study conducted by Craig Haney[32] found that the death qualification process—the procedure by which prospective jurors with disqualifying attitudes toward the death penalty are identified and excluded—itself renders the jury more likely to believe the defendant is guilty and that the sentence of death is appropriate.[33]

Defense attorneys associated with the NAACP Legal Defense Fund decided that in view of the wealth of new empirical data relating to the prosecution proneness issue, the time was ripe for relitigating it. In *Grigsby v. Mabry*,[34] a case originally involving three defendants, the Legal Defense Fund lawyers litigated the prosecution proneness issue in the federal district court and were able to obtain the first unequivocal ruling that a death-qualified jury violates a capital defendant's right to a fair determination of the issue of guilt.[35] The federal district court ruled that death qualifying the jury before the guilt phase of a capital case violates both the capital defendant's right to a jury selected from a fair cross-section of the community and his right to an impartial jury.[36] On appeal, the Eighth Circuit Court of Appeals affirmed.[37] This ruling set the stage for the Court's decision in *Lockhart v. McCree*.

As a result of the efforts exerted by both the litigators in *McCree* and the social scientists who generated data relevant to the prosecution proneness issue, the record before the Court in *McCree* stood in stark contrast to the meager record that confronted it in *Witherspoon*. At the hearing in the federal district court, the defendants presented the final results of the three studies that were cited to the Court in *Witherspoon*.[38] In addition, they presented eight post-*Witherspoon* attitude surveys,[39] three post-*Witherspoon* conviction proneness studies,[40] the Haney study relating to the effect of the death qualification process on the jury, and national and Arkansas-specific demographic data relating to the proportion of the relevant populations that would be excluded by the current system of death qualification.

In addition, three expert witnesses, Edward Bronson, Craig Haney, and Reid Hastie, testified about the studies and the conclusions that could be drawn from them. Based on the studies relating to prospective jurors' attitudes, the experts concluded that, in their opinions, "persons excluded by the process of death-qualification share sets of attitudes toward the criminal justice system that set them apart and distinguish them collectively from those not excluded by that process."[41] The experts also concluded that the same studies showed that death qualification significantly decreases the proportion of women and blacks eligible to serve as jurors. Moreover, they testified that the conviction proneness studies showed that people eligible to serve on a death-qualified jury

> are substantially more likely to convict a defendant charged with a
> serious crime than would be prospective jurors who are not
> qualified to serve because of their adamant opposition to the death
> penalty but who could, nevertheless, fairly try the guilt-innocence
> issue in capital cases.[42]

And finally, Haney testified that in his opinion the death qualification procedure has a biasing effect on jurors who survive the voir dire challenge.[43]

The district court credited and accepted all of the expert opinions, finding them "to be based upon reliable empirical data, reason, and common sense."[44] The court concluded that the defendants had demonstrated infringements on their Sixth Amendment right to jury trial. In addition, it concluded that the state did not have adequate justification for the death qualification procedure, because it could protect its legitimate interests by requiring one jury to determine a capital defendant's guilt and, if needed, a second jury to determine penalty.[45]

In dealing with the record in *McCree,* the Supreme Court was once again confronted with both an empirical question and a legal one. The lower court's findings were empirical as well as factual.[46] Was the Supreme Court willing to accept the lower court's conclusions about the effects of death qualification? If so, the legal issues reserved in *Witherspoon* would have to be considered. The Court could avoid the legal issues if it decided the empirical question against the defendant. Conversely, the Court could avoid the empirical question if it assumed arguendo that the lower court's findings were correct but decided the legal issues against the defendant. In fact, however, the Court chose to consider both the empirical and the legal questions. It is worthwhile to examine its treatment of the two questions separately.

The Empirical Question

The Court focused on the lower court's finding that death qualification produces juries that are "more prone to convict" than non-death-qualified juries.[47] In dealing with this empirical question, the Court engaged in an exercise of reductionism that evoked memories of the nursery rhyme Ten Little Indians. Instead of reducing ten little Indians to one, the Court reduced fifteen studies to none.

Ignoring the expert testimony, the Court focused exclusively on the "fifteen studies that were presented into evidence."[48] It said that the eight studies that examined correlations between attitudes toward the death penalty and other aspects of the criminal justice system were "at best, only marginally relevant."[49] It then dismissed the Haney study, which examined the biasing effect of the death qualification process, with the observation that counsel admitted at oral argument that that effect "would not, standing alone, give rise to a constitutional violation.[50] The fifteen studies thus quickly became six.

Next, the Court whittled these six down to three. Although it admitted that all six studies directly examined whether a death-qualified jury is conviction prone (in the sense that it is more likely than a non-death-qualified jury to convict a capital defendant), it observed that three of the six had been before the *Witherspoon* court when it concluded that the empirical data were "too tentative and fragmentary" to establish the prosecution proneness thesis. The Court concluded that if these studies had been "too tentative and fragmentary" in 1968, "the same studies, unchanged but for having aged some eighteen years, are still insufficient to make out a claim in this case."[51]

Turning to the three remaining studies, the Court observed that they too had problems. First, it noted that all three examined the responses of individuals who were not actual jurors dealing with actual capital cases. The majority expressed "serious doubts about the value of these studies in predicting the behavior of actual jurors."[52] The Court also noted that two of the three studies did not attempt to simulate the jury deliberation process and that none of them were able "to predict to what extent, if any, the presence of one or more '*Witherspoon*-excludables' on a guilt-phase jury would have altered the outcome of the guilt determination."[53]

Finally, the Court pointed out that only one study—the Cowan, Thompson, and Ellsworth examination of jury deliberations[54]—took account of the fact that nullifiers (people who state that their views on capital punishment would render them unable to decide a capital defendant's guilt fairly and impartially) would not be eligible to consider a capital defendant's guilt. In the Court's view, the two other studies'[55] failure to take account of "nullifiers" rendered them "fatally flawed."[56] Thus, the fifteen studies were reduced to six, to three, and finally to one. The Court concluded its discussion of the empirical evidence with the apparently reasonable suggestion that a sweeping constitutional rule should not be based on the results of a single study.[57]

The major problem with the Court's analysis was not so much that it was disingenuous—which it certainly was in places[58]—or that it neglected to discuss important issues—which it certainly did[59]—but rather that its approach to evaluating empirical data was fundamentally misguided. It essentially discarded each study that did not precisely focus on the extent to which the modern system of death qualification affects a jury's proneness to convict, and such a process is antithetical to a rational inquiry into the consequences of death qualification.

In their classic study of jury trials, Harry Kalven and Hans Zeisel observed, "Social science more than natural science is forced to operate at a remove from the reality it studies. It must work, therefore, through a chain of inferences."[60] No social science experiment designed to examine the effects of death qualification can expect to precisely replicate the situation that takes place in the real world.[61] Even the simulated trials used in the most complete study—the Cowan-Thompson-Ellsworth jury deliberation study—differed significantly from real jury trials. As the Court emphasized,[62] the study did not involve actual jurors who were required by law to decide an actual case. Moreover, whereas an actual murder trial might be expected to last for several weeks, with jury deliberations continuing until the jury either became hopelessly deadlocked or arrived at a verdict, the simulated murder trial lasted two and one-half hours, and jury deliberations were limited to one hour.[63] As the Court indicated,[64] the other simulated trial experiments mirrored reality even less precisely.[65]

But in dealing with social science data, the focus should not be on whether the data precisely replicate real world situations but rather on whether the data are helpful in identifying a phenomenon that exists in the real world. Moreover, the inquiry should include examination of any data that provide further insight into the phenomenon at issue. Thus, in examining the differences between death-qualified and non-death-qualified juries, the Court should consider any data that shed further light on the effects of death qualification.

The Court followed this approach in *Ballew v. Georgia*.[66] In examining the differences between twelve-person juries and five-person juries, it did not limit its inquiry to simulated experiments that compared results obtained by five-person juries and twelve-person juries—in fact, there were no such experiments; instead, it tried to make use of any empirical data that would shed light on the empirical question at issue. It even considered some data that were not directed toward comparing results obtained by juries of different sizes. It relied on psychological studies of groups, for example, to infer that "progressively smaller juries are less likely to foster group deliberation."[67] The Court also relied on various types of statistical analyses to assess the extent to which reducing jury size would reduce a minority group member's chances of being represented on the jury.[68] In addition, the majority sensibly concluded that simulated experiments finding that twelve-person juries reach more consistent results than six-person juries could be extrapolated to support the conclusion that a similar phenomenon would exist if results from twelve-person and five-person juries were compared.[69]

By making a similar analysis of the relevant data relating to the differences between death-qualified and non-death-qualified juries, the Court could have obtained a much clearer picture of the effects of death qualification. To begin with the conviction proneness studies, it was highly unreasonable for the Court to discard altogether the studies that were not directed toward examining the precise legal issue involved in *McCree*. In assessing the impact of death qualification, one of the critical questions is whether veniremen who are otherwise eligible to serve as jurors at the guilt phase of a capital case but are excluded because of their views on capital punishment would behave differently from the rest of the population in adjudicating guilt. Any evidence correlating jurors' attitudes toward capital punishment with their propensity to convict would obviously be significant to this problem. Just as simulated experiments comparing results reached by twelve-person and six-person juries shed light on the differences between twelve-person and five-person juries, in the present context, data comparing the conviction propensity between people in group one and those in groups two, three, and four[70] or between people in groups one and two and those in groups three and four[71] illuminate differences in conviction propensity between people in groups one and two and those in group three. In other words, any data that examines the relationship between a person's favorable attitude toward capital punishment and her likelihood to vote for conviction in a real or simulated jury trial is relevant to the empirical question at issue in *McCree*.

Properly evaluated, the six conviction proneness studies provide strong confirmation of the prosecution proneness thesis. The simulated trial experiments are remarkable for their consistency. They all show that the more strongly a person is opposed to capital punishment the less likely he is to vote for conviction. This same phenomenon is present regardless of the number of experiments,[72] the sophistication of the simulation techniques employed,[73] or the extent to which the subjects of the experiment accurately reflect the population from which a jury would be drawn.[74] Moreover, the results Hans Zeisel obtained by questioning actual jurors[75] provide another important link in the chain of evidence by suggesting that the phenomenon identified by the simulated experiments is one that is, in fact, translated into reality.

Taken as a group, the studies establish a correlation between prospective jurors' opposition to capital punishment and their proneness to vote for acquittal in a particular capital case. It follows that people belonging to *either* group three (the *Witherspoon* excludables) or group four (the nullifiers) will be less likely to vote for conviction than people belonging to groups one and two. Thus, the data indicate that in any particular case *Witherspoon* excludables who are not nullifiers are less likely to vote for conviction than people who are eligible to serve on a death-qualified jury. Accordingly, the Cowan-Thompson-Ellsworth study, which showed impressively that juries with *Witherspoon* excludables who are not nullifiers are more likely to acquit,[76] or to convict for a lesser offense,[77] than are juries without excludables, is strongly corroborated by the results from the other conviction proneness studies.[78]

The majority's characterization of the attitude studies as "at best, only marginally relevant" to the constitutional issues before the Court was also singularly inappropriate. Even aside from the question of whether the *Witherspoon* excludables group's distinctive attitudes should have a bearing on the cross-section issue,[79] the studies' findings that jurors belonging to groups one and two have a cluster of attitudes that are relatively favorable to the prosecution and jurors belonging to the automatic life imprisonment group have attitudes that can be characterized either as more neutral or as relatively favorable to the defense[80] seem to bear directly on one of the principal questions defined by *Witherspoon*: whether a death-qualified jury is "less than neutral with respect to guilt."[81] *Witherspoon* did not define a jury that is neutral with respect to guilt; but *Witherspoon*'s logic suggests that the non-death-qualified jury used in noncapital cases is an appropriate benchmark.[82] If the death-qualified jury is selected by a process that is likely to cause it to be comprised of individuals who are less favorably disposed toward the defendant than individuals who sit on a normal criminal jury, then a death-qualified jury would certainly appear "less than neutral with respect to guilt." The attitude surveys' findings that in comparison to the automatic life imprisonment group, those eligible to serve on a death-qualified jury are less favorably disposed toward the defense with respect to such questions as (1) whether the defendant's testimony should be credited,[83] (2) whether the defendant's refusal to testify should be viewed as evidence of guilt,[84] and (3) whether the judge's instructions to ignore evidence damaging to the defense should be followed[85] provides a good basis for concluding that the death-qualified jury is "less than neutral with respect to guilt."

Finally, the Court's dismissal of the Haney study of the biasing effect of the process of death qualification allowed it to ignore a separate dimension of the problem. In addition to relying on counsel's concession at oral argument,[86] the Court stated that it was rejecting the claim that the death qualification process violates the Constitution because the prosecution must be permitted to question prospective jurors about their views on the death penalty in order to identify the nullifiers, those "whose opposition to the death penalty is so strong that it would prevent them from impartially determining a capital defendant's guilt or innocence."[87] By taking this position, the Court was exercising a curious form of pseudologic. In effect, it was saying that since *some* inquiry into veniremen's views on capital punishment is necessary to identify nullifiers, the inquiry required to exclude veniremen who belong to the automatic life imprisonment group cannot be unconstitutional.

This analysis was either naive or disingenuous. Anyone familiar with capital trials knows that there is a vast difference between the type of questioning necessary to identify nullifiers and the type used to identify those belonging to the *Witherspoon* excludables group. To identify nullifiers, the prosecutor needs only to ask whether a venireman's attitude toward capital punishment would prevent him from impartially determining a capital defendant's guilt or innocence. On the other hand, in order to determine whether a potential juror belongs to the automatic life imprisonment group, the prosecutor will question her extensively as to whether she would be willing to vote for the death penalty in the event the defendant is convicted of a capital offense. This questioning not only presents the hypothesis that the defendant *will be convicted* of the capital offense but also at least intimates that a venireman who is strongly opposed to voting for the death penalty is not qualified for jury service.

Haney's study took account of the fact that some death qualification must be permitted to exclude nullifiers. In his experiment, both tapes presented to subjects asked whether their views on the death penalty would render them incapable of returning an impartial verdict, but only one asked whether they would be willing to vote for the death penalty in the event the defendant was convicted of the capital offense.[88] Haney's study concludes that the voir dire questioning directed toward excluding those belonging to the automatic life imprisonment group suggests to prospective jurors (1) that the judge, defense counsel, and prosecutor all believe that the defendant is guilty of the capital charge and (2) that the law disapproves of people who are opposed to capital punishment.[89]

Haney's results are scarcely surprising. Common sense suggests that the death qualification process would communicate these messages to the prospective jurors. The communication that the defendant is believed to be guilty stems from the anomalous discussion of penalty before the commencement of trial. Veniremen are asked whether they would be able to vote for the death penalty in the event the defendant is found guilty of a capital crime. By its very nature, this question suggests that the questioner believes that it is likely the defendant will be found guilty of the capital crime. The prospective juror would have to wonder why the judge and lawyers would ask so many questions about penalty if they didn't believe the issue was likely to arise.[90]

The process's communication that the law disapproves of people who are opposed to the death penalty is perhaps even more obvious. In *Witherspoon* the trial judge expressed the law's attitude in stark terms when he said, "Let's get these conscientious objectors out of the way, without wasting any time on them."[91] The clear message was that the criminal justice system has no use for people who are opposed to the death penalty. Under the present system of death qualification, the same message is still communicated by the court's actions, if not in words. A venireman who witnesses the process in operation or is subjected to extensive questioning to determine whether he belongs to the automatic life imprisonment group does not have to be unusually astute to realize that people who are unwilling to vote for the death penalty will not be permitted to serve on the jury. Therefore, regardless of the tone of the questioning, veniremen will inevitably be left with the impression that opposition to the death penalty is a view that is in some sense contrary to law.[92]

Thus, the empirical studies, taken together, certainly provided stronger support for the prosecution proneness thesis than the Court suggested. The conviction proneness studies consistently indicated that there is a direct correlation between a person's opposition to capital punishment and his willingness to vote for acquittal in a real or simulated criminal case. Thus they show that in any given capital case, a death-qualified jury will be more likely than a non-death-qualified jury to vote for conviction. The attitude studies confirmed Oberer's original claim that those eligible to serve on death-qualified juries have attitudes that separate them from the rest of the community.[93] Indeed, in view of the resources that have been expended to identify personality types that are likely to be favorable, as jurors, to one side or the other,[94] it is somewhat remarkable that the empirical data indicate that a person's attitude toward capital punishment is the best known index for determining whether his attitudes toward issues relating to the determination of guilt or innocence are relatively pro-prosecution or relatively pro-defense.[95] And finally, a study relating to the effects of the death qualification process indicates that the process itself will have the effect of biasing the jury against the defendant, whether or not prospective jurors are excluded.

The Court's failure to consider the implications of the studies seemed to foreshadow a negative answer to the empirical question. But after disparaging the studies, it said that it would assume for purposes of the present decision that the studies "establish that 'death-qualification' in fact produces juries somewhat more 'conviction-prone' than 'non-death-qualified' juries."[96] The Court then went on to resolve the legal issues against the defendant. By taking this approach, the Court in effect said that the answer to the empirical question no longer mattered. Its reductionist approach seemed to purposely obscure the picture of the death-qualified jury presented in the studies. And it ended by making it clear that new data on the effects of death qualification would not be legally significant. In contrast to the clear implications of *Witherspoon,* the Court in *McCree* decided that the empirical question was no longer relevant to the legal issues.

The Legal Issues

Only a few years ago, civil libertarians had reason to be hopeful when the Court heard a case that concerned the question of whether a capital defendant was entitled to a procedural safeguard. Not only was the Court likely to decide in favor of the capital defendant, but in some cases its decision would be on grounds that expanded the protections of other defendants as well.[97]

In *McCree,* however, the Court reversed the process. It decided the procedural issue against the capital defendant, and in the course of its decision it made statements that seemed to diminish Sixth Amendment protections in general. For example, in rejecting defendant's claim that death qualifying the jury violated his right to a jury representing a cross-section of the community, the Court held that the fair cross-section principle does not "invalidate the use of either for-cause or peremptory challenges to prospective jurors, or . . . require petit juries, as opposed to jury panels or venires, to reflect the composition of the community at large."[98] Taken literally, the first part of the Court's statement suggests that the safeguards provided by the cross-section requirement could be defeated if the prosecution were merely allowed to challenge certain groups for cause. Thus, a state provision allowing the prosecution to challenge all blacks or women for cause would not violate the fair cross-section requirement, because it would not affect the composition of the jury panels or venires. The state would be free to engage in discrimination so long as it did not do so at the outset of the jury selection procedure.[99]

In dealing with the claim that death qualifying the jury violated defendant's right to an impartial jury, the Court took an even more expansive approach. It held in effect that the defendant's constitutional right to an impartial jury only encompasses the right to be tried by jurors who are not biased against him.[100] Indeed, the Court suggested that any other rule would be illogical: "[I]t is hard for us to understand the logic of the argument that a given jury is unconstitutionally partial when it results from a state-ordained process, yet impartial when exactly the same jury results from mere chance."[101] If taken seriously, the Court's conclusion means that juries selected with the exclusion of particular groups (or even with the inclusion of only certain groups) would not violate the defendant's right to an impartial jury trial so long as no member of the jury could actually be shown to be biased against the defendant. Thus, if the state provided that in certain types of cases[102] only Republicans, only people who belonged to certain civic organizations,[103] or even only people whose score on psychological tests marked them as authoritarian personalities[104] would be eligible to serve as jurors, a defendant convicted by such a jury would apparently have to be satisfied with the explanation that the jury that convicted him was not unconstitutionally partial because even if the jury had been selected from the total population, the same jurors could have been selected by "mere chance."

In supporting this position, the Court found it necessary to distinguish its holdings in *Witherspoon* and *Adams v. Texas*.[105] The defendant argued that since *Witherspoon* and *Adams* preclude the state from using a jury that is predisposed toward imposing the death penalty at the penalty stage, the state should also be barred from using a jury that is predisposed toward conviction at the guilt stage. The Court rejected this argument on two grounds.

First, it distinguished *Adams* and *Witherspoon* from *McCree* on the ground that in the present situation the state "excludes from the jury only those who may properly be excluded from the penalty phase of the deliberations."[106] The importance of this distinction is that it shows that the state has a legitimate reason for removing the automatic life imprisonment group before the guilt phase—that is, the state's legitimate reason for using a process that predisposes the jury in favor of conviction is simply that it prefers to use the same jury at the guilt and penalty stage. Although *Witherspoon* had suggested that the state's interest in having capital cases decided by a single jury should be balanced against the defendant's interest in having "a completely fair determination of guilt or innocence,"[107] *McCree* rejected the idea of a balancing test. Without assessing the strength of the state's interest in maintaining a single jury, the Court merely concluded that the state's justification for using the death-qualified jury was sufficient.[108]

The Court's second basis for distinguishing *Witherspoon* and *Adams* was even more sweeping. It concluded that those cases only apply to juries responsible for capital sentencing and not to juries that are assigned the "more traditional role of finding the facts and determining the guilt or innocence of a criminal defendant."[109] Thus, the state's justification for its method of jury selection need not be considered. The state is simply permitted to have a conviction-prone jury at the guilt stage, even though it is not permitted to have a hanging jury at the penalty stage.

This conclusion—and the Court's supporting analysis—is curious in several respects. First, it is surprising that without discussion, the Court rejected one of *Witherspoon*'s basic premises. *Witherspoon*'s holding that it is unconstitutional for the state to have a pro-prosecution jury at the penalty stage sprang from the following reasoning:

> It is, of course, settled that a state may not entrust the determination of whether a man is innocent or guilty to a tribunal "organized to convict." . . . It requires but a short step from that principle to hold, as we do today, that a state may not entrust the determination of whether a man should live or die to a tribunal organized to return a verdict of death.[110]

Thus, *Witherspoon* accepted the proposition that it is unconstitutional to have a pro-prosecution jury at the guilt stage as the *starting point* in its analysis. The problem for the Court—and post-*Witherspoon* commentators viewed it as a greater problem than the Court did[111]—was to move from that starting point to its conclusion. *McCree,* on the other hand, was unable to move from *Witherspoon*'s conclusion back to its starting point. The 1986 Supreme Court was unwilling to accept a proposition that the 1968 Court viewed as uncontroversial.[112]

The *McCree* majority defended its position by asserting that the penalty jury's broader range of discretion gives rise to "greater concern over the possible effects of an 'imbalanced' jury."[113] But as the dissent pointed out,[114] in view of the Court's decision in *Adams,* the guilt and penalty juries cannot validly be distinguished on this basis.

In *Adams* the Court applied *Witherspoon* to the Texas death penalty scheme. In Texas, once a jury finds a defendant guilty of a capital offense, it hears additional evidence at a penalty stage and then answers three questions. If it finds beyond a reasonable doubt that the answer to each of these questions is yes, the defendant is sentenced to death; otherwise, the sentence is life imprisonment. The first and third questions address circumstances of the crime. Did the accused kill "deliberately and with the reasonable expectation that" the victim's death "would result"? Did the defendant act "unreasonabl[y] in response to the [victim's] provocation"? The second question is: Is there "a probability that the defendant would commit criminal acts of violence that would constitute a continuing threat to society"?[115]

As the dissent pointed out,[116] in answering these questions the Texas penalty jury is fulfilling exactly the same function as the Texas guilt jury. Indeed, the first and third questions "could well have (and may have) been answered when the jury deliberated culpability."[117] The middle question allows the jury a considerable breadth of discretion, but no more, perhaps, than the jury exercises when it decides between different levels of culpability.[118] Thus, Justice Rehnquist, dissenting in *Adams,* stated that he could "see no plausible distinction between the role of the jury in the guilt/innocence phase of the trial and its role, as defined by the State of Texas, in the sentencing phase."[119] Since this is so, distinguishing the guilt and penalty juries on the ground that the latter exercises a greater degree of discretion seems totally inconsistent with the Court's decision in *Adams.*

Finally, the Court's analysis is curious for what it fails to discuss. In a long line of decisions, it had articulated a concern for enhancing reliability in capital cases. On numerous occasions, it had struck down procedural rules that were perceived as "diminish[ing] the reliability of the sentencing determination."[120] In *Beck v. Alabama,*[121] the Court said that "[t]he same reasoning must apply to rules that diminish the reliability of the guilt determination."[122] Applying this rule, the Court in *Beck* struck down Alabama's practice of requiring the jury to convict or acquit of the capital offense without considering the alternative of convicting for a lesser included offense.

The present case certainly involves a rule that bears on the reliability of the guilt determination in capital cases. The Court had before it a procedural rule applied only in capital cases that it assumed would increase the likelihood of conviction. A rule that increases the likelihood of conviction changes the fact-finding process either for better or for worse. In other words, it either increases or diminishes the reliability of the guilt determination. In view of its prior decisions, the Court's failure to even consider whether the practice of death qualification diminishes the reliability of the guilt determination in capital trials seems remarkable.

If the Court had considered this issue, it might have been hard-pressed to avoid the conclusion that death qualification does diminish the reliability of guilt determinations in capital cases. In *Beck* the Court's conclusion that Alabama's practice diminished the reliability of guilt determinations was premised on its assumption that failing to give the jury the option of convicting for a lesser included offense "enhance[d] the risk of an unwarranted conviction."[123] In other words, the Court assumed that under the Alabama practice, a defendant who might "properly" have been convicted of second-degree murder, for example, if that option had been available, would have been more likely to be convicted of the capital offense by a jury confronted with the choice between convicting the defendant for that offense or acquitting him.

In the present case, the assumption that the practice in question will increase the likelihood of conviction is more firmly grounded than it was in *Beck*. In *Beck* the Court merely exercised its intuition to assume that some cases in which a jury would convict a defendant of a lesser included offense if that option was available would end up as convictions for the capital offense rather than acquittals or hung juries. In the present case, however, the majority's assumption that a death-qualified jury is more likely to convict than a non-death-qualified one is supported by a wealth of empirical data.

The majority might argue that even though using a death-qualified jury increases the likelihood of conviction, it does not increase the "risk of unwarranted conviction." The fact that death-qualified juries convict more often than non-death-qualified ones does not determine which of the two types is more accurate in its results. It could be, for example, that death-qualified juries will convict a higher percentage of defendants than non-death-qualified ones but that both types will convict only defendants who are in fact guilty.[124]

But this argument misconceives the significance of a jury verdict. In the real world, it is generally impossible to determine whether a particular jury verdict is factually correct.[125] Thus, the only proper yardstick for gauging the accuracy of jury verdicts is the normal pattern of verdicts produced by juries that normally sit in criminal cases. As the Court recognized in *Ballew v. Georgia*,[126] if an aberrant procedure like death qualification or reduction in jury size alters the normal pattern of jury verdicts, by definition that procedure is impairing the accuracy of jury verdicts.[127] The same logic shows that if the aberrant procedure increases the likelihood of conviction, it is increasing the "risk of an unwarranted conviction."

There is more to the present case than simply abstract, logical arguments, however. The empirical data presented in *McCree* demonstrated overwhelmingly not only that death-qualified juries are more likely than normal juries to convict but also that they are less likely to provide protections that should be available to every criminal defendant. For example, as the dissent noted, the empirical data shows that "[d]eath qualified jurors are . . . more likely to believe that a defendant's failure to testify is indicative of his guilt, more hostile to the insanity defense, more mistrustful of defense attorneys, and less concerned about the danger of erroneous convictions."[128] In addition, the Cowan jury deliberation study found that subjects who sat on normal (*i.e.*, non-death-qualified) juries remembered facts presented at the simulated trial "more accurately than subjects serving on juries composed of only death-qualified persons."[129] Thus, the empirical studies indicate that the reason death-qualified juries are conviction prone is that death qualifying jurors reduces the extent to which they will provide protections that stem from constitutional principles, rules of law, and the jury's traditional attributes.

Moreover, the empirical evidence indicates that the magnitude of the risk of unwarranted convictions is not insignificant. Justice Rehnquist's assertion that the studies cannot predict the extent to which "the presence of one or more '*Witherspoon*-excludables' on a guilt-phase jury would have altered the outcome of the guilt determination"[130] is, of course, correct. As Stephen Gillers has said, even if the studies accurately reflect a phenomenon that exists in the real world, there is no reason to believe that the voting patterns produced in particular simulated cases "will reappear in other cases."[131] Every case is different, and the cases used in the studies are in no sense representative of the capital cases that are tried in real life. Thus, the fact that particular studies show a certain differential between the conviction rates of death-qualified and non-death-qualified juries does not mean that the same differential will exist in a given capital case.

Nevertheless, the differential revealed by the Cowan jury deliberation study suggests that at least in certain types of cases, death qualifying the jury will substantially increase the risks of an unwarranted conviction. The Cowan subjects watched a two-and-one-half-hour videotape reenactment of an actual Massachusetts murder trial that included appropriate jury instructions.[132] Afterward, each subject was asked to vote for one of four verdicts: (1) guilty of first-degree murder, (2) guilty of second-degree murder, (3) guilty of voluntary manslaughter, or (4) not guilty. Then the subjects were assigned to juries that were either death-qualified or non-death-qualified (that is, including from one to four "jurors" who belonged to the automatic life imprisonment group but were not nullifiers) and asked to deliberate for an hour. The subjects then filled out a questionnaire in which, among other things, they again voted for one of the four verdicts.

On both the predeliberation and postdeliberation ballots, the *Witherspoon* excludables were significantly more lenient than the nonexcludables. Considering only guilty and not guilty votes, the study showed nearly a 25 percent greater guilty vote by death-qualified subjects on the predeliberation ballot (77.9 percent compared to 53.3 percent for the excludables) and more than a 20 percent differential on the postdeliberation ballot (86.3 percent for the death-qualified subjects compared to 65.5 percent for the excludables). Even without any further statistical analysis,[133] these figures are sufficient to suggest that in certain cases the impact of death qualification will be very significant.

Thus, the Court's treatment of the legal issues was extraordinary in that in several respects it seemed to reverse directions. In dealing with *Witherspoon*, the Court accepted its holding but refused to accept the premise underlying it. In dealing with *Adams,* Justice Rehnquist, the author of *McCree,* refused to accept implications that he had earlier stamped as unmistakable. Most importantly, the majority ignored its prior commitment to safeguarding capital defendants from rules that diminish reliability in capital sentencing. Indeed, instead of providing greater protection to capital defendants than to noncapital defendants, the Court seemingly reversed its priorities. It held that states may death qualify the jury in capital cases, even though this unique means of jury selection creates juries that may be significantly more likely to convict and significantly less likely to honor constitutional protections than juries that are used in criminal cases in which the death penalty is not at issue.

The Broader Implications of *Witherspoon* and *McCree*

Both *Witherspoon* and *McCree* in a sense provide a barometer of the Court's attitude toward capital punishment. Though the cases deal exclusively with procedural issues, the Court's approach to those issues reveals a good deal about its perception of the role it should play in regulating our system of capital punishment.

Given its historical context, the *Witherspoon* decision can best be characterized as a bold step forward. Before *Witherspoon,* the Court had largely avoided issues relating to capital punishment. It had certainly never invalidated a procedure applied in capital cases.[134] But by invalidating death sentences imposed by juries selected by means of excluding veniremen who stated that they were opposed to the death penalty or had conscientious scruples against imposing it, the Court called into question nearly every death penalty imposed by a jury.[135] Its sweeping decision, moreover, served notice that other aspects of capital punishment would not be immune from scrutiny.

Witherspoon set the Court on the path that led to its decision in *Furman.* Indeed, the holding in *Witherspoon* may have helped to precipitate *Furman.* As a result of *Witherspoon,* hundreds of death penalties were vacated, with the defendants in many cases being resentenced to life imprisonment; on the other hand, death penalties imposed in cases involving crimes that were no more heinous were left undisturbed for the seemingly fortuitous reason that the death penalty was not imposed by a jury or was imposed by one from which no scrupled veniremen were excluded. The Court's awareness of the different treatment afforded seemingly similar capital defendants in this context may have been an important step toward its realization that the then-existing system of capital punishment imposed the death penalty arbitrarily. That realization culminated, of course, in the *Furman* decision.

In its treatment of the prosecution proneness issue, *Witherspoon* was more circumspect. Even in 1968, the existing empirical data strongly suggested that Oberer's thesis was correct. Moreover, even before 1968, prosecutors routinely acted on the assumption that death-qualified juries were more likely to convict than non-death-qualified ones.[136] If the Court had chosen to take an activist approach—as it had, for example, in *Miranda v. Arizona*[137] or *United States v. Wade*[138]—it could have easily accepted the prosecution proneness thesis on the basis of empirical evidence, intuition, or both.[139] If it had, then, as a logical extension of the views it expressed in footnote 18,[140] it would presumably have gone on to safeguard a capital defendant's right to a fair trial by holding that death qualification before the guilt phase of a capital case would not be permitted.

The Court's failure to take this approach may be attributed at least in part to its awareness of the immediate impact of such a decision. A holding that convictions returned by death-qualified juries were unconstitutional would have likely had a much greater impact than the Court's decisions in *Witherspoon* and *Furman*. It would have called into question the convictions of not only hundreds of defendants who had been sentenced to death but also thousands of others who, although not sentenced to death, had been convicted of heinous crimes. The Court is sensitive to the consequences of its decisions and to the way the public may perceive them. Rather than placing itself in a position where it might be perceived as imposing a staggering blow upon law enforcement,[141] the Court opted for caution.

But even while opting for caution, the Court made it clear that it was willing to monitor procedures employed in capital cases. It did not decide the prosecution proneness issue in favor of the defendant, but it did not foreclose a future favorable decision. Indeed, Justice Black read the Court's discussion of the issue as "a thinly veiled warning to the States that they had better change their jury selection procedures or face a decision by this Court that their murder convictions have been obtained unconstitutionally."[142] At the least, *Witherspoon* seemed to indicate that if new empirical data were generated, the prosecution proneness issue would have to be reconsidered and that in considering that issue or any other issue affecting the rights of capital defendants, the Court would decide the question before it on the merits, providing capital defendants with at least the same protection as noncapital defendants. Thus, the Court's approach served notice that it would monitor procedures employed in capital cases and that as a result, the then-existing system might have to be modified.

As I said in the beginning, the *McCree* case was decided in a different era of capital punishment. Between its decisions in *Witherspoon* and *McCree*, the Court had held that the jury discretionary system of capital punishment was unconstitutional,[143] and by endorsing the principle that death is different,[144] it had also expressed a commitment to providing special protections for capital defendants. Given this context, the contrast between *Witherspoon* and *McCree* in their respective treatments of the prosecution proneness issue is particularly striking.

If *Witherspoon*'s discussion of the prosecution proneness issue constituted a "thinly veiled warning" to prosecutors, *McCree*'s treatment of the issue communicated the strongest possible reassurance that the present system of jury selection in capital cases is constitutional. Even though the record before the Court in *McCree* was far more complete than in *Witherspoon,* the Court could have decided that the existing empirical evidence was still too "tentative and fragmentary" to form the basis for a constitutional holding. Indeed, the majority intimated that this was its position.[145] Nevertheless, the Court decided the case on the basis of its assumption that death-qualified juries are in fact more prone to convict than non-death-qualified ones. Thus, the Court seemed to be going out of its way to decide the prosecution proneness issue finally and forever. Prosecutors need no longer fear that convictions imposed by death-qualified juries are going to be declared unconstitutional by the Supreme Court.[146]

In commenting on the Court's decision, Justice Marshall said that he could not "help thinking that [the defendant] would have stood a far better chance of prevailing on his constitutional claims had he not been challenging a procedure peculiar to the administration of the death penalty."[147] Given the Court's expressed commitment to providing special protection for capital defendants, that is an extraordinary statement.

Yet Justice Marshall's charge may be accurate. In recent times, the Court has indicated—sometimes by its decisions[148] and sometimes in statements by individual justices[149]—that it does not want to frustrate the operation of the system of capital punishment. At the time of the ruling in *McCree,* most of the important issues concerning the administration of capital punishment had been decided; realistically, only two major challenges remained: the claim that the death penalty violates the Constitution because it is applied discriminatorily,[150] and the claim considered by the Court in *McCree. McCree*'s decision eliminated one of the two and provided a clear signal to the states that executions—many of which had been stayed pending the Court's decision in *McCree*—could resume.[151]

To read *McCree* as suggesting that the Court desires to withdraw from its role of regulating our system of capital punishment would be an exaggeration, however.[152] In the same term that it decided *McCree,* it decided *Skipper v. South Carolina,*[153] a case that significantly expanded a capital defendant's right to present mitigating evidence at the penalty trial.[154] Over the past few years, the Court has decided several other cases that reaffirm its commitment to providing special protection for capital defendants.[155] Nevertheless, *McCree* does show that the Court is very reluctant to take any action that would even temporarily frustrate the operation of the system of capital punishment. The Court has retained a position from which it will be able to closely monitor procedures employed in capital cases. But in contrast to the *Witherspoon* court, which had not even stated a special concern for protecting the rights of capital defendants, the present Court holds that maintaining the smooth functioning of our system of capital punishment is a higher priority than protecting the rights of capital defendants.

NOTES

1. 106 S. Ct. 1758 (1986).
2. See N.Y. Times, May 11, 1986, § A at 22.
3. The voir dire is the stage at which prospective jurors are questioned to determine their eligibility to sit on the jury. The prosecutor and defense counsel are each permitted a specified number of peremptory challenges and unlimited challenges for cause.
4. 391 U.S. 510 (1968).
5. Id. at 522–23 n.21.
6. Oberer, Does Disqualification of Jurors for Scruples Against Capital Punishment Constitute Denial of a Fair Trial on Issue of Guilt, 39 Tex. L. Rev. 545 (1961) [hereinafter cited as Oberer].
7. See, e.g., Spenkellink v. Wainright, 578 F.2d 582, 593 (5th Cir. 1978).
8. 391 U.S. 510.
9. 106 S. Ct. 1758.
10. For a compilation of many of these cases, see Gillers, Proving the Prejudice of Death-Qualified Juries After Adams v. Texas, 47 U. Pitt. L. Rev. 219, 254 (1985) [hereinafter cited as Gillers, Proving Prejudice].
11. 391 U.S. 510.
12. See generally Oberer, supra note 6, at 560.
13. 391 U.S. at 515.
14. Id. at 514.
15. Id. at 514.
16. See supra text following note 6.
17. In United States v. Wade, 388 U.S. 218 (1967), for example, the Court decided that suggestive identification procedures often lead to mistaken identifications. The Court decided this empirical question without even discussing some empirical data that could

have been relevant to its resolution. See generally Gross, The Neutrality of Death Qualified Juries, 8 Law & Hum. Behav. 7, 20 (1984).
18. 391 U.S. at 517.
19. Id. at 518.
20. See, e.g., Furman v. Georgia, 408 U.S. 238 (1972) (White, J., concurring) (deciding, on basis of his own exposure to capital cases, that death penalty is arbitrarily applied); United States v. Wade, 388 U.S. 218, 229 (1967) (deciding, without discussion of empirical data, that suggestive identification procedures lead to mistaken identifications).
21. See, e.g., Ballew v. Georgia, 435 U.S. 223 (1978) (using social science data to determine that five-person jury denies criminal defendant right to jury trial guaranteed by the Sixth and Fourteenth Amendments); Brown v. Board of Education, 347 U.S. 483, 494 n.11 (1954) (citing empirical evidence to support proposition that segregated education will inflict psychological damage on black students).
22. 391 U.S. at 518.
23. Id. at 520 n.18.
24. See infra text at note 25.
25. 391 U.S. at 518.
26. Id. at 520 n.18.
27. Id. at 518.
28. See Gillers, Deciding Who Dies, 129 U. Pa. L. Rev. 1, 83 (1980).
29. Finch & Ferraro, The Empirical Challenge to Death-Qualified Juries: On Further Examination, 65 Neb. L. Rev. 21, 24 (1986) [hereinafter cited as Finch & Ferraro].
30. Compare, e.g., Goldberg, Toward Expansion of Witherspoon: Cap-

ital Scruples, Jury Bias and Use of Psychological Data to Raise Presumptions in the Law, 5 HARV. C.R.–C.L. L. REV. 53 (1970) [hereinafter cited as Goldberg] *with* Cowan, Thompson & Ellsworth, *The Effects of Death-Qualification on Jurors' Predisposition to Convict and on the Quality of Deliberation,* 8 LAW & HUM. BEHAV. 53 (1984) [hereinafter cited as Cowan et al.]. The Goldberg study presented sixteen written descriptions of homicide and assault cases to 100 black and 100 white college students. The students were asked to select a verdict and penalty in each case. Each student was also asked whether he or she had conscientious scruples against the use of the death penalty. In contrast, the Cowan, Thompson, & Ellsworth study required a group of adults to watch a two-and-one-half-hour videotape of a simulated homicide trial. After hearing the evidence and the arguments, the subjects issued an initial verdict. They were then divided into twelve-person juries and were given one hour to deliberate. Half the juries were comprised solely of death-qualified jurors, and the remaining juries were made up of primarily death-qualified jurors but also included from one to four excludables. After deliberation each juror completed an extensive questionnaire that was designed to examine aspects of the juries' functioning.

31. The later studies, *see infra* notes 38–39, have begun to examine a whole new range of issues relating to death-qualified juries. For example, they have looked at how different jurors (excludable v.

death-qualified) interpret the same evidence and also at how these two groups differ in their interpretations of the standard of proof required in criminal cases. For further discussion of the range of issues considered in the post-*Witherspoon* studies, see text at notes 72–89.

32. Haney, *The Biasing Effects of the Death-Qualification Process,* 8 LAW & HUM. BEHAV. 121 (1980) [hereinafter cited as Haney].

33. *Id.* at 129.

34. 569 F. Supp. 1273 (E.D. Ark. 1983).

35. For the first *equivocal* ruling that a death-qualified jury is more conviction prone than a non-death-qualified jury and is less likely to afford the defendant a fair determination on the issue of guilt, *see* Hovey v. Superior Court of Alameda County, 28 Cal. 3d 1, 616 P.2d 1301, 168 Cal. Rptr. 128 (1980). The California Supreme Court decided that based on the empirical data presented, a death-qualified jury is more likely to find a defendant guilty than a non-death-qualified jury. The court refused to invalidate California's use of the death-qualified jury, however, on the ground that the data presented by the defendant failed to establish the non-neutrality of his jury or other California juries. Under California law, all jurors who would either automatically vote for or against the death penalty are excludable. The court said that the relevant comparison to be made was between juries used in noncapital cases and juries in which people who would automatically vote for or against the death penalty are excluded. Since the experiments presented to the court failed to

make this comparison, the court ruled that defendant had not established that the California death-qualified jury was conviction prone.

36. 569 F. Supp. at 1304.
37. 758 F.2d 226 (8th Cir. 1985) (en banc).
38. Goldberg, *supra* note 30; H. ZEISEL, SOME DATA ON JUROR ATTITUDES TOWARD CAPITAL PUNISHMENT (1986) [hereinafter cited as ZEISEL]; Wilson, Belief in Capital Punishment and Jury Performance (unpublished manuscript, University of Texas, 1964).
39. The following attitudinal surveys were introduced: Bronson, *On the Conviction Proneness and Representativeness of the Death-Qualified Jury: An Empirical Study of Colorado Veniremen,* 42 U. COLO. L. REV. 1 (1970); Bronson, *Does the Exclusion of Scrupled Jurors in Capital Cases Make the Jury More Likely to Convict? Some Evidence from California,* 3 WOODROW WILSON L.J. 11 (1980); Fitzgerald & Ellsworth, *Due Process vs. Crime Control: Death Qualification and Jury Attitudes,* 8 LAW & HUM. BEHAV. 31 (1984); Thompson, Cowan, Ellsworth & Harrington, *Death Penalty Attitudes and Conviction Proneness,* 8 LAW & HUM. BEHAV. 65 (1984).
40. The following post-*Witherspoon* conviction-proneness surveys were introduced: Jurow, *New Data on the Effect of a "Death Qualified" Jury on the Guilt Determination Process,* 84 HARV. L. REV. 567 (1971) [hereinafter cited as Jurow]; Cowan et al., *supra* note 30; Louis Harris & Associates, Inc., Study No. 2016 (1971) [hereinafter cited as 1971 Harris Poll].

41. 569 F. Supp. at 1293.
42. *Id.* at 1294.
43. *Id.* at 1292.
44. *Id.* at 1293.
45. *Id.* at 1313.
46. The district court's findings were ostensibly factual findings that were subject to review under the "clearly erroneous" standard of Federal Rule of Civil Procedure 52(a). As the Supreme Court said, however, the district court's findings related essentially to legislative facts and applying the "clearly erroneous" standard to legislative findings creates difficulties, because different lower courts may make different findings with respect to the same legislative facts. 106 S. Ct. at 1762 n.3.
47. *Id.* at 1762 (quoting 569 F. Supp. at 1323).
48. *Id.*
49. *Id.*
50. *Id.*
51. *Id.*
52. *Id.*
53. *Id.*
54. Cowan et al., *supra* note 30.
55. Jurow; 1971 Harris Poll, *supra* note 40.
56. 106 S. Ct. at 1764.
57. *Id.*
58. For example, the Court's statement that the pre-*Witherspoon* conviction-proneness studies were obviously entitled to no more weight in 1986 than they were at the time when *Witherspoon* was decided was disingenuous. In *Witherspoon,* the Court concluded that the data presented by the defendant were too "tentative and fragmentary" because the studies relied on were neither published nor presented into evidence, see *supra* text at note 19, not because the studies' conclusions

were insufficient. By the time *Mc-Cree* was decided, two of the three pre-*Witherspoon* studies had been published. Moreover, in *McCree* itself, all of the pre-*Witherspoon* studies were introduced into evidence, and experts presented testimony with respect to their implications. The Court purposely chose to ignore these significant developments, however.

59. For example, the Court failed to consider whether the results from the attitude studies established that death-qualified juries are "less than neutral with respect to guilt." 391 U.S. at 520 n.18. For a succinct discussion of this issue, see *infra* text at notes 79–85.

60. H. KALVEN & H. ZEISEL, THE AMERICAN JURY 11 (Phoenix ed. 1971).

61. As Michael Saks has observed, "[U]nlike problem-solving tasks used in much research on decision-making, the jury's task is one in which there exists no objective criterion against which to compare the decisions of differently structured juries. The 'true' verdict can never be known. If it were, there would be no need for a jury decision." M. SAKS, JURY VERDICTS (1977) [hereinafter cited as SAKS].

62. 106 S. Ct. at 1763.

63. *See* Cowan et al., *supra* note 30, at 65, 66.

64. 106 S. Ct. at 1764.

65. *See, e.g.,* Jurow, *supra* note 40, at 577–83. In Jurow's study, 211 employees of the Sperry-Rand Corporation were given written tests to determine their attitudes on capital punishment. After the tests, the subjects listened to audiotapes of two simulated murder trials and were instructed to think about each case for a while and then vote guilty or not guilty. The study revealed that those subjects who according to the written test would not be excludable under *Witherspoon* were more likely to vote guilty than those who would be excludable. As Jurow noted, the earlier conviction-proneness experiments involved written summaries of cases. Neither written summaries nor audiotapes involve the subjects in the intense way that a real jury trial would.

66. 435 U.S. 233 (1978).

67. *Id.* at 232.

68. *Id.* at 236.

69. *Id.* at 235.

70. *See supra* authorities cited at note 38.

71. *See supra* authorities cited at note 40.

72. *Compare, e.g.,* Goldberg, *supra* note 30 (sixteen simulated cases used) *with* Cowan et al., *supra* note 30 (one simulated trial used).

73. *See supra* note 30.

74. *Compare, e.g.,* 1971 Harris Poll, *supra* note 40 (using nationwide random sample of 2,068 subjects) *with* Goldberg, *supra* note 30 (using 100 black and 100 white college students).

75. *See* ZEISEL, *supra* note 38, at 28–29. This study was designed to compare the death penalty attitudes and behavior of people who had actually served as jurors. Zeisel asked the subjects three questions: (1) What was the first ballot vote of your jury as a whole? (2) What was your own first ballot vote? (3) Do you have conscientious scruples against the death penalty? The first question was designed to measure the overall strength of the prosecutor's case. Zeisel grouped the

first ballot responses into eleven categories, of guilty/not guilty splits, ranging from eleven guilty and one not guilty vote to eleven not guilty and one guilty vote. These groupings were designed to control the weight of the evidence against the defendant, so that the response to the third question could be analyzed without fear that the strength of the prosecutor's case would effect the results. Zeisel generalized that if five different juries voted eleven guilty and one not guilty, then those jurors' responses to the third question could be analyzed with the knowledge that the prosecutor's case was comparably strong in all five trials. The results of the study found that in nine of the eleven groupings, jurors without scruples against the death penalty voted guilty more often than did jurors with scruples; also, in ten of the eleven groupings jurors without scruples voted not guilty less often than jurors with scruples.

76. *See* Cowan et al. *supra* note 30, at 68. Almost half (46.7 percent) of the excludable jurors voted for acquittal on the first ballot. Of the death-qualified jurors, less than a quarter (22.1 percent) voted initially for acquittal. When the jurors were examined after one hour of deliberation, the acquittal figures decreased for both groups: 34.5 percent of the excludables and 13.7 percent of the death-qualified jurors voted for acquittal.

77. *Id.* at 68, 69. On the initial ballot 70.2 percent of the death-qualified jurors voted for conviction of either second-degree murder or manslaughter, while just 50 percent of the excludable jurors voted for conviction as to a lesser offense. On the post-deliberation ballot 85.3 percent of the death-qualified jurors voted for conviction on one of the lesser charges, while 62.1 percent of the excludable jurors did the same.

78. *See generally* W. WHITE, LIFE IN THE BALANCE 119–20 (1984) [hereinafter cited as WHITE]; Finch & Ferraro, *supra* note 29, at 52–54.

79. The Court observed that "groups defined solely in terms of shared attitudes that would prevent or substantially impair members of the group from performing one of their duties as jurors . . . are not 'distinctive groups' for fair cross-section purposes." 106 S. Ct. at 1765. Thus, the Court was deciding that the automatic life imprisonment group's shared attitudes need not be considered, because of the group's inability to fulfill its legal responsibility at the penalty trial. But as Finch and Ferraro have said:
This view is not only peculiarly formalistic, it is irreconcilable with Witherspoon *itself. Witherspoon expressly recognized that the propriety of death qualification presents distinctive issues depending on whether the guilt or the penalty phase of a trial is examined. The very point of the challenge to death qualification under* Witherspoon *is that the two phases are discrete events: one in which death qualification is appropriate, and the other in which it may be questionable. . . . Therefore, the . . . refusal to examine the impact of death qualification on the guilt-determination phase of a trial, based on the asserted ground that excludable jurors are unfit to serve during*

the sentencing phase, begs the legal question.
Finch & Ferraro, *supra* note 29, at 32.

80. For example, in comparison to death-qualified jurors, excludables are less likely to have faith in the ability of the police to arrest the right person, less likely to place a negative interpretation on the defendant's failure to testify at trial, and more likely to accept an insanity defense as legitimate. In the procedural sphere, excludables are less likely than death-qualified jurors to trust the police or to feel courts are mistakenly relying on too many procedural technicalities. *See supra* studies cited in note 39.

81. 391 U.S. at 520 n.18.

82. This jury is a logical benchmark because it is used in the vast majority of criminal cases, and it is representative of the community in the sense that it is surrounded by procedures designed to ensure that it will be selected from a fair cross-section of the community. No better benchmark could be found.

83. *See, e.g.,* 1971 Harris Poll, *supra* note 40, at question 6 (26 percent of those eligible to serve on a death-qualified jury said they would trust what the defendant had to say "only a little or hardly at all"; 19 percent of those who could never vote for the death penalty said the same).

84. *See, e.g., id.* at question 13 (34 percent of those eligible to serve on a death-qualified jury said that a defendant's failure to testify would prevent them from finding the defendant innocent; 27 percent of those who could never vote for the death penalty gave the same response).

85. *See, e.g., id.* (in response to a hypothetical in which "the defendant made a confession but the judge wouldn't let it be introduced because the defendant had no lawyer there when he made it," 41 percent of those eligible to serve on the death-qualified jury said they would not find the defendant innocent; 31 percent of the automatic life imprisonment group made the same response).

86. 106 S. Ct. at 1767.

87. *Id.*

88. Haney, *supra* note 32, at 124 n.3.

89. *See* Haney, *Examining Death Qualification: Further Analysis of the Process Effect*, 8 LAW & HUM. BEHAV. 133, 144 (1980).

90. *See* People v. Keenan, Criminal Case No. 100402 (Nov. 1982) (Recorder's Transcript, p. 567) (judge instructing jurors at beginning of trial that "there are two parts to this case"); State v. Foster (Jan. 1982) (Recorder's Transcript, p. 337) (prosecutor telling veniremen, "[Y]ou know all that you are going to have to go through in the second phase"). *See* Haney, *supra* note 89, at 137.

91. 391 U.S. at 514.

92. Sometimes this message is explicit. *See, e.g.,* Cave v. State, 476 So. 180 (Fla. 1985) (in questioning two veniremen opposed to capital punishment, trial judge stated that it is the right of every American citizen to disagree with the law and that he respected their right to disagree).

93. *See* Oberer, *supra* note 6, at 555. In making this claim Oberer presented a particularly striking metaphor. He said, "[T]he vision impelled for the advocate is of twelve Madame DeFarges, knitting while they deliberate with equal impartiality on the ques-

tions of guilt and punishment!
Or, as the psychologists might
put it, twelve authoritarian
personalities."

94. *See* Brosnahan, *Jury Selection,* in
J. WING, THE JURY 1984 p. 19
(1984):
*In recent years defense lawyers
have been aided in their jury selection processes by psychologists
and sociologists who have done
studies on identifying pro-defense
jurors. These studies involve
questions concerning a potential
juror's marital status, income,
age, sex, race, religion, occupa-
tion, and education. This information is compared with other
information obtained from these
same potential jurors concerning
their feelings on: crime generally,
punishment, rehabilitation, procedural safeguards, honesty of attorneys, and the criminal justice
system as a whole. By comparing
this information defense lawyers
can see which groups (age, sex,
race, etc. . . .) are more likely to
convict and which are more likely
to acquit.*

95. *See* Cowan et al., *supra* note 30,
at 55.
96. 106 S. Ct. at 1764.
97. *See, e.g.,* Estelle v. Smith, 451
U.S. 454 (1981). In *Smith* the
Court held that at the penalty
trial using disclosures made by a
capital defendant during a pretrial
psychiatric examination violated
the Fifth and Sixth Amendments.
In so holding, the Court expanded the scope of both Miranda
v. Arizona, 384 U.S. 436 (1966)
(by making it clear that *Miranda*
applies to situations that do not
involve a police-dominated atmosphere, 451 U.S. at 466–69) and
the defendant's Sixth Amendment
right to counsel (by making it

clear that at least in some situations consultation between the
defendant and his attorney will be
indispensable to a valid waiver of
the defendant's Sixth Amendment
right, 451 U.S. at 471). *See generally* WHITE, *supra* note 78, at
215.

98. 106 S. Ct. at 1764.
99. The second part of the Court's
statement constructed a straw
man. The defendant never argued
that his petit jury should reflect a
cross-section of the community.
As the Court recognized later in
its opinion, 106 S. Ct. at 1767, he
was not arguing that the composition of the particular jury that
convicted him was unconstitutional. Instead, he was saying
that his constitutional rights were
violated, because he was denied
the possibility of having a member of the automatic life imprisonment group on the jury. In a
sense, the defendant was claiming that he was denied the luck
of the draw. In most criminal
cases, the jury selection procedure provides the prosecution
and defense with roughly equal
chances of obtaining jurors that
are favorably disposed toward
their respective points of view. In
capital cases, however, eliminating the automatic life imprisonment group stacks the selection
procedure against the defense because, given the prodefense perspective of the excludables, the
defense's opportunity to obtain
jurors favorably disposed toward
the defendant is reduced.

100. 106 S. Ct. at 1767.
101. *Id.*
102. *Cf.* Fay v. New York, 332 U.S.
261 (1947) (5-4 decision upholding the constitutionality of New
York's blue ribbon jury). New

York's trial judge had discretion to require that cases of special "importance or intricacy" be tried before blue ribbon juries.

103. *But cf.* Glasser v. United States, 315 U.S. 60, 84 (1942) (defendant's right to an impartial jury would be violated if jury was selected by a process that allowed on jury only members of Illinois League of Women Voters, who had attended "'jury classes whose lecturers presented the views of the prosecution'").

104. *Cf.* Oberer, *supra* note 6, at 552 (observing that death-qualified juries are likely to be composed of people who are authoritarian personalities).

105. 448 U.S. 30 (1980).

106. 106 S. Ct. at 1769.

107. 391 U.S. at 520 n.18.

108. The Court did include some discussion of the state's interest in maintaining a single jury. It suggested that the state has three justifications: first, the same jury should decide guilt and punishment, because the questions are necessarily interwoven; second, requiring two juries would be inefficient, because much of the evidence presented to the guilt jury would also have to be presented to the penalty jury; third, using a single jury might be advantageous to the defendant, because the jury's "residual doubts" about the evidence presented at the guilt phase might lead it to spare the defendant at the sentencing phase. Obviously, the first two justifications are essentially the same. To the extent that the questions of guilt and penalty are interwoven, evidence presented to the guilt jury would have to be presented again to the penalty jury. But once all the relevant evidence was presented to the penalty jury, it would be in at least as good a position to decide the question of penalty as the guilt jury would have been. Thus, the state's only interest is in avoiding the administrative costs involved in selecting a second jury and presenting some of the same evidence to two different juries. Administrative interests of this kind have traditionally been held insufficient to justify the impairment of Sixth Amendment rights. *See, e.g.,* Ballew v. Georgia, 435 U.S. 223, 241 (1978) (administrative interests held insufficient to justify reducing jury size to five).

As the dissent indicated, the third interest identified by the Court should not be entitled to any weight whatsoever. "[A]ny suggestion that the current system of death qualification may be in the defendant's best interests, seems specious unless the state is willing to waive this paternalistic protection in exchange for better odds against conviction." 106 S. Ct. at 1787 (dissenting opinion of Marshall, J.) (quoting Finch & Ferraro, *supra* note 29, at 69).

109. 106 S. Ct. at 1769.

110. 391 U.S. at 521.

111. *See, e.g.,* A. BICKEL, THE SUPREME COURT AND THE IDEA OF PROGRESS 74 (1970). Bickel argued that under the Court's prior decisions, fixing the punishment for a given offense was a legislative function, not a judicial one. Since the legislature could impose mandatory capital punishment, there was no obvious reason for precluding it from delegating the death penalty decision to a group that was more favorably disposed toward the

death penalty than the community at large.

112. In support of its position, *Witherspoon* relied on dicta in Fay v. New York, 332 U.S. 261, 294 (1947), where the Court said, "No device, whether conventional or newly devised, can be set up by which the judicial process is reduced to a sham and courts are organized to convict." In *Fay* the Court indicated that statistics showing that special (or blue ribbon) juries are significantly more likely than ordinary juries to convict "might, in absence of explanation, be taken to indicate that the special jury was, in contrast to its alternate, organized to convict." 332 U.S. at 286.

113. 106 S. Ct. at 1769.

114. *Id.* at 1776 (dissenting opinion of Marshall, J.).

115. TEX. PENAL CODE ANN. § 12.31(b) (Vernon 1974); *see* Adams v. Texas, 448 U.S. 30, 42 (1980).

116. 106 S. Ct. at 1776 (dissenting opinion of Marshall, J.).

117. Gillers, *Proving Prejudice, supra* note 10, at 219, 244.

118. For example, in many jurisdictions, first-degree and second-degree murders are distinguished on the basis of whether the killing was premeditated. But as Justice (then Judge) Cardozo said more than fifty years ago in distinguishing between premeditated and unpremeditated killings, the legislature is essentially requiring the jury to exercise discretion: "What we have is merely a privilege offered to the jury to find the lesser degree when the suddenness of the intent, the vehemence of the passion, seems to call irresistibly for the exercise of mercy." Cardozo, *What Medicine Can Do for Law,* in B. CARDOZO,

LAW AND LITERATURE AND OTHER ESSAYS AND ADDRESSES 99–100 (1931).

119. 448 U.S. at 54 (dissenting opinion of Rehnquist, J.).

120. Beck v. Alabama, 447 U.S. 625, 638 (1980); *see, e.g.,* Lockett v. Ohio, 438 U.S. 586 (1978); Gardner v. Florida, 430 U.S. 349 (1977).

121. 447 U.S. 625 (1980).

122. *Id.* at 638.

123. *Id.* at 637.

124. Alternatively, two commentators have suggested that the death-qualified jury's proneness to convict does not indicate that death-qualified juries' verdicts in general will be less accurate than non-death-qualified juries' verdicts. See Finch & Ferraro, *supra* note 29, at 68.

125. *See supra* note 61.

126. 435 U.S. 223 (1978).

127. In finding that the verdicts of five-person juries are less accurate than those of twelve-person juries, the Court relied upon Saks's finding (*see* SAKS, *supra* note 61, at 107) that twelve-person juries were more consistent than six-person ones in arriving at the same verdict when dealing with simulated trials.

128. 106 S. Ct. at 1772 (dissenting opinion of Marshall, J.).

129. Grigsby v. Mabry, 569 F. Supp. 1273, 1305 (1983)

130. 106 S. Ct. at 1764.

131. Gillers, *Proving Prejudice, supra* note 117, at 233.

132. *See* Cowan et al., *supra* note 30, at 63–64. The videotape used in the study was based on the transcript of an actual Massachusetts homicide trial. The witnesses were played by actors, the lawyers were played by experienced criminal lawyers, and the judge was portrayed by a real California

judge. Each lawyer was asked to develop the case as if it were a real trial, and witnesses were asked to study their testimony so that it was firmly planted in their minds. The only significant modification was that the judge's instructions to the jury in the actual trial were based on Massachusetts law, but in the simulation they were replaced by instructions based on California law. The instructions were taken from *California Jury Instructions, Criminal* (1970) and were assembled after consultation with trial attorneys and law professors. The judge took half an hour to read the instructions to the jury, and he explained each possible verdict (first-degree murder, second-degree murder, manslaughter, acquittal).

133. Assuming that the jury-eligible population was made up of 17.2 percent *Witherspoon* excludables, Ellsworth calculated that in a case similar to the one portrayed in the experiment the systematic exclusion of excludables "would result in 31% fewer initial votes to acquit." Grigsby v. Mabry, 569 F. Supp. 1273, 1301 (1983).

134. *See generally* Francis v. Resweber, 329 U.S. 459 (1947) (second electrocution, conducted after first had failed to kill defendant, held permissible as it did not amount to cruel and unusual punishment under Eighth Amendment); Andres v. United States, 333 U.S. 740 (1948) (hanging held a permissible form of execution); Wilkerson v. Utah, 99 U.S. 130 (1878) (shooting held a permissible form of execution).

135. At the time that *Witherspoon* was decided, most states provided for death-qualified juries and either specifically allowed exclusion of scrupled veniremen on much wider grounds than those authorized in *Witherspoon* or in practice allowed challenges for cause of scrupled veniremen where the strict *Witherspoon* requirements were not met. *See generally* Comment, *Jury Selection and the Death Penalty: Witherspoon in the Lower Courts*, 37 U. CHI. L. REV. 759 (1970).

136. *See* Oberer, *supra* note 6, at 549.

137. 384 U.S. 436 (1966).

138. 388 U.S. 218 (1967).

139. *See supra* text at notes 20–21.

140. Footnote 18 strongly intimated that both the state's interest in obtaining an appropriate penalty determination and the defendant's interest in obtaining a fair guilt determination could be accommodated "by means of a bifurcated trial, using one jury to decide guilt and another to fix punishment." 391 U.S. at 520 n.18.

141. The Court could have reduced the burden on law enforcement by limiting the retroactive effect of its decision. At the time *Witherspoon* was decided, however, decisions that related to the integrity of the fact-finding process were generally retroactively applied. *See* Williams v. United States, 401 U.S. 646, 653 (1971); Berger v. California, 393 U.S. 314, 315 (1969) (per curiam); Roberts v. Russell, 392 U.S. 293, 294 (1968) (per curiam); Witherspoon v. Illinois, 391 U.S. 510, 523 n.22 (1968).

142. 391 U.S. at 539 (dissenting opinion of Black, J.).

143. *See* Furman v. Georgia, 408 U.S. 238 (1972).

144. *See, e.g.,* Lockett v. Ohio, 438 U.S. 581, 604 (1978); *see also* Woodson v. North Carolina, 428 U.S. 280, 305 (1976).

145. *See supra* text at notes 47–57.
146. A state court could, of course, decide that this system of jury selection violates its state constitution. To date, none has done so.
147. 106 S. Ct. at 1782 (dissenting opinion of Marshall, J.).
148. *See, e.g.,* Barefoot v. Estelle, 463 U.S. 880 (1983), discussed in chap. 1.
149. *See* Justice Powell's May 10, 1983, speech to federal judges. This speech is discussed in chap. 1.
150. The Court has accepted certiorari in a case posing this issue. *See* McCleskey v. Kemp, 106 S. Ct. 3331 (1986). For a discussion of this issue, see chap. 6.
151. After the Court's decision in *Lockhart v. McCree,* the pace of executions did increase. *McCree* was decided on May 5, 1986. During the next two months, there were five executions.
152. *Cf.* Weisberg, *Deregulating Death,* 1983 SUP. CT. REV. 305 (reading the Court's 1982 decisions as "announc[ing] that it was going out of the business of telling the states how to administer the death penalty phase of capital murder trials").

153. Skipper v. South Carolina, 106 S. Ct. 1669 (1986).
154. *Id.* at 1673. The Court in *Skipper* held that the exclusion from the sentencing hearing of testimony of jailers and a regular visitor regarding defendant's good behavior during the seven months he spent in jail awaiting trial deprived him of his right to place before the sentencer relevant evidence in mitigation of punishment.
155. *See, e.g.,* Ford v. Wainwright, 54 U.S.L.W. 4799 (1986) (Eighth Amendment prohibits state from inflicting death penalty on prisoner who is insane); Caldwell v. Mississippi, 105 S. Ct. 2633 (1985) (death sentence is unconstitutional when sentencer has been led to believe that final responsibility for determining appropriateness of defendant's death rests elsewhere); Ake v. Oklahoma, 105 S. Ct. 1087 (1985) (indigent defendant who has made a preliminary showing that his sanity at time of offense is likely to be significant factor at trial is entitled to psychiatrist's assistance on this issue).

Table of Cases

Index